excellence in

Procurement

How to optimise costs and add value

excellence in

Procurement

How to optimise costs and add value

Stuart Emmett & Barry Crocker

First edition published by Cambridge Academic, The Studio, High Green, Gt. Shelford, Cambridge CB2 5EG.

ISBN 1-903-499-40-2
978-1-903499-40-5

Printed and bound in the United Kingdom by
4edge Ltd, 7a Eldon Way Industrial Estate, Hockley, Essex, SS5 4AD.

Contents

About the Book

In writing this book, we have made best-efforts endeavours not to include anything that, if used, would be injurious or cause financial loss to the user. The user is, however, strongly recommended before applying or using any of the contents, to check and verify their own company policy/requirements. No liability will be accepted by the authors for the use of any of the contents.

It can also happen in a lifetime of learning and meeting people, that the original source of an idea or information has been forgotten. If we have actually omitted in this book to give anyone credit they are due, we apologise and hope they will make contact so we can correct the omission in future editions.

About the Authors

Stuart Emmett

My own journey to "today", whilst an individual one, does not happen, thankfully without other people's involvement. I smile when I remember so many helpful people. So to anyone who has ever had contact with me, then please be assured you will have contributed to my own learning, growing and developing.

After spending over 30 years in commercial private sector service industries, working in the UK and in Nigeria, I then moved into Training. This was associated with the, then, Institute of Logistics and Distribution Management (now the Chartered Institute of Logistics and Transport).

After being a Director of Training for nine years, I then choose to become a freelance independent mentor/coach, trainer and consultant. This built on my past operational and strategic experience and my particular interest in the "people issues" of management processes. Trading under the name of Learn and Change Limited, I now enjoy working on five continents, principally in Africa and the Middle East, but also in the Far East, Europe and South America.

Additional to undertaking training, I am also involved with one-to-one coaching/mentoring, consulting, writing, assessing and examining for professional institutes' qualifications. This has included being Chief Examiner on the Graduate Diploma of the Chartered Institute of Purchasing and Supply and as an external university examiner for an MSc in Purchasing and Logistics.

Married to the lovely Christine and with two adult cute children, Jill and James; James is married to Mairead, who is also cute. We are additionally the proud grandparents of twin girls (the totally gorgeous Megan and Molly).

I can be contacted at stuart@learnandchange.com or by visiting www.learnandchange.com. I do welcome any comments.

Barry Crocker

Barry is a lecturer in the Salford Business School at the University of Salford. He is currently Programme Leader for the MSc Purchasing and Logistics and MSc Supply Chain Management. Previously, he has had many years industrial experience in various management positions in the field of transport, warehousing and physical distribution. He has been an assistant chief examiner for the professional stage of the CIPS Diploma.

His previous publications include, as co-author with Stuart, The Relationship Driven Supply Chain (2006) and Procurement Principles and Management by Bailey, Farmer, Crocker, Jessop and Jones (2008)10th Edition.

Like Stuart, Barry has conducted many training sessions for multi-nationals in Africa, the Middle East and the Far East in the field of Logistics and Supply Chain Management.

1.0. Procurement Policies and Processes

In this first part of the book we explore the objectives and the five rights of procurement. We then look at procurement in organisations and examine its role in the supply chain. The benefits of taking a supply chain view are then illustrated.

We continue by looking at the evolution of procurement and the strategic management of procurement, especially procurement strategy in the supply chain. We then look at supply/demand planning, inventory and the managing of supplier relationships. Finally strategy alternatives are examined and our vision for procurement is revealed.

Procurement objectives and the five rights

A classic definition of procurement is the five rights:

"Securing supplies, materials, and services of the right quality in the right quantity at the right time from the right place (source) at the right cost."

It should be appreciated that the Five Rights (quality, quantity, time, place and price) are inter-related and are not mutually exclusive. Using them however, ensures that all aspects have been considered and the priority by which the rights are applied can also be dictated by organisational strategy and requirements of the business. Meanwhile another aim for procurement is:

"To obtain bought-in goods/services at the lowest acquisition cost."

The total acquisition cost (TAC) concept emphasising that more than the cost price is involved and we shall be examining this important concept soon but let's first look at each of the five rights.

The Right Quality

Quality is the degree of level of excellence as perceived by the customer; meanwhile it may also be viewed as the product or service being "fit for purpose". Quality is also "performing right first time every time" and involves:
*   Meeting requirements
*   Fitness for purpose
*   Minimum variance
*   Elimination of waste
*   Continuous improvement culture

The right quality should be agreed by the buyer with the customer. Whilst the customer will be restricted by design, performance or safety factors, the buyer will be restricted by costs and market competition. From the buyers' perspective, the quality agreed should allow competition between suppliers.

The Right Quantity

The right quantity to be ordered by the buyer and sold by the supplier, will attempt to balance the requirements of both parties. If taking a wider procurement/supply chain management view, then possibly collaboration or partnership methods may well be used in the supplier/customer relationship to better balance the requirements.

Lower prices can be negotiated for larger quantities, but this may conflict with storage capabilities and production requirements. Dependent or independent demand should be established prior to assessing the quantities needed. The different methods of replenishment for these two distinctive types of demand are covered in section 3.0.

The Right Time (to buy and to deliver)

The right time to buy will be influenced by the following factors:
* Availability
* Market conditions
* Competition
* Procurement policies
* Customer Demand

The right time to deliver will be influenced by:
* Supply lead time (from "initial need" to "available for use")
* Organisational requirements
* Customer demand

In a production environment, the right time to deliver will need to coincide with production schedules, where any failure/lead time variability could have consequences to the schedules and also to the raw material inventory levels. In a retail environment, the right time to deliver will ideally be organised to coincide with low to zero stock holding in the retail store so that non-availability "on-shelf" does not occur.

The Right Place

Procurement needs to ensure that the products or services are bought from the right supplier upstream in the supply chain. Once the source has been identified, the market conditions will need to be assessed and a formal supplier appraisal may be needed, depending on spend, volume and risk.

Downstream, it is also often, the responsibility of procurement to ensure that the materials, products or services are delivered to the right place. So for example, procurement will need to ensure that the correct delivery details are provided by the user/customer and that the supplier has the comprehensive delivery details.

The Right Price

Information on prices should be gathered to allow full analysis of market prices. For example, raw material prices could be monitored, not only for the purchase of the actual raw materials, but also for when raw material prices may affect the cost of products that are being bought. Key factors in the total price need to be understood and broken down and these would include direct and indirect costs along with the profit margin.

Where capital equipment is being purchased a Total Cost of Ownership approach (TCO) should be applied.

Total Cost of Ownership

This is a costing philosophy that also includes value, as the Total Cost of Ownership viewpoint sees the benefit of ownership will only come when the value added to the business through owning the asset, is greater than, the TCO. Conceptually therefore:

TCO = Price +total acquisition cost (TAC) + life-cycle costs (LCC) or whole life costs (WLC).

Both TAC and WLC are examined below.

Total acquisition cost (TAC) is the Price Paid plus all other costs, for example:
- Quality   e.g. errors, defects, returns
- Delivery   e.g. modes, time scales
- Delivery Performance   e.g. non availability, unreliability
- Lead Time   e.g. stock financing
- Packing   e.g. point of display re-pack
- Warehousing   e.g. extra handling
- Inventory   e.g. product deterioration
- New Supplier   e.g. start-ups, assessments
- Administration   e.g. order processing

The question to be answered is: Exactly what are all these costs, beyond the price paid?

Whole life costing (WLC) is the same as Life-cycle costing and can be defined as:

"The systematic consideration of all relevant costs and revenues associated with the acquisition and ownership of the asset."

Essentially therefore, WLC is a means of comparing options and their associated cost and revenue over a period of time. The elements to be costed include:

- Initial capital/procurement costs; e.g. design, construction, installation, purchase, or leasing fees and charges
- Future costs; e.g. all operating costs (rent, rates, cleaning, inspection, maintenance, repair, placements/renewals, energy, dismantling, disposal, security, and

management). It should be noted that unplanned and unexpected maintenance/ refurbishment may amount to more than half of the initial capital spent

- Opportunity costs; e.g. the cost of not having the money available for alternative investments, which would earn money, or the interest payable on loans to finance work

The importance of TCO, TAC and WLC is that they go beyond looking only at the cost price and emphasise that there is more involved than say the lowest cost. As has been said, if everyone purchased on a lowest price basis, then every car on the road would be a (whatever model is the lowest priced car).

The Five Rights and Supplier/Buyers

The five rights connect buyers and suppliers and the following common features can be identified.

Quality

Clarity with suppliers will better enable the meeting of quality requirements. Customers who are very clear on their specific requirements may generate a response from their suppliers that gives them some alternative options. Sharing of requirements is therefore useful; after all, suppliers "do not know what they do not know." Suppliers can then deliver the appropriate quality required and in accordance with a negotiated "right price." Quality needs to be designed into products or services before they are supplied, for as has been said, you cannot inspect quality into a product.

Quantity

It is the placing of an order quantity that triggers the buyer/supplier relationship. Order size differences between the parties will require discussion. It may be that allowing supplier's access to demand information and forecasts, will enable them to better plan their production and stock levels and enable them to better match the buyers requirements for smaller more frequent deliveries.

Time

In the total supply lead time, the suppliers lead time only starts, after the all of customer's internal processes has been completed. If therefore, buyers/customers are reporting delays or variations in supply, then it may not be always the "fault" of the actual supplier. An examination of lead times will therefore indicate all the process involved in the lead time "chain." We will fully examine supply lead time later in the book.

Place and delivery

There can be an assumption that the supplier is only interested in producing/selling a product and that it will be the customers responsibly to "come and get it." Meanwhile, the customers may require goods delivered to them including payment of all the duties/taxes etc. To enable full comparisons between these two extremes, goods will need to be costed at the place where they are to be consumed/used. This can be a negotiation point as some customers do find an advantage in buying from suppliers on ex works terms. Here they then get clearer lead time visibility and control of both the transit lead times and freight/logistics cost prices. We will consider more fully later in the book.

Delivery has common key performance indicators (e.g. on time, in full) for both the supplier (on the outbound delivery) and the customer (on the inbound delivery). If both parties are able to record these on a per transaction basis and then share such measurements openly and periodically, they will find that this enables better communications and understanding. It also will prevent any juvenile "you did/I did not" debates between suppliers/customers that may well eventually lead to mistrust and feelings that "they" are unreliable.

Cost/price

If total cost of ownership evaluation approaches are used, then there is really little to stop the sharing of the results with suppliers. Again, this can mean that they may be able to better suggest alternatives and options. It will also show "fairness," which is what many suppliers look for.

Procurement structuring in an organisation

The terms of reference for the procurement and the supply function will depend upon specific company strategy. Sometimes buying will be carried out separately from inventory or the stores/warehouse functions. In other organisations some integration will have taken place with these functions and a more supply chain view will be taken; perhaps using a procurement and materials or logistics title. Meanwhile others will have the procurement/buying function remaining "independent" but with "supply chain coordinators" looking after day to day ordering and scheduling of replenishment as/when the organisation requires.

Procurement as a centralised or decentralised function

These are the two broad extremes that can be considered in organising the procurement function. The advantages put forward for centralisation include:
*   economies from bulk buying
*   avoiding competitive buying of short supply items from within the organisation
*   specialist product/service buyers and more research/development into alternative sources
*   fewer larger orders are placed
*   common procedures, documents and specifications
*   simpler supplier relationships as a single point of contact
*   more opportunity for spreading of best practice and learning
*   centralised stock control with reduction in overall stock levels
*   procurement is seen as a key business function

The advantages for decentralisation will include:
- closer contacts with other departments in the organisation
- more day to day "hands on" contact and control
- local buyers are better informed about local supplier market conditions
- local buyers have more specialised knowledge of the local products being manufactured by the organisation
- clearer responsibilities to local management

Structure and matching company circumstances

An organisations structure will follow a specific strategy; therefore there cannot be one "fit all" structure. Examples of these differences can be found as follows:

Company circumstances	Example	Procurement Structure
Single product with multi sites	Third party distribution companies	Centralised procurement to leverage procurement power
Multi and related product with multi sites	Detergent manufacturer	Common items could be centralised, with specific items purchased locally
Multi and unrelated product with multi sites	Wines and spirits conglomerate	Divisional level procurement
Multi national	Car Assembly	Global overviews for policy with much local or regional autonomy, dependant upon circumstances
Public sector	Local government	Local procurement with some centralised consortia buying to leverage procurement power

Case Study: Smurfit Eire, and centralised Procurement

Today, Smurfit's extensive Irish operations are part of the Smurfit Kappa Group and fully realises the importance of bottom line efficiencies. Both figuratively and literally speaking, purchasing is positioned central to current and future needs.

The Group has annual sales in excess of over Euro 7 billion, operations at some 400 locations and over 40,000 employees. It is the European leader in containerboard, solid board, graphic board, corrugated and solid board packaging. The Group operates in 20 European countries, nine Latin American countries and in the US, Canada, Singapore and South Africa.

In 1999, following the implementation of SAP, Smurfit Kappa in Ireland established a Shared Services Centre and three years later Central Purchasing was set up as a department within the Shared Services offices.

Michael Binchy is general manager of the Shared Services Centre and heads Central Purchasing, which provides a service to the 12 Smurfit Kappa plants in Ireland. He is a

Certified Accountant and has been with the Group for 22 years, mainly on the financial side.

Shared Services functions include purchasing, SAP processing, master data management, treasury and various other financial functions. It has a staff of eight, two of whom are in Central Purchasing. "My function is to apply management skills to the procurement process and to drive it, " says Binchy.

Smurfit Kappa's annual purchasing spend in Ireland is around Euro 60 million. Paper used in the manufacture of corrugated board is predictably the biggest category, followed by transport. Being a commodity, paper prices are market driven and market forces such as demand, capacity and inventory levels determine global prices. The biggest issue is ensuring source and supply. Most of Smurfit Kappa's paper is bought internally from its Dills across Europe.

European procurement strategy is fairly straight forward- product categories are put to tender across the European supplier base. Benchmarking plus negotiation results in a shortlist of preferred suppliers.

In the European procurement operation, category managers are assigned to the main categories that are common across Smurfit Kappa corrugated plants and mills. Their responsibility is to meet pan-European suppliers and negotiate prices at of pan European level. "They communicate that back to country coordinators " says Binchy, "and it s our responsibility to implement those prices across the plants in our respective countries. This process gives us transparency of pricing across Europe over a wide range of product categories. There is two-way dialogue; we obviously feedback to the category managers on how we are progressing or what difficulties or challenges that we may be facing with suppliers here; it works well."

Everything feeds down from Europe, through Shared Services to the individual Irish plants, each of which has its own purchasing coordinator with responsibility for local tenders from suppliers or for goods that are unique to that plant. The role of the plant purchasing coordinator varies with the size of plant. In some of the larger plants, it is a full time role, whereas in smaller plants, it is part time.

"Quarterly meetings are held with our local Irish plant purchasers to ensure European policy is implemented, to monitor progress on local purchasing initiatives and provide training so that all users are aware of the tools within SAP that will assist the purchasing functions. What I'm trying to do is consolidate and leverage our spend and adopt best practices across the plants. Prior to SAP, every plant managed its own procurement and selected its own suppliers. What we have done is coordinate all expenditure, review existing suppliers and reduce their number and leverage off the consolidated spend with the aim of getting better value." But Binchy sees cost as only one element. "We are looking for three things from suppliers - good product, good service, all at the right price."

In a company of the size of Smurfit Kappa, working' capital is exceptionally important, so Central Purchasing looks at what suppliers can offer in areas such as consignment stock, often terms, payment terms, how often they can they make deliveries into a plant, what kind of quantities they can deliver, minimum orders, and similar issues. We take all these factors into consideration because they affect our working capital. The ultimate strategy is to achieve cost savings and improve working capital," he says. According to Binchy, the biggest challenge has been changing the mindset not only of the purchasers in the local plants on what their function should be but function getting department managers to see what Central Purchasing is aiming to achieve. "With support from plant general managers, the focus has been to get buy-in from all departments including maintenance, production, finance, inventory control - everyone needs to be involved in the process and fully commit to it."

From the outset, Binchy strongly believed that Central Purchasing needed to be viewed, not just as a cost centre, but as adding value to the organisation and the plants. It took a while for this message to get across and initially there was a tendency to view Central Purchasing as an unnecessary layer of administration. We needed to show that Central Purchasing saves money. In the past, purchasing didn't really sell itself. What we have achieved is to raise the profile of the purchasing function within Smurfit Kappa and demonstrate the results it can deliver. "We're not just punching in purchase orders - that's not saving money. We're adding value to the organisation and generating tangible savings that we can actually measure. So we focus very much on selling to the general management across the plants the concept that we actually help them achieve savings. We are able to show lands what we've saved during the year.

"I'm fortunate in having Tom Dalzell as my colleague. He a strong technical background so he works closely with the engineers and production people in the plants in rolling out new tenders. We arrange for our suppliers to meet with Tom and the maintenance manager at the plants to see where efficiencies and improvements can be made.

"As a result, we develop good teamwork between Central Purchasing, the plant managers and key suppliers big enough to be important to the supplier. That comes from experience, says Binchy. "Where our orders are worth abound 10% to 15% of a supplier's business, we are big enough a customer in their eyes that they will give us top service, and when we pick up the phone they respond. In the past, we've given business to major UK suppliers and found that our business was far too small for them and we were not getting the level of service we required. So we brought the business back .to an Irish supplier. Our order was substantial in their books and they gave us a level of service that reflected this.

"Conversely, if our business dominates a supplier, it can become a problem, particularly if the supplier goes out of business. There are not many where that is the case, but it is something that we would be careful of and watch. The last thing we want is to enjoy attractive prices this year and next year the supplier is out of business or cannot sustain the same level of pricing and are forced to raise prices back to or even above previous levels. We have the cost of change and we lose the investment we have made in building a relationship.

"Changing suppliers can be a costly business, especially in our case where we have twelve plants and we have to manage this change across the twelve plants. So, we try to develop a relationship with these suppliers where it is open and honest. Where both sides can put their cards on the table and we both know where we are going. We tend to stay with suppliers unless their service levels fall, or product quality drops, or they increase their prices beyond what is acceptable to us."

Suppliers are asked to be proactive and come back with new ideas. "They need to work with us to achieve further cost savings and deliver efficiencies to the production process. They are the people with the product knowledge and they are best placed to come to us with ideas and new developments that are relevant to us -because if they are not doing it, their competitors may well do it."

That said, it usually difficult for new suppliers to get business from Smurfit Kappa if an incumbent supplier is performing well. Central Purchasing benchmarks suppliers. "We inform suppliers that they will be benchmarked during the period of the contract. We go back out to the market and make sure that the pricing levels are still competitive. Once a contract is created within SAP, it can be subsequently downloaded and enabled to other potential suppliers. From the responses can see how our existing supplier is performing."

Apart from paper and machinery OEMs most purchasing is local. "Over the years, Irish suppliers have become more professional," notes Binchy. "They understand our business well, they know our needs and they know the people within the plants. They are invariably more flexible than overseas suppliers. Where they have a premium on the price, that premium is justified by the level of service that they are giving. They have come a long way and are adapting well to our business and are being more proactive and in providing information back from their side."

Source: "Purchasing and Supply Solution" The Irish Journal for Supply Chain Management Best Practice, undated in 2007.

Procurement and the supply chain

Procurement is an important element in supply chain management and must therefore be integrated through all of the strategic, tactical and operational levels in organisations. Procurement may cover all of the following aspects:

- The acquisition/procurement of what is needed by spending money externally, so as to satisfy the needs of internal customers/users or external customers
- Following up on the delivery from suppliers

9

- Providing information and services to internal customers (e.g. production/ manufacturing/retail shops etc.)
- Liaising/integrating and coordinating the internal supply chain

The Supply Chain Philosophy

The Supply Chain is the process, which integrates, coordinates and controls the movement of goods, materials and information from a supplier through to a customer to the final consumer/ user.

The essential point here is that the supply chain links, all the activities between suppliers and customers to the consumer in a timely manner. Supply chains therefore involve the activities of buying/procurement, making/manufacturing, moving/distributing, and selling/marketing. The supply chain "takes care of business" following from the initial customer/consumer/user demand. Nothing happens with supply until there is demand represented by an order; it is the order that drives the whole process. Indeed some people logically argue that the term supply chain could be called the demand chain.

So the Supply Chain bridges the gap between the fundamental core business aspects of Supply & Demand, as shown below:

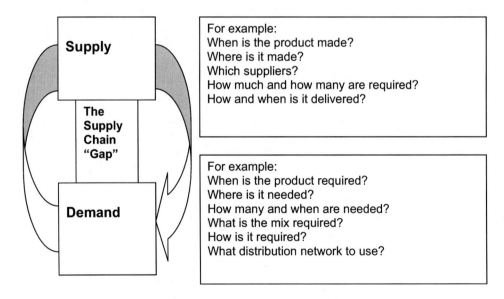

The philosophy of Supply Chain Management is therefore to view all these processes as being related holistically so that they:

- Integrate, coordinate and control the movement of materials, inventory and information, from suppliers through a company to meet all the customer(s) and the ultimate consumer/user requirements, in a timely manner.

A diagrammatic view follows, where it will be seen that the flows of products and the flows of information are represented by ideas, order creation, and cash/orders:

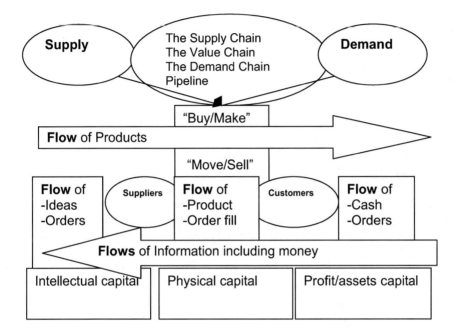

In this diagram:
*   The demand chain represents the creation of demand, for example, marketing and selling with product development
*   The supply chain represents fulfilment, for example, procurement and buying, production and making with distribution and moving
*   The value chain represents performance, for example, financial measures and capital in both the internal value chain and the "extensions" upstream and downstream to the value chains of:
    -   the upstream first level suppliers
    -   the first level suppliers supplier and so, upstream
    -   the downstream customers
    -   the downstream users and final consumers

The above activities of Buying-Making-Moving and Selling take place in business operational functions of Procurement, Production, Distribution and Marketing.

Supply chain networks

Each company therefore has not one supply chain, but many, as it deals with different suppliers and has different customers. For each individual finished product or line item, whilst some of the buying, making, moving and selling processes will be identical or very similar, the total supply chain for each product will be different and will involve often a complex network. This goes, for example, far beyond the first supplier and includes the supplier's supplier, then that supplier's supplier and so on.

Many companies in their supply chain management do not work on the supply chain in this way and often stop with the first level supplier; in so doing they ignore that the supply chain is effectively a large network of many and varied supplier/customer players.

Supply chain differences

Additionally, different types of business and industry sectors will have different views of what the supply chain is about for them, for example:
*   Retailers are driven by end consumer demand creation and the "on the shelf" availability/fulfilment of a variety of products
*   Oil exploration and production companies are driven by pumping oil, so the supporting production by the supply side is critical
*   Car assemblers are end consumer demand driven, meaning developing a closer integration of both the supply and the demand sides of the business so that demand flows "seamlessly" through to suppliers for JIT supply followed by assemble to order production methods

Business may be classified, as shown below, which shows the influences of the operating environments and the key competence/key performance indicators:

	High Complexity	Low Complexity
High Uncertainty	Capital intensive industries: Aerospace Shipbuilding Construction **Key: Fitness for purpose** (of product)	Fast moving consumer goods: Cosmetics Textiles Food and drink **Key: Time to market**
Low Uncertainty	Consumer goods: Automotive White goods Electrical goods **Key: Value for money**	Staple primary industries: Paper Glass Simple components **Key: Price** (from production productivity)

Supply chains differ and therefore multiple supply chain management is perhaps a better description but it is a cumbersome one. At a simple level, consider the following multiple supply chain (part only) for Lee Cooper jeans:

Customers: World wide via agents, wholesalers and retailers, from a factory in Tunisia, which gets its supplies of:
*   Denim cloth from Italy, who use dye from West Germany and cotton from Benin, West Africa and Pakistan
*   Zips from West Germany, who use wire for the teeth from Japan and polyester tape from France.
*   Thread from Northern Ireland, who use dye from Spain and fibre from Japan

- Rivets and Buttons from USA, who use zinc from Australia and copper from Namibia
- Pumice (used in stone-washing) from Turkey

Economic sectors

With supply chain management therefore, there are many different supply chains to manage. These wide reaching supply chain networks will contain companies from all of the main economic sectors:

- Primary sector: Raw materials from farming/fishing (food, beverages, and forestry), quarrying/mining (minerals, coals, metals) or drilling (oil, gas, water)
- Secondary sector: Conversion of raw materials into products; milling, smelting, extracting, refining into oils/chemicals/products and then maybe; machining, fabricating, moulding, assembly, mixing, processing, constructing into components, sub-assemblies, building construction/structures and furnitures/electronic/food/paper/metal/chemicals and plastic products
- Service or tertiary sector: Business, personal and entertainment services, which involve the channels of distribution from suppliers to customers, via direct, wholesale or retail channels. Services include packaging, physical distribution, hotels, catering, banking, insurance, finance, education, public sector, post, telecoms, retail, repairs etc.

Companies will therefore have many supply chains both internally and externally that interact through a series of simple to complex networks.

Supply Chain History

In the UK, the history of the supply chain can be viewed as passing through three phases. However, with any such stereotyping there is much overlap but an "ideal-typical" view can be provided which enables the key areas to be viewed more clearly (continues overleaf):

Attribute	Functional Supply Chains To the 1980s	Responsive Supply Chains The 1990s	Adaptive Supply Chains The Naughties
Integration focus	Over the wall	Transactional	Collaboration
	Reactive/Quick fixes	Responsive	Decision/ Proactive
	Monopoly suppliers	Competition in suppliers	Joined up networks of enterprises
Customer focus	Customer can wait	Customers wants it soon	Customer wants it now
	"You will get it when we can send it	"You will have it when you want it"	"You will get it"

Organisation focus	Departmental and ring fencing	Intra-enterprise. "Internal" involvement.	Extended enterprise involvement.
Product positioning	Make to stock	Assemble to order	Make to order
	Decentralised stock holding	Centralised stock holding	Minimal stock holding
			Whatever is needed
	Store then deliver	Collect and cross dock	
Management approach	Hierarchical	Command and control	Collaborative
Technology focus	Point solution	ERP	Web connected
Time focus for the business	Weeks to months	Days to weeks	Real time
Performance focus	Cost	Cost and service	Revenue and profit
Collaboration	Low	Medium	High levels
Response times	Static	Medium	Dynamic

The Benefits of a Supply Chain Management Approach

Competitive advantage

The real competition in business comes not just from companies competing against each other, but increasingly comes from competing supply chains. Here there is a growing approach to maximise benefits, from the supply chain, beyond the first level suppliers.

Competitive advantage is to found by doing things better or by doing thing cheaper. Looking for these advantages really means extending from within a company, towards, the supply chains. This means looking to remove sub functional conflicts from all the interdependent processes, whether these processes are internal or external to a business. Accordingly, it is the supply chain that can now provide the competitive advantage for a business.

This will also mean taking a collaborative supply chain approach to examine and total the costs of all the functions, matched to the service levels. If this is not done, and by continuing to minimise the costs for each sub function, then this could mean:
- Buying in bulk from multiple sources (Procurement is only being optimised); but for example, this will give high storage costs
- Making few products with long production runs (here Production is only being optimised); which means limited ranges, poor availability etc.
- Moving in bulk (Transport only being optimised); but gives infrequent delivery etc.
- Selling what produced (Marketing only being optimised); but it may not be needed

Supply chain structures and benefits

The way the supply chain is structured and managed is therefore critical. Some reported benefits of following a supply chain approach follow; it will be noted that different approaches give different results:

	No Supply Chain: Functional Silos	Internal Integrated Supply Chain	Plus, External Integration to the first level only
Inventory days of supply Indexed	100	78	62
Inventory carrying cost % sales	3.2%	2.1%	1.5%
On time in Full deliveries	80%	91%	95%
Profit % Sales	8%	11%	14%

To get these benefits, organisations will need to more away from a functional silo approach and whether it is procurement that leads the internal integrated supply chain will actually depend on each specific organisation. However, it will be seen that with a supply chain integrated approach; inventory costs do fall, profit and the service fulfilment do increase. This represents the "best of both worlds" for any organisation undertaking the approach.

Additional benefits from supply chain management will only usually come when there is a joint examination of all costs/service levels with all the players; so as to obtain reduced lead times and improved total costs/service for all parties in the network. This means therefore, going beyond the first tier of suppliers and looking also at the suppliers' supplier and so on. To undertake such an extended view of the supply chain, then this may well require a total Supply Chain Re-thinking; a topic addressed more fully in "Excellence in Supply Chain Management" Stuart Emmett (2008).

However, working and collaborating fully with all players in the Supply Chain is the only way to find the optimum/"ideal" cost/service balance. A key area here is to balance the service aspects with the costs as 30 to 70 percent of an organisations cost may be in the Supply Chain; indeed, cost will be a common language to anyone in the supply chain.

Managing efficiently and effectively the flows of goods and information across the supply chain networks are therefore essential in bringing about the optimum cost/service balance. A big promise and often never an easy approach but this can result in the perfect ideals of:
- Increased/improved service, reaction times, product availability etc.
- Reduced/improved total cost, total stock levels time to market etc.

All activities in the supply chain, including procurement, have a part to play in achieving such ideals.

Procurement evolution and history

Procurement evolution

Having looked at the history and benefits of the supply chain philosophy we will now look specifically at procurement. Procurement has evolved through the following stages:

- Stage one: Product-centred procurement concerned with tangible products and outcomes
- Stage two: Process-centred procurement that has moved beyond stage one into process measurement
- Stage three: Relational procurement that has expanded into purchaser/supplier relationships
- Stage four: Performance-centred procurement that focuses on best product management and integrates relationships, processes and outcomes, which are jointly resourced with suppliers

Procurement and the internal offer

Procurement can be seen here as a part of the supply chain philosophy and indeed in many organisations Procurement does occupy a strategic role that:

- recognises buying gives both value for money and cost reduction
- takes more whole/holistic views over a longer term
- uses a more integrative process approach
- builds internal and external relationships
- coordinates flows from suppliers into the company to meet lead time and availability requirements of users/customers

Many organisations however, actually operate their procurement activities, sub-optimally and in a silo. This is because suppliers, organisations and internal business are not integrated in any meaningful way.

The organisation therefore needs aligning to its core business drivers, such as customers "needs." This in turn impacts on the core organisational competencies and capacity and will require external and internal integration.

The following Case Study illustrates very simply some of the needed internal integration aspects.

Case Study: Board room scenario

MD to Procurement Director:
"How much obsolete stock have you bought today?"
Procurement Director:
"None"

MD to Production Director:
"How much obsolete stock have you made today?"
Production Director:
"None"

MD to Sales Director:
"How many week's stock have you got?"
Sales Director:
"Three week's"
MD to Sales Director:
"How many week's stock do you need?"
Sales Director:
"One week's."

MD comments:
"Sales does not want the next two weeks production, and Production does not want what procurement is planning to buy tomorrow."

The simple lesson:
All internal operations should be integrated, coordinated and controlled

In procurement, "doing the deal" alone and incrementally, is not enough, as value, risk, cost, service etc. are all involved in a complex series of trade-offs that attempts to optimise the "whole" business/supply chain.
Procurement should be a part of this optimisation.

Strategic and Corporate Procurement

Corporate strategy

Strategic development of a procurement function can be seen as moving from a passive stage one, through independence and supportive stages to stage four, integrative. This development also parallels the above discussion on the overall Supply Chain development of the functional – responsive - adaptive stages.
Corporate strategy links down to business strategy and in turn links to functional strategy, for example of the procurement function. Meanwhile the following points can be noted on the links and connections between strategies:

- Strategy is long term, broad in scope and can be determined at corporate, business or functional levels
- Strategy is best applied by establishing a mission or goals, assessing the organisation, assessing the environment, identifying strategic options, implementing strategy to achieve the chosen option(s)
- Continuous improvement will be needed to gain competitive advantage in times of dynamic change in global markets, shortened product life-cycles and more demanding customers

- Value is essentially that perceived by the customer and is some thing they are prepared to pay for

Corporate strategy is therefore a concept of an organisations business, which provides a unifying theme for all its activities by asking three basic questions:
- What is the mission: what will we do and for whom will we do it (what business are we in)?
- What objectives do we want to achieve (what are the goals)?
- How will we manage the activities to achieve the chosen objectives?

Strategic management of procurement

Strategic management of procurement will therefore need to include the following:
- Reviewing existing suppliers related to risk and spend
- Identifying a number of potentially strategic suppliers
- Examining existing activities to see if they can be outsourced
- Developing strategic alliances, collaborations and partnerships
- Developing strategic performance criteria

The strategic management of procurement will need to be related to the corporate strategy and the needs of the business. For example, a business involved in trading will need to look for new products to sell; a business selling fast moving consumer goods will look for fast, reliable suppliers. Businesses involved in continuous production will require raw material to be always available; a local public sector authority will need to demonstrate public accountability.

These differences can come from differing types of:

- Organisations; in the earlier identified primary, secondary or tertiary sectors
- Purchases; from these three sectors
- Organisation ownership; for example the private and the public sectors. The former is usually profit driven and therefore procurement will be required to contribute to this goal. In the public sector, a similar role to the private sector may be found in those quasi independent/public owned organisations, such as the UK Post Office. However, the central and local government organisations, such as the NHS, are responsible to the countries population and required to obtain maximum value for a given level of cost, along with, transparency and public accountability

Taking a more strategic view of procurement involves the following differences:

Operational procurement	Strategic procurement
Transactional order placers	Value added facilitators
Short term	Long term
Cost focus	Customer/user focus
Internal view	External views
Performance statistics	Benchmarking
Technical processes	Business process

Procurement by the strategic requirements of the product

Once a need has been identified, next is to determine the importance which is applied to the product or material that is required. ABC/Pareto analysis provides a basis to identify where the spend is the greatest and where most effort should be directed to reduce costs. Here, the 80/20 rule states that, in most cases, 80% of purchase value is concentrated within 20% of the items purchased. Additionally, risk and other factors are involved.

These risk factors can be viewed from high to low, against the following criteria:
- Experience with product /service (high risk for a new, untried products to a lower risk for repeats)
- Supply/demand balance (short supply /excess capacity)
- Supply chain complexity (many parties involved to "direct" purchases)
- Financial aspects of supply disruption (high to negligible costs)
- Safety consequences of disruption (high to low hazards)
- Design maturity (new to established designs)
- Manufacturing complexity (complex to simple)

The other factors can also be rated from high to low against the following criteria:
- Market structure (many sources to a monopoly supplier)
- Value of spend (high to low spending)
- Supply/demand balance (spare to no capacity)
- Efficiency of buying process (identical for all, to tailored buying)
- Development of buying process in the company (users agree specifications to cross functional reviews)
- Knowledge of suppliers pricing (cost plus to market based pricing)?

To account for both spend and risk from non supply (due to there being few suppliers); based on the work of Kraljic, the range of purchased items can be broken down into four categories:

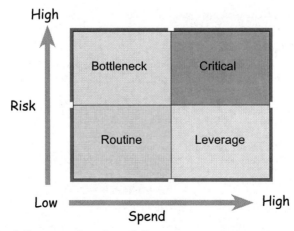

This indicates that different products have different strategic requirements to a business. It also gives a broad indication of how buying and the supplier relationships can be conducted into the following four basic strategies:

- Routine items: Routine buying of commodities, needing efficiency. Relationships may be conducted at "arm's length" for these low value items
- Leverage items are those where a high volume is purchased with a high level of supplier numbers giving competition. Here therefore the lowest cost can easily be found
- Bottleneck items: The need here is to ensure the supply and reduce the risk of non supply and disruption to the business. Suppliers are often few in number, for example, a monopoly
- Critical items require closer supplier relationships to ensure they are always available. These will involve usually involve longer term relationships and partnering approaches with suppliers

Some examples of different products from the oil and gas and chocolate confectionery industries, for each of these categories, are as follows:

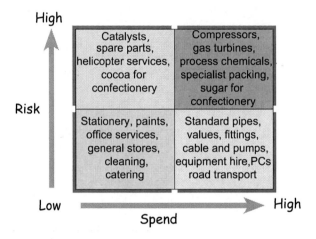

In general terms the following will be involved:

Leverage; Low risk, high spend items
- There would be a need to create competition in the market place for these items to drive down price. The supply market is competitive with many available sources, hence buyers are able to leverage by maximising economies of scale and by offering large spends.

Routine; Low risk, low spend items
- Minimal effort is needed for sourcing these items due to the relatively little impact purchasing can make to reducing purchase costs. Therefore acquisition costs are targeted by the use of credit cards, EDI, internet ordering and call-offs with users directed to place orders direct with the selected supplier; who reports on usage.

Critical; High risk, high spend items
- These items rank high in the Pareto analysis of spend but are also difficult to source

due to low numbers of suppliers or complex logistics. Close supplier relations are needed with possible use of joint working and multi-functional teams.

Bottleneck; High risk, low spend items
- These items would not rate as important when analysing spend alone, but due to difficulties in sourcing there would need to be concentrated effort to secure supply of these items as the supplier often has the power, for example, OEM spare parts.

Levels of risks

As will have been seen from the above discussion, risk is the impact of uncertainty and results from:
- an unexpected event
- false assumptions
- human failure

The sources of risk can be as follows:
- lack of planning
- lack of competent resources
- unrealistic timescales
- evolving technology
- poor communication
- insufficient task definition
- financial restrictions
- legislative requirements

The level of risk will depend on a variety of factors, such as those already covered above (the strategic requirements of the product, spend and the usage) and an acceptable level of risk will therefore vary from contract to contract. Risk can rarely be eliminated, but, it can be managed or transferred to another party; the key principle is that risk should be allocated to whichever party can best manage it.

In conducting business then commercial risks will often need to be taken. Specifically for procurement, the following are examples of commercial risks:
- supplier liquidation
- delayed delivery
- supplier failure to meet environmental requirements
- cost and/or price inflation
- changes in law

Risk factors must be identified and then the probability of each risk occurring should be estimated. Risks can then be placed in rank order and the likely impact of each risk on success factors determined. The risk assessment process therefore has the following four stages:
- identify potential problems and causal factors
- consider possibility of problems arising
- weight factors and assess impact
- devise strategies to control risk

Procurement Strategy in the Supply Chain

As noted earlier, many companies actually operate procurement sub-optimally. Value, risk, cost, service etc. are actually all involved in a complex series of trade-offs that must be examined with all relevant parties to optimise the "whole" business/supply chain.

Therefore suppliers, customers and the internal business must be integrated in a meaningful way. Many organisations therefore need aligning to its core business drivers, such as customers "needs." This in turn impacts on the core business competencies and capacity and will then require internal integration ("win the home games first") and the removal of functional silos. Externally, this will mean developing a clear strategic view and fit of suppliers using, for example, the above Kraljic purchasing portfolio analysis.

Any approach to doing this, will mean getting answers to the following questions:
*   What are the steps and stages in the supply chains?
*   When last did we process map these supply chains?
*   What are the cost and value adders?
*   What are the risks and vulnerabilities?
*   What opportunities are there for reducing, simplifying processes?
*   How can the number of steps and stages in the supply chains be reduced?
*   What are the opportunities for containing and reducing costs in each process?
*   Where can improvements be made in quantity, quality, time and place?
*   How can risk and vulnerability be reduced?

Such an approach attempts to bring a balanced yet integrated view and will involve:
*   Lead times being fully examined
*   ICT integration
*   Product designs examination
*   Service improvements
*   Zero defects "rules" instead of quality inspections/assurance
*   Suppliers involvements
*   Continuous improvement philosophy
*   Inventory and stock holding levels

We return again to procurement strategy soon, but next we look at inventory and stock holding, an often poorly managed aspect.

Procurement, Inventory & Supply/Demand Planning

Inventory in the supply chain

Inventory is the common component throughout the Supply Chain and is held as either raw material, sub-assemblies/work in progress or as finished goods (which are often held at multiple places in the supply chain). In the supply chain, the flows of goods and information will need to be coordinated so as to optimise the required inventory levels to meet the required level of service at an acceptable cost to satisfy the users demand.

But who does this and who is responsible? Is it a procurement function, a logistics function or a finance function or a production function or a marketing function?

No straight answer here as it depends on the organisation and how it is structured. However it must be someone's responsibility and it also will need to be a cross functional activity. Where it is not recognised this way, then inevitability too much stock will be held. Additionally due to poor understanding and control, stock-outs may occur regularly of the wrong products, whilst high levels of deteriorating and obsolete stocks will be found. Inventory is therefore an important component that has to be understood.

Procurement's role

The format of inventory and where it is held should therefore be of common interest to all supply chain players and be jointly investigated and examined. Procurement can however have a key part to play here in discussions with suppliers and in agreeing fixed reliable lead times.

The importance of inventory must be appreciated by procurement people as their role should be more than merely placing orders without regard to inventory aspects. Too often orders are "blindly" placed with for example, scant regard to lead time reliability, resulting in variability and inevitably, extra stock holding and dissatisfied customers who also experience poor stock availability. Procurement must not ignore the cost/service availability issues of having appropriate stock levels to satisfy the users demand; however inventory is often not well understood by procurement people.

Inventory management has the movement and product flow as a key concept and attempts to achieve the required service level at an acceptable cost. When the flow stops, then cost will be added (unless the stored product is one that appreciates in value over time).
Key aspects that have to be considered in inventory management are therefore as follows:
* Determining the products to stock and the location where they are therefore held
* Maintaining the level of stock needed to satisfy the demand
* Maintaining the supply
* Determining how much and when to order?

The placing of orders will generally include an amount that is ordered for stock holding. The procurement department may not of course be the ones who decide this. In for example retail organisations, procurement/trading will source suppliers, undertake evaluation and selection, but the ordering and stock levels will be decided by a supply chain department or by an inventory control department. In other organisations however, procurement will be involved in determining stock levels and the subsequent ordering and may also have an expediting section that is used to order progress chase with suppliers. We will examine expediting more fully later.

Why hold stock?

The following is a summary of the reasons why stock is held:
* De-couples supply and demand; here the following examples of stock maybe found:
  - Raw material stock to enable the production process

       - Work in progress and semi assembled items, for customising into finished products
       - Finished goods stock for immediate demand order filling

- Safety/Protection, for example:
       - to protect against supplier uncertainty
       - to cover for non forecasted demand
- In anticipation of demand, for example:
       - promotional or seasonal build up
       - bulk supply price discounts
- To provide service to customers (internal, external), for example:
       - cycle stocks of finished goods
       - availability from safety stock for non forecasted demand

There may also be pipeline inventory in the supply chain. This would be stock in transit either from suppliers and/or to customers. The time in "the pipeline/in transit" may be considerable if goods are undergoing a long sea journey.

In financial accounting, stock improves the company balance sheet. Stock is therefore an asset in financial terms. However, holding stock also carries costs (as we shall see later), which will appear in the financial profit and loss accounts. The turnover of inventory also means sales and profits to a trading business, as the faster the inventory turns, then the greater the profitability. In inventory management, stock comprises of two components, cycle stock and safety stock and the differences between these two components of stock can be noted as:

- Cycle stock is that held to cover the normal in/out movements from normal order policies; it is also known as replenishment stock.
- Safety stock is that held to cover the expected use during the supply lead time, any uncertainty in supply, and/or in demand and to provide a higher levels of stock cover for availability. It is also known as buffer stock.

Inventory and uncertainty

A key aspect for procurement staff to understand is that inventory management is dealing with uncertainty. This is not only uncertainty with the supply and the customer or with end consumer demand, but also in asking whether the uncertainty is "real." For example, is it caused by the dynamic aspects of the supply chain, or, is it caused by institutionalised and out-dated/ill-informed procedures and lack of communication within the organisation, and/or in the supply chain? These latter aspects can be found for example, when institutionalised demand distorts the real demand as it passes down a supply chain where each player in the supply chain is viewing demand as being random and independent.

These uncertainties and distorted demand can cause fluctuations and dependencies that can limit subsequent events occurring as these depend on the last previous dependencies and are therefore being influenced by the fluctuations of the preceding dependencies. Where the supply chain is long with no end to end visibility, the length of dependencies in turn, increases, and means each dependency "struggles" to undertake its activities due to the fluctuations. They "struggle" with the capacity as the demand and the flow are not in balance. This results in higher inventory carrying in the chain and in slower product movements.

Demand

The supply chain exists to satisfy demand and this is found in two basic forms that have different replenishment methods:

- Independent or random demand is independent of all other products; e.g. tyre manufacturer for puncture repairs. It is the classic consumer driven demand for "end use" products or services and therefore is more random with uncertainty being found. It uses reorder point/level (ROP/ROL) methods or systems for inventory.

- Dependant or predicative demand is that derived from consumer demand which produces "end use" products or services. For example, tyre manufacturer for new cars which is driven by the derived requirement for new cars and is planned for by the car assembler based on their view of the independent demand from consumers. With dependant demand, this means that the previous event has to happen first and that subsequent events will then depend on the ones preceding them. Dependant demand is therefore more certain for suppliers and for procurement, enabling some degree of anticipation; for example the tyre manufacturer obtains from the car assemblers their forward planning on production. It uses requirement/resource planning systems (such as MRP)

ABC Analysis

A useful step is to conduct an ABC Analysis exercise which will analyse, the products being ordered and stocked in terms of fast/slow movers. This involves the classic Pareto analysis named after the 1890s Italian economist who reckoned that 80% of the wealth lay in the hands of 20% of the population. A high incidence in one set of variables equates to smaller incidence in a corresponding set of variables; as shown below:

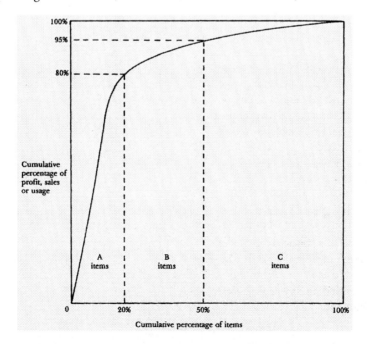

25

The results of a product analysis on a volume throughput usage basis will, classically, show that:
- A items – fast movers = high volume, few lines
- B items – medium movers = medium volume, medium lines
- C items – slow movers = low volume, many lines

If the ABC analysis is undertaken on a product value basis, then the following procurement/ stocking situation may apply in a manufacturing company:
- A high value items require a low stock holding needing continuity in supply/JIT or periodic review replenishment system (explained later). Bulk chemicals are examples here.
- B medium value items use minimum/maximum or continuous review replenishment system (see later) with supplier weekly check on stock/reorder. An example could be protective paints.
- C low value items can use a two bin system replenishment system (see later) for items like nuts, washers etc.

As an example, the following stocking policy is for inbound supplies to serve production and is based on product values:
- A items (by value) are tightly controlled with orders only for known requirements. Continual accurate records/progressing with less than two weeks safety stock being held.
- B items are moderately controlled with ordering against forecast based on historic demand. Safety stocks of 6-8 weeks were held
- C items are at a lower control level with larger levels of safety stocks around 12 weeks Clearly here the high valued items have minimal stock levels and this therefore lowers the costs to the business.

It will be seen therefore, that both the ordering and the replenishment policies are central and these must be fully understood by buyers and procurement personnel.

Inventory Costs

Many different internal activities and departments of a company cause these costs; additionally, many of the costs may be hidden from view.
The following cost items can be involved:
Capital Investments:
- Value of Stock holding
- Warehouse investment
- Warehouse equipment investment
- ICT systems investments

Plus...Product-holding costs
- Storage/handling (if not in above)
- Obsolescence
- Deterioration /damages to stock
- Insurance

Plus...Ordering costs
- Procurement
- Warehouse receiving
- Finance payments

All these individual cost items will equal the total cost of inventory i.e.:
Total Cost of Inventory = Total of Capital investment @ Cost of borrowing money per annum,
+ Holding total costs per annum,
+ Ordering costs per annum,
+ Any other, specific, annual costs (such as stock checking)

Inventory Service

This centres around the level needed (the availability) to satisfy demand. This will usually be a strategic decision of the business, but it also can be a decision taken at a lower level and one being taken to provide cover against complaints and "noise" factors. Inventory management is a dynamic and interactive process, so such anti "noise" low level decision making can be reflections that inventory it is not fully understood in a business and that sub-optimal decision making is actually occurring.

The levels of stock being held to satisfy demand should be a company policy decision based upon an objective view of the requirements of users and customers. In a market situation, then what the competition is offering will also have an input into the strategic decisions.

Inventory and Lead Time

Lead time is critical when making procurement (and the resultant related inventory) decisions, as the following simple example illustrates:

If use 70 items per week, and the supply lead time (SLT) is 2 weeks; then, the maximum stock is 140 items.

But if the SLT is variable by +/- one week, then, the maximum stock is 210 items and the minimum stock is 70 items.

But, people may understandably decide to "play it safe" and hold 210 items.

This is not the best decision but an understandable one for those who are left to base replenishment decisions on protecting against personal "noise" factors when past stock-outs have occurred. In such cases, then clearly management is not being involved both strategically and operationally in the business.

It needs to be realised here that the supply lead-time is the total time from the start, of determining the need, to the end, of the product being available for use. This is shown overleaf.

Supply and Supplier Lead Times

- Time decide need
- Time place order
- Time order received
- Time order despatched
- Time product received $\Big\}$ Supplier LT
- Time available for issue
- Time payment is available to supplier $\Big\}$ Supply LT

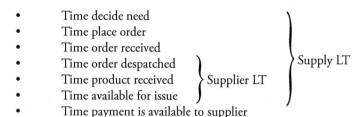

Supply lead time therefore involves many processes such as:
- internal processes of determining when to order, requisitions and authority "signing off" up to, the placing of an order.
- the external supplier lead time from order receipt, to the delivering of the goods
- the internal process of receiving, checking and placing into store and notifying the system and users that the product is available for issue

Supply lead-time is a therefore a topic that procurement is actively involved in; not only with much of the above processing but also in dealing with the external suppliers.

Service levels/availability

In determining order quantities, especially for random/independent demand, what is important is the effect on the level of safety stock required, as shown below.

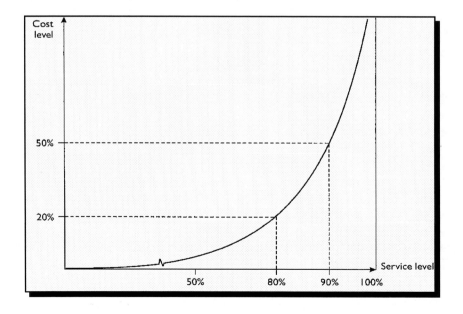

For example, a service level availability increase from 95 to 98% (plus 3%) means a 25% increase in the extra safety stock to be carried to satisfy the random demand.

Increasing service levels gives an exponential curve relationship in the extra safety stock required, as the relationship is not a straight line; for example, a 3% increase in stock does not equal a 3% increase in the extra safety stock required. For example, there is a huge increase of 226.8 % when moving from 95% to towards the mythical 100% (or 99.99% in statistics, as there is always the probability).

Higher service levels for stock availability with random demand mean proportionately far higher levels of safety stock are carried. The subjective 100 percent availability that is commonly stated as a requirement is therefore a myth for random demand. This must be known about by all people in a company, then, the varied levels can be more objectively accessed.

Of course, the idea of anyone setting say a 90% service level for stock availability is fraught with problems for customers and for internal sales/marketing departments. All they rightly expect is 100% service and levels below this mean little to them. The key aspect here is that customers will always get there demand requirements satisfied and how we deal with the other say 10%, will influence how the level is set in the first place, what the extra costs are for maintaining higher levels stock and also how the supply chain is operated. With the acceptance of back-ordering this will often provide an acceptable service for non-stocks with a firm date for delivery.

In many companies the majority of profit will also come from a relatively small number of lines; the 80/20 rule again. So here safety stock levels can be set to minimise the value that may be on back order and minimises the cost to the company. Lost sales for retail companies are however extremely difficult to analyse and some companies may see it is better to let a competitor have such sales to prevent the high cost of stocking relatively slow moving low profit lines.

How much stock should be held?

Looking at this simply, there are three basic aspects to be considered here by procurement (or by who ever places the orders):

1) If decoupling supply/demand, then we need enough to cover for the difference between the input and output rates. This is called bulk or quantity (Q) stock and is the inventory to be used for routine demand consumption.

2) If uncertainty with supply, then we need to have cover for the expected use during the supply lead time. This is called safety stock (SS) and is held to cover the supply.

3) If uncertainty with demand, then we need enough to provide availability until the next delivery. This is also called Safety stock, and is being held here to cover the demand.

Any one or all of the above three situations may be involved and also illustrates the two types of stock that were identified earlier:
- Cycle stock (or replenishment or lot size stocks). These are held as a result of the in and out movements and involve decisions on order quantity and frequency

- Safety Stock (or buffer or fluctuation stocks). These are held as a "cushion" between supply and demand (either or for both) and involve decisions on Supply Lead Time (SLT), any Supply Lead Time Variability (SLTV) and the amount of demand that will occur during the SLT/SLTV

It should be appreciated that these two types of stock are not held separately, but are only separated out in the calculation for the when and how much to order stock decisions. Meanwhile, inventory is given a wider consideration in the book, "Excellence in Inventory Management; how to minimise costs and maximise service" (2007) by Emmett and Granville. We will also return to inventory shortly when we look at the ordering activity in the procurement cycle.

Managing supplier relationships

Many companies need to remember that they are only as good as their suppliers. After all what comes in to an organisation does eventually create what goes out; the "rubbish-in-rubbish-out" analogy again. This means therefore that relationships with suppliers require managing effectively and this needs to be done on a selective basis; as we examine below.

Managing short-term relationships

Short-term relationships should require only a minimum involvement from procurement as the onus could be placed on the supplier to maintain control. For example with routine items, the supplier should offer or suggest ways of managing the quality and supply of the goods or materials being delivered. Where items being purchased are routine and commodity type items, then there is competition in the marketplace meaning the supplier could be willing to do this as a source of their competitive advantage.

Spot-buys will be based on primary requirements for low risk items. There will not be such a great emphasis on comprehensive specifications or standards. In these circumstances, suppliers should be encouraged to provide reports on their progress and suggest improvements. These reports should be broken down to list key criteria including delivery performance and where appropriate, cost savings.

Managing long-term relationships

Long-term relationships will need to be established to ensure supply, to reduce costs and to add value to both organisations. In a production environment, failure to establish these relationships will result in restricted productivity and added costs.

With bottleneck and critical items, security of supply with reliable fixed and known supply lead times is important, especially where, as with bottleneck items, there are only a few suppliers or where, for example with global markets, there may be risks in guaranteeing the supply. In relation to the total goods and services being procured, there will be relatively few relationships and in relation to spend and risk, the number of items or materials may be relatively few in comparison to the total number of products being procured.

Long-term relationships will require total commitment from the buyer, their organisation and supplier. Detailed plans will need to be produced to ensure both parties understand their responsibilities, objectives and targets. Initially the customer/user, in liaison with the buyer, will draw up these plans. Milestone events and timings should be included.

An open and honest approach to the relationship must be maintained to ensure that maximum benefit is achieved for both parties. Both parties must be motivated towards each other. The supplier must be motivated and focused towards the buyer's goals and both organisational structures and cultures should lend themselves to support this motivation.

Supplier development

Supplier development follows a series of steps designed to get the best from a supplier and is especially useful for the high risk critical and bottleneck items. It will therefore be considered for the more strategic supplier relationships. This topic is of major importance in terms of improving procurement and supply chain performance; we have therefore devoted a whole chapter to it in section 4.0.

Case study: Philips

Philips is a global operator in the electronics market with factories all over the world. In order to compete and to ensure customer satisfaction, Philips has to manage its quality and procurement strategy very carefully. The company recognises that customer satisfaction depends on the quality of what happens on the production line, which in turn depends on the performance of suppliers. If any of the links in the chain break down or fail to meet the required standard, then all the glossy advertising in the world is not going to make up for the customer's disappointment in a product that is unavailable, or does not work properly, or fails to meet their technical expectations. Total quality, therefore, is an ingrained philosophy throughout Philips' operations, resulting in better products and better processes. 'Philips Quality' has five simple, but important principles:

(a) Strive for excellence
(b) Customer first
(c) Demonstrate leadership
(d) Value people
(e) Supplier partnership

Directly or indirectly, many of these principles could not be properly implemented without good relationships with the right suppliers. Philips cultivates supplier relationships based on trust and Cooperation, sharing experience and expertise to benefit not only the buyer and the supplier, but also the end customer. Together, Philips and its suppliers develop technology, solve problems, learn from experience and try to avoid errors and misunderstandings.

Clearly, Philips cannot develop and maintain deep relationships with every one of its suppliers. Instead, it assesses its suppliers to discover which ones are the most important in terms of their strategic significance to Philips' business. These receive the most attention and investment in relationship building. Philips has three categories of supplier:

1. Supplier-partners: this might be the smallest group, but these are the most important suppliers and Philips builds intense, involved relationships with them. An important focus of the Cooperation is innovation, the development of new expertise and new opportunities. These suppliers might well have essential knowledge and/or expertise that Philips could not otherwise access or develop for itself. This makes these suppliers extremely significant strategically as their loss could seriously undermine Philips' current business and future direction.

2. Preferred suppliers: these suppliers are less important, but there is still good reason for Philips to work closely with them on issues such as quality, logistics and price to gain mutual benefit. The supplier does adapt itself to suit Philips' requirements, to some extent, but there is not the same mutual dependence as in the first category.

3. Commercial suppliers: these are the least important suppliers and although Philips will encourage better performance in terms of quality etc., it is unlikely to get involved in helping the supplier to achieve it.

Philips also emphasises the importance of supplier revaluation as a basis for improving future performance. A supplier's actual performance is measured against mutually agreed targets in terms of quality, logistics, costs and responsiveness.

Procurement: an outline strategy

The following "ideal-typical" view presents an overview and outline strategy for procurement. As with all ideal typical views, it is not "absolute" but is intended to demonstrate the alternative methods available and that "one size does not fit all":

Aspect	Bottleneck items	Critical items	Routine items	Leverage items
Overall aim	Ensure and secure supply. Reduce the risk by looking for new sources so that can diversify from the bottleneck suppliers	Form closer relationships to get competitive advantage from the supply chain and ensure continual supply	Reliable and efficient supply using simplified ordering processes: Multi sourcing and simplifying/ automating the ordering process	Exploit buying advantage, buy at lowest cost: Multi sourcing for standard, easily available products.
Risks from non supply	High to medium	High	Low	Medium to Low
Suppliers numbers	Few specialist suppliers, possibly a monopoly market	More suppliers	Many suppliers	Many competing suppliers
Power	With supplier	Inter-dependant	Independence	With buyer

Supplier Relations	Close and collaborate with preferred suppliers.	Long term "partnerships" and collaborate with few trustworthy and reliable suppliers.	Short term with procurement "Setting up the deal" with orders/ transactions direct between users/suppliers.	Short term "deals" with possible buying consortiums, alliances, reverse auctions etc; whatever gives the greater leverage.
Buyers requirements	Certainty of supply.	Secure and continuity of supply.	Simplify product variety and the order/ supply process.	Low cost supplies.
Inventory	Repeat predictable usage. Need reliable long term forecasting. Maybe hold large stocks as insurance.	Repeat predictable usage. Work close together to minimise stock holding. Maybe hold large stocks as insurance.	Low stocks with JIT Supply. Maybe hold consignment stocks.	Low stocks with possible 2 bin or VMI and JIT and consignment stocks.
Staffing	Hi level buyers with market knowledge and contingency plans	Top level buyers for the start up, implementation and monitoring	Low level buyers, procurement maybe contracted out.	Medium level buyers
Procurement methods	Elemental questionnaires, RFI/RFQ. Negotiation. Supply agreements.	Comprehensive questionnaires. Competitor analysis. Negotiation. Blanket agreements.	RFI/RFQ with ITT and competitive bidding.	Some RFI/RFQ. Elemental questionnaires. ITT and competitive bidding and reverse E auctions.
Orders handled	Standard POs, Framework agreements, medium term contracts. Quick responses.	Call offs	User direct call offs with agreements; otherwise spot buys / self managed	Standard POs.

Procurement: our vision

There are many things we would like to see happen to improve the performance of procurement and in so doing, the standing of the function in organisations.

Whilst we see some organisations are already involved in areas covered in our vision below, unfortunately the majority are still sometime away and regrettably many of these, still, show no movement towards our vision. As visions are meant to inspire, then our hope is that the following views may provide such inspiration:

- Procurement will champion early involvement with customers and will be proactive to meet anticipated customer requirements. Procurement is far more than the reactive placing of orders and the passing around of paperwork to execute the requisitions of users.

- Procurement will provide customers with value by delivering a quality product at the right time and at the right price. Procurement involves more than buying at the lowest cost
- Procurement will not call suppliers vendors, as vendors are those who only seek to match the specification. Procurement will therefore recognise that suppliers are critically important in the provision of new ideas, innovation and value that can increase the performance of the organisation
- Procurement will share with suppliers a joint common agenda; to meet customer requirements. Procurement will recognise that its own organisations performance is indelibly connected to the performance of its suppliers
- Procurement will be committed to its key suppliers for mutual benefit and gain over the medium to long term and will work together for continuous improvements year on year by having a joint restless search for inter-linked improvements
- Procurement will ensure that "fit for purpose," supplier selection and evaluation is undertaken and that this key activity is not rule bound or covered by restrictive bureaucratic procedures that are now out of date
- Procurement will recognise that the supply chain is a series of internal and external cross functional processes and procurement will be an active and willing and leading member of the internal cross functional structure that connects to all of the external supply processes
- Procurement will join with the rest of the organisation in recognising:
    - Profit and success only comes from customer satisfaction
    - The organisation and its supply chain are run by people working with other people. How people relate is therefore the key to success.
- Procurement will actively encourage and embrace as the norm:
    - Selective use of technology, for example, E-commerce is used as appropriate for the organisation.
    - Education and training and professional standing with professional certification will be a requirement (as is found with accountancy, legal professions etc).
    - Measuring of supply lead time, their improvement and the removal of all supply lead time variability by negotiating fixed, known and reliable supply lead times with both internal and external parties.
    - Outsourcing of all non core activity, including where required, part or all, of tactical procurement.
    - Continuously review its own activities and practice continuous improvement including searching for procurement best practices in all sectors.
- Procurement will be the sponsors of honest and ethical dealing within their organisation. Procurement will not be seen as "the free lunch guys" or will be involved in any corrupt practices and "under the table deals" that denigrate personal morality, an organisation and society. In this regard we would personally support and commend the honesty and openness shown in the following article.

Case Study: Administrative corruption undermines development

Administrative corruption is undermining development plans and confidence of citizens, according to a police study. "Administrative corruption is one of the most devastating behaviour as it runs counter to development drive," said a study conducted by the Abu Dhabi Police's Centre for Security Research and Studies.

The study, "Security in the face of administrative corruption", cited psychological, environmental and administrative factors as well as poor control and supervision systems, lenient judicial deterrence and weak security organs as main reasons behind administrative corruption.

"Administrative corruption poses real threats not only to the security and stability of the international community but also to its democratic institutions, moral principles, justice, socio-economic and political development and rule of law," the study noted. "Rampancy of bribery, nepotism, embezzlement and abuse of power lead to failure of development projects and hamper socio-economic development," the study said. The Abu Dhabi Police's control and supervision departments are working hard to cut out roots of corruption. Special anti-corruption sections were set up out of the belief that reform of the society depends on the level of fighting the phenomenon of corruption.

The study called for adoption of integrated strategy for administrative reform based on fighting red tape and introduction of strict penalties against corrupt people.

Source Gulf Today 2 August 2005

Case Study: IBM & Procurement

One of the world's largest organisations, IBM, has transformed itself over the years to stay competitive in its industry. Specifically, since the early 1990s, the procurement organisation has gone through a transformation, including a phase of process design, a phase of deployment, and a phase (ongoing) of Web integration.

Company Information
IBM Procurement worldwide consists of more than 3,700 individuals, with a presence in 72 countries. Currently, the structure of IBM Procurement is in three main sections:
- sourcing component
- client component (sourcing for those clients who have outsourced their procurement
  to IBM)

- centralised operations centre

Global spend managed is approximately $40 billion, of which about one third is in Europe.

Operations

One exciting aspect of IBM Procurement operations, implemented in the past three years, is this centralised operations centre in Budapest, Hungary, supporting the European, Middle East, and African (EMEA) regions (for all indirect spend).

While the sourcing groups have strategic responsibility, including global commodity councils and managing the supply base, the operations centre executes all the steps related to building the purchase order and ensuring everything is communicated to the supplier. It also handles all questions related to purchase orders and invoices.

The centre operates in 26 languages, with various individuals assigned to each supported country For example, there are two people supporting all the requests coming out of Belgium. The procurement organisation in Belgium has specified individuals who interface with the operations centre to field questions or help it understand requisitions that come through. The operations centre is essentially the purchase competency centre.

Because this model is relatively new, there is still a learning curve to determine what spend elements are handled in country, versus, the Budapest operations centre. There are some instances where, for legal reasons, a buy must be generated locally, so then the operations centre is not utilised.

One powerful tool that is used by the operations centre is a sourcing feed database (SFD). Through this database, IBM collects as much information as possible from suppliers, such as potential pricing. IBM might send out requests to multiple suppliers asking them to quote all sorts of materials and services. This data then goes through the SFD to the Budapest operations centre.

Then, as purchase orders come through (from any supplier, whether or not it was one that responded with earlier data), the centre can determine if that price is within the reasonable range or appropriate. Twice a year, price standards are reviewed as "reality check" for actual versus negotiated prices.

In addition, the information gathered through the SFD becomes extremely valuable when the sourcing group renegotiates contracts or does strategic sourcing activities.

Source: Roberta J.Duffy, the Centre for Advanced Purchasing Studies in Purchasing and Supply Solutions, undated, in 2007, article entitled "Operational Excellence in Procurement"

Action Time: VMC Ltd.

VMC Limited produces specialised medical equipment. Previously the company has been highly profitable but recently has suffered from the arrival of new competitors and a reduction in the market share. At the same time, costs have been increasing and current sales of £42 million are declining. This combination is potentially disastrous and if allowed to continue, may result in the collapse of the organisation.

At a senior management crisis meeting, the MD put the position into sharp focus and established a survival plan which included the following:
* VMC must break even in the final period of this year
* Next year, profits need to be 5%, increased sales of 20% with substantial economies in labour, material and overheads

Later that day the MD called in the procurement manger. Procurement was told they would have to be the driving forces in the survival effort as it would be at six months before sales would get moving. Every aspect of materials was to be considered and every opportunity for savings was to be explored, including negotiations, inventories, contracting out, in fact, anything, that would generate savings and reduce cost immediately.

The procurement manager started with a review of the procurement organisation. The annual spend was £24 million. VMC buying a wide range of materials and components, with a major spend being on components for printed circuits, circuit boards, stainless steel components, non-ferrous casings, stampings, fasteners and sub-assemblies. A wide range of suppliers was used with a supplier base of 2600 suppliers. All items are sourced competitively with at least two suppliers for each item.

VMC also produced its own printed circuit boards in house from the purchased components and blank boards. They have never looked at outsourcing to a specialist circuit board manufacturer, which would eliminate the assembly work and all the associated costs.

The next executive committee of the organisation meeting was in one week's time and the procurement manager then, has to produce the outline plan.

Task
Discuss the ways in which the procurement function can improve the supply chain of the organisation.

Action Time: Anglo Oil

Recently, Anglo Oil decided to seek the advice of a team of procurement consultants. Their advice was quite simple. "What you are doing, you are doing well, but you need to be more strategic". Anglo Oil took this advice seriously and asked their procurement teams to put together a procurement strategy.

The Company was organised along geographical lines. HO was in London and then there were overseas offices in the United States, Africa, the Far East and Middle East. Each overseas office had a supply manager who reported to the local Head of Operations and who also had a dotted line responsibility to the Head of Supply based at HO.

At the next procurement get-together following the consultants' report, the over seas supply managers each agreed to submit their thoughts on what the strategy should be. It was quite clear, following the debate which took place at the meeting, that they had different ideas on the way forward. The Head of Supply agreed to review the strategies and then discuss them with the Head of Operations before agreeing the next steps.

The Submissions

When the submissions came in, they were different. Different formats, different ideas, different directions for the Company to take.

The Far East submission was based on a form of devolution. The key theme was that centralisation was not policy at the moment that in other sectors people were moving towards empowerment and, therefore, each of the overseas procurement operations should be empowered to do their own thing.

The African view was totally different. As the organisation was buying essentially the same things, it made sense to centralise. All of the contracting should be done at the centre and the role of the regions was to call off against the contracts, handle the few local arrangements and manage stock.

The team from the Gulf had heard of something called the Centre Led Action Network (CLAN). Although no-one could find an example of one that really worked well, what it involved was some form of co-operative arrangement driven by the centre who would act as facilitators and co-ordinators.

The US team were into outsourcing. Their view was that supply was not a core activity and therefore it should be market tested. There is any number of organisations who would do the supplying for a fee and this would then free up resources to do more important things for the Company. Obviously, the strategy submissions were more detailed than this. They also covered a lot more ground; development needs, policies, approaches and techniques, information systems, etc., but the bare bones are as described above.

Task

Put yourselves in the position of the Head of Supply and the Head of Operations at HO. You have received four strategy submissions, all pulling the organisation in different directions. You are required to do two things:

1. Explain how you believe the two heads should assess the four strategies.

2. Explain the steps you think should be taken when putting a procurement strategy together.

2.0. The procurement cycle: the preorder steps

This part of the book will examine the stages in the procurement cycle and start by looking at the needs and total cost models. We continue with specifying, specifications and standards before considering supplier and market conditions and sourcing requirements and options. We next look at enquiries by tendering, evaluation and appraising by using weighting factors and we then finish this part of the book with a look at negotiations.

The procurement cycle stages

The procurement process follows the following procurement cycle:

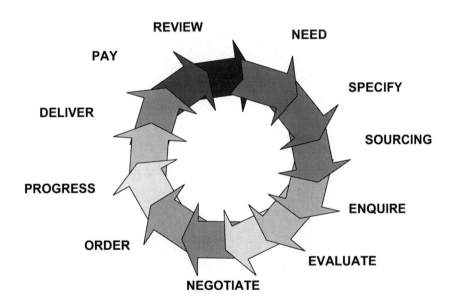

The procurement process cycle therefore involves the following three stages:

The Preorder stage

Need/Requirements – Specify – Sourcing – Enquiry – Evaluation – Negotiation/Selecting (these are covered in this section).

The time taken to complete this preorder stage can be long, especially with contract approvals for new projects.

The following example from a company in the Oil & Gas sector illustrates their contract approval lead times.

Contract Approval Stage	Involves	Time
Receipt of the requisition.	Agreeing the specification / scope of work (SOW)	8-12 weeks
The strategy approval of the scope of work/specification.	Internal approval	1 week
	Partner approval	6-8 weeks
	Government approval	12-16 weeks
Supplier/ Market approach e.g. with ITT	Sending to receiving the ITT response.	Variable, but say 1-4 weeks
Receipt of the ITT to the award recommendation. e.g. use of Tender committees	Internal approval	1 week
	Partner approval	6-8 weeks
	Government approval	12-16 weeks
The contract award	Contract placed	1 week
Total Time scale		48-67 weeks

After the preorder stage, the following stages are involved:

The Order stage
Ordering – Progressing/Expediting – Delivery/Receipt (these are covered in chapter 3.0.)

The Post order stage:
Payment/Invoice verification – Reviewing (these are also covered in chapter 3.0.)

Needs

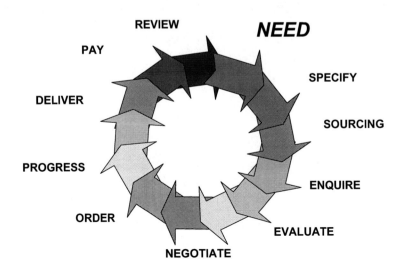

Handling Orders and Requisitions

An initial requisition may be used to identify the user or customer needs by for example, simply defining the product coding required.

As a simple and cost effective form of ordering, requisitions may also be used for low to medium spend items, for example, in a production environment, as shown later, the Bill of Materials in MRP will form the basis for production requirements. The details on a requisition include:

- Name and details of the customer/user. This ensures that costs are internally allocated correctly, a contact is also available should there be any queries.
- Item details. This needs to be provided in enough depth to enable sourcing from a competitive market. Too much detail will restrict the buyer's ability to identify potential sources.
- Delivery details. This will be required either direct to customer or into storage. It will include the time of delivery and instructions regarding changes and late arrivals.
- Signature of authority. Procurement will maintain a list of those with the authority to spend budgets and where applicable the spend limits that apply.

However, more complex project and contract plans will be used for high value, high-risk contracts. In these cases a thorough analysis will be carried out prior to making the final requests for products and materials.

Products or services

There are some important differences between products and services. Products are those things bought and owned that will satisfy a want or need and will have the following characteristics:

- Features; are those characteristics beyond the product's basic functioning
- Performance; is the designed output levels that may have been engineered into the product to give a specific level of reliability for given operating conditions
- Conformance; this is how far the product's design and operating characteristics match the requirements
- Durability; is the product's expected operating life
- Reliability; the probability that a product will not malfunction or fail within a specified period of time
- Reparability; the ease of fixing a product that malfunctions or fails
- Style – how well the product looks and feels to the buyer

Services are the performance or act from one to another that does not result in ownership. Services are an intangible exchange that may or may not be connected to a physical product; they are perishable and cannot be stored. Compared to products, the performance of services may be often highly variable and unreliable, as products can be engineered and certified/tested to give a standard and known reliable performance.

Services have the following characteristics:
- Are intangible:
  - cannot really be seen, tested, touched, felt etc.
  - have to be experienced/bought
- Are produced and consumed at the same time
- May have a variable performance
- Are perishable and cannot be stored

Services involve the following:
- Delivering; how well the product or service is delivered to the customer
- Installing; the work done to make a product or service operational in its planned location
- Training; ensuring the customer's employees can use products properly and efficiently
- Consulting; data, information systems and advising services that the seller offers
- Repairing – describes the quality of repair service available to buyers of the company's product.

Specify

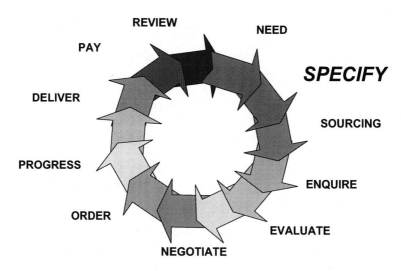

Specifications and Standards

Product and service specifications and standards will need to be identified in liaison with the user or customer.

Specifications are a description of what a customer/user wants and therefore communicate what is required, to meet the needs. They are a statement of need from internal sources that is to be satisfied by the procurement of external resources.

Specifications do need to be clear and to communicate; they may therefore take the form of industry used standards, or of coding/classifying products; they can also identify potential sources to provide materials and products.

Standards differ from specifications. Whilst every standard is specification, not every specification is a standard as standards are all about obtaining the expected performance or the expected output from the use of a product or service. Standards have also often been originated by organisations such as The British Standards Institution (BSI), The International Standards Organisation (ISO) as well more industry led bodies such as with drugs (e.g. BPC), insurance (e.g. Lloyds), and mechanical engineering (IMechE). Where such standards are found, it will usually imply that there are many supply sources; it can however also mean that the use of such a standard may preclude other suppliers, which in turn, may be against legislation on preventing competition.

Where standards are a part of specifications, it is useful to check that the current version is being used as standards are often regularly updated.

Product coding

A company may have a method of identifying products through the use of some form of coding system. The coding system maybe a unique one (for example, the Materials and Equipment Standards and Codes (MESC) 10 numbers coding used worldwide within the Shell group, see below) or it may be a coding system that conforms to industry standards (for example, the UK food industry bar code labelling of products).

Whatever coding method is used, the reasons for it are universal:
- Provides a unique identifier per product line/item
- Prevents duplication of stocks; for example by ensuring coding is used by suppliers and customers/users
- Provides standardisation; for example, coding a "new" product for the first time can identify that similar products already exist and therefore possible duplication is avoided
- Simplifies product identification for all suppliers, customers and users
- Can help in determining stock locations; for example within a store holding engineering items where all those products in one main coding category are kept together
- Assists in pricing and costing; for example with food supermarkets EPOS systems

Example: Shell Material Equipment Standards Code (MESC)
Materials understood across +130 world wide companies in 94 countries covering over 125,000 items:

To classify:
- Main group XX
- Sub group XX
- Sub-sub group XX

To identify:
* Item number XXX

To categorise e.g. Who created, special conditions etc:
* Indicator X

Example for item 76.05/39.120.1
> 76 = fittings and flanges
> 05 = screwed API steel
> 39 = elbows 90 degrees
> 120 = 2 inch. class 3000
> 1= item is centrally coded

Determine the specification types

Specifications should comply with the following criteria:

* Are the requirements stated clearly, unambiguously and with only the essential characteristics stated?
* Will it enable suppliers to decide and cost their offer?
* Will the suppliers offer be able to be evaluated against the specification?
* Does the specification enable opportunity for all suppliers to make an offer?
* Does it include any legal requirements?

The development of specifications will usually require liaison between users, procurement and maybe potential suppliers. Trade associations and other users can also help, as can independent people who can check and verify the final draft specifications.

Specifications may take the form of the following:

* Technical specifications: such as a highly detailed description; e.g. engineering products
* Sample specifications: such as to assess the suitability of chemicals or fabric
* Brand specifications: such as a specific brand which may denote the customer's preference and identify a standard. As this will however limit the supplier options, then any such use will need to have been specially justified
* Design specifications: such as to identify dimensions and outlines
* Functional specifications: such as to ensure the product performs 'fit for purpose' or what it has to achieve
* Form specifications: such as shape and appearance
* Performance specifications: such as the output range within which the item must function

Role of procurement

From the users' specifications or by using existing coding, procurement is then better able to:

- Provide information on available supply
- Provide a supplier appraisal
- Identify risks on suppliers and products
- Identify where the business able to standardise

Ultimately, procurement aims to procure products and materials which are fit for purpose and the characteristics that give this, may be determined by the specification. Once the product or service requirements have been established /specified, it is important to summarise the details with the user or customer to confirm that what is being sourced is to the specification they require. Additionally, lines of communication will need to be established to ensure there are minimum delays should problems occur and areas of responsibility, should be highlighted and confirmed.

Performance specifications/contracts

The nature of the product/service being procured may determine that a performance related specification is required, perhaps becoming part of the formal final contract. Performance being, the output(s) required from the product or service, therefore, the aim here is to provide a clear and objective view of the expected output.

The following questions can be asked. The answers will assist in determining the objective performance outcomes, such as the following:
- Clarity; what has to be done? This must be very clear as well as, who is accountable with clear levels of responsibility and authority.
- Competence; do the knowledge and skills exist?
- Consequences; why is it being done? These must be clear.
- Competition; what other tasks are there to do? Prioritising may be needed.
- Cooperation; who else is to be involved?
- Control; how is it known that a desired and satisfactory end has been reached?
- Commitment; do they have the confidence to do it willingly and well?
- Context; are the right surroundings and support available?

On performance specifications, in the UK public sector for example, the provision of services such as ambulance, police, hospitals and fire rescue, have used performance contracts widely in recent years. The aim here is to ensure that government objectives can be maximised by the setting of targets to be achieved that will bring improved performance.

These expected conditions can however fail to materialise when for example, managers with information and bargaining power and with no strong incentive to "comply", can manipulate targets to ensure performance is judged satisfactorily.

For performance specifications to work correctly therefore, objectives must be explicitly stated with assigned weighting and priorities translated into clear and agreed performance improvement targets, perhaps also with clear incentives and disincentives about compliance.

Performance contracts

Performance contracts are an enforceable agreement between suppliers and buyers as they link incentives and disincentives to the contractual performance outputs. The supplier is required to provide guarantees, for example, a timely completion of a project and for the achievement of performance specifications, for example on quality and cost.

Liquated damages may be a part of such contracts; this is a pre-determined estimate of loss by the buyer and payable by the supplier in the event of failure to meet agreements. Liquated damages for delays are determined by a time scale (e.g. daily) and normally will equate to the buyers financial loss. Liquated damages for failure to meet performance are normally based on an amount for each percentage point the failure falls below the guaranteed performance level.

Differences between Technical and Performance Specification

The following shows the important differences between the two types of specifications:

	Technical specifications	Performance specifications
Supplier	Receives an exact and clear specification.	Responds to the outcomes required in the required operating conditions and environment
Buyer	Certainty of what is being bought. However these may not the "best", as other options that may satisfy the need are excluded	Must very clearly specify the requirements and outcomes needed
Technical risk	With the buyer	With the supplier
Supplier Innovation	Low/little	Higher/likely
Examples	Simple and branded products	Complex projects

It should be noted that the above technical specifications and the subsequent, technical assessment in the evaluation process, are different.

As we will see later, the technical assessment looks at things such as compliance with the specification (and this is either the technical or the performance specification), and also the performance parameters of the specification.

Sourcing

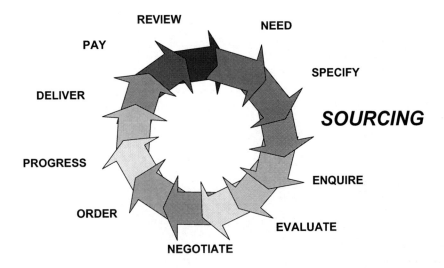

Supplier & Market Conditions

The number and location of suppliers will influence the price of the goods in the marketplace. There are often other buyers for materials and products and this will ensure a review by the supplier of how "attractive" the buyer could be as a customer. For example, markets may be expanding or contracting, this will influence the number of suppliers. The power of each party also has a part to play, for example:

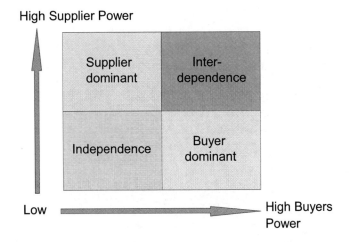

Whilst we return to this power aspect in the final part of this book, the following differences can be seen:

Where the buyer is dominant there is:
- A small number of big buyers
- Buying of a large percentage of a sellers output
- Ease for buyer to switch
- Many sources of supply
- Low transaction costs
- A "take it or leave it" view from the buyer

Where the seller is dominant there is:
- A small number of big sellers
- Supplying to many buyers
- Difficulty for buyers to switch
- Few sources of supply
- High transaction costs
- An "enforced" view from the supplier

Supplier Availability

Procurement needs to be aware of the expansion or contraction of the markets from which they are procuring. There may be several reasons why the markets appear unattractive to suppliers including:
- The standards that need to be met
- The amount of competition
- The investment that needs to be made
- A low profit level

It should also never be assumed by buyers that every supplier is "desperate" to supply them with products or service. Suppliers also have a view of their market and therefore this will affect a suppliers positioning towards buyers, for example:

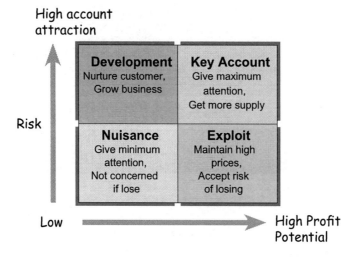

PESTLE Analysis

Once procurement is aware of the number of suppliers and buyers vying for business in the market place, along with the entry and exit of possible suppliers, they will need to consider factors that affect the sectors in which they are buying. PESTLE analysis maybe used here, this involves the following:

- **P**olitical considerations, such as government policies in the countries from which they are buying.
- **E**conomic considerations, regarding the employment of finite resources and the effect on supply and demand.
- **S**ocio-cultural considerations, for the people employed to produce and manufacture the materials and products along with the customer base.
- **T**echnological advancements and the possibility of alternatives.
- **L**egal requirements and contractual documentation and processes.
- **E**nvironmental considerations and policies of the suppliers and the procurement organisation.

Many of these factors interrelate, as the following discussion shows:

- Political Issues: Governmental decisions will influence the economy of the countries where suppliers are located, and also, possibly, in the country of the buyers.
- Economic Issues: The levels of trade, inflation, unemployment and exchange rates will all influence costs, price and profit; for example, countries controlling key raw materials such as oil/gas, will carry greater economic power.
- Socio/Cultural Issues: Core cultural values will influence people's attitudes to what and where they buy. Attitudes toward foreign cultures will influence trade as do ethical buying polices.
- Technological Issues: Procurement will be concerned with technological advancements to remain competitive. Alternative technology will be considered for value add or cost reduction.
- Legal Issues: Procurement must understand the laws under which the contracts they make are governed. The terms and conditions, which have been applied, must safeguard the buying organisation.
- Environmental Issues: Environmental procurement policies can offer differentiation in the market place.

Once information has been gathered on the market conditions, it will be possible to compare this to the internal capabilities, as opportunities may exist to contract out non-core activities or services, such as a make or buy decision.

Make or Buy?

Strategic make or buy decisions will involve the overall organisational strategy; tactical make or buy decisions will however involve the need for external investment and the Total Cost of Ownership may be applied. Operational make or buy decisions however, will be based on the capacity and capability of the buying organisation, relative to, the analysis by the procurement department of the potential suppliers.

Sub-contracting may be appropriate where the internal resources are finite, as the costs and risks will here clearly indicate that this option is the most viable. Alternatively, the sub-contractor may have greater experience. Buyers will need to ensure that performance measures have been clearly defined for sub-contracting and that all legal considerations have been covered in the contract.

Procurement Options from Economic Sectors

Prices will overall be governed by normal economic supply and demand elasticity.
In the primary sector that covers raw materials from farming/fishing (food, beverages, and forestry), quarrying/mining (minerals, coals, metals) or drilling (oil, gas, water); then, a dictated market price may be found. This in turn works through into the secondary sector in the conversion of these raw materials into products, therefore affecting the price make-up of components and finished products.

Purchasers from the manufacturing sector require a good understanding of cost breakdowns, so that a realistic price is negotiated; whereas, procurement from the service sector requires greater emphasis on performance definition and measurement. We look at price analysis later in chapter 4.0.

Procurement Options of Existing or New Sources

Some of the advantages of using existing suppliers are that they can provide information on performance from the existing historical data. Additionally they will have knowledge of the normal practices policies and expectations.

If changing to a new supplier, then there are costs of changing, as well as, an element of risk. However, new suppliers need not be seen as "disadvantaged" and markets need to be monitored so that opportunities can be developed where spend, risk or usage mean a change is needed.

Procurement Options of Local or Global Solutions

Local suppliers have the advantage of offering reduced lead times and lower transport costs, against with the risks and costs associated with global logistics. Global suppliers however, do offer opportunities in lower prices achieved from the use of cheaper resources, materials and components. Fluctuating exchange rates would need to be taken into account along with lead time and legal aspects (foreign business law can be complex).

Procurement Options of Single or Multiple Sources

Multiple sourcing encourages competition and innovation; it also protects against the risk of having "all ones eggs in one basket". Single sourcing should only be considered where:
*   The market dictates there is only one supplier
*   The value and usage defines the material or product as critical
*   A long-term relationship can be negotiated.

Procurement Options: conclusion

The available options for sourcing will be affected by the product or service being sourced, its availability, location, the number of suppliers, and buyers along with market growth. New opportunities for sourcing must always be considered for materials and products that are critical to the company. As global markets are becoming the norm for larger organisations, then this offers potential new suppliers and possibilities of negotiation for larger volumes. Additionally, the growing trend for smaller supplier bases with closer links requires a more intensive supplier management with longer-term relationships.

Enquiry & Evaluation

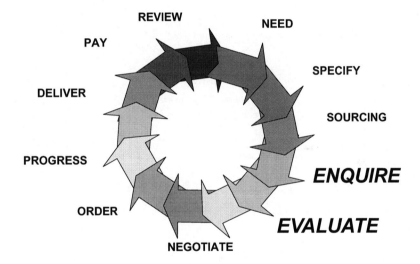

Enquiry by requesting for information

This may take the form of pre-qualifying suppliers and is used to invite suppliers to apply for potential business. It ensures that supplier conform to certain required criteria, before, further detailed information is provided to them. It uses a standard request form that should make clear to all who receive it:
- The mandatory conditions to be fulfilled
- Which parts require a response
- The form and length of responses required

Questions can be asked that will require explanation answers, so that the ability of the supplier can be better judged against the following criteria:
- Financial position
- Previous experience
- References

An example follows of a pre-qualification that covers the supplier capability for offering a freight forwarding service:

1.0. Companies outline of requirements:
(This is to give the suppliers an indication of what is on offer and what is required from them)

2.0. Supplier details
(This is to get basic supplier details such as contacts, company structure, and professional qualification/affiliations)

3.0. Financial details
(This is to get details on financial support/backing, insurance covers/liability)

4.0. Equipment and Facilities
(This is to get details on the necessary equipment and facilities)

5.0. Management Skills
(Key Contacts and their skills/experience of the people who will be handling our business on a day to day basis, Training and development policy, technical questions may be asked here to "test" the management capability)

6.0. Referees/references

7.0. Customer Service/reliability
(Statement of how you would prefer to work with us, IS 9002 or other external accreditations, methods to improving service/performance)

In making and dealing with enquiries to suppliers, then approaches need to be seen as ethical and a "level playing field" must be maintained for all proposals. A set procedure should be laid down to deal with the response proposals based on size and spend. Analysis of the proposals can include commodity value, delivery, quality, technical merit, after sales service, security of supply, health and safety and environmental polices.

Enquiry by tender

Tendering is defined as:

"The procedure, by which potential suppliers are invited to make a firm unequivocal offer of the price and term which, on acceptance, shall be the basis of the subsequent contract."

If tendering is required, then an appropriate tendering method must be used. This may be subject to specific directives, for example, from government in the public sector.

Competitive tendering is a formal process involving the following steps:
- identification and selection of suppliers from whom to seek bids
- issue of invitation to tender (ITT) documentation to the selected suppliers
- receipt and assessment of tenders
- selection of a preferred tender

Competitive tendering aims to obtain compliant tenders from qualified tenderers in a single round of tendering. The invitation to tender document may be only sent to those who have been pre-qualified (as discussed above); a procedure that will often save much time and effort for both parties. To achieve this, the best available information must be prepared and issued under identical conditions to all those being invited to tender. The key principles for tender invitation and submission are as follows:
- conditions for all tenderers should be the same
- confidentiality should be respected by all parties
- sufficient time should be allowed to prepare tenders
- sufficient information should be provided for the preparation of tenders
- the terms and conditions of contract should be clearly specified

All the purchaser's requirements should be set out in the Invitation to Tender (ITT) document and is made up as follows:
- instructions to tenderer
- form of tender
- contract award criteria
- technical specification
- drawings
- health and safety plan
- pricing schedules
- terms and conditions of contract

The formal procedure for the tender must be stated in the instructions provided to the suppliers with the same instructions provided to all tenderers, along with identical details regarding the buyer's requirements.

There are three general methods used to obtain tenders, as follows:
- Open tenders; these invite everyone and are only really useful where a small number of suppliers are expected to respond
- Selective tenders; invite those few suppliers who can meet the selecting criteria and have been pre-qualified. Here the number of responses is controlled, saving the high costs of dealing with a large number of responses, as is found with open tenders
- Single tenders; invite one tender to be negotiated. This may be where the technical complexity of the product being bought restricts the marketplace, or where there is a monopoly

Public sector tendering procedures use the following three methods:
- Open tenders; this process may be used where there are few suppliers or the buying organisation is attempting to develop new sources

- Restricted tenders; this limits the number of suppliers to tender, but, according to EU regulations, there must be a sufficient number invited so that the tender is seen as competitive.
- Negotiated tenders; here the buying organisation may negotiate with selected suppliers. This would be used where no tenders had been received through the other methods available, or where a monopoly exists.

Specific timescales will be set and the suppliers informed. Registered post or recorded delivery should be used to return tenders, however email returns being now more widely accepted. Late bids will be rejected unless an extension is given to all applications. This ensures the process is seen to be fair.

In the public sector, two individuals, who should not be involved in the evaluation, will be appointed to open the tenders/access the emails. Tenders should be registered and recorded, with complete details of the supplier. Next, the tenders are examined against the technical and commercial checklist and at this stage; any offers that do not meet these criteria are eliminated. Tenders should be treated as confidential with access restricted to the tender panel with documentation being maintained in its original condition. Tender boards may be multiple in number with varied levels dependant varied dependant on the spend, as per the following example

Example of tender procedures in a Government-owned oil exploration and Production Company:

Spends of over £50000 go via Tender Committees at three levels:
- Internal Tender Committee (ITC); Spend over £50000 to £2 Million. Sign-offs are dependant on managerial grades with break points of up to £500K, up to £1 million and up to £2 million.
- Higher Tender Committee (HTC); £2 to £10 million. Sign off by committee made up of managing directors of government owned companies
- Central Tender Committee (CTC); over £10 million. Chaired by Government and signed off by the Oil Minister.

Where strict and "open" tender procedures are being used, for example in the public sector, then it should be noted that any anomalies in the above tender principles could result in the tender being revoked and the process being re-started.

Evaluation of tenders

These should be conducted as a joint technical and commercial assessment exercise that allows for all criteria that meet requirements. Whilst the assessment process depends on the scope and nature of the contracts, normally there will be a technical assessment and a commercial assessment. The technical assessment looks at things such as:
- compliance with the specification (and this is either the technical or the performance specification)
- performance parameters
- quality

56

- maintenance over the operating life

The commercial assessment will look at things such as:
- terms of payment
- programme risks
- any commercial qualifications

The objective of the tender assessment is for the purchaser to establish which the best offer is. If price is the only criterion, then the tenderer submitting the lowest price should be awarded the contract. It is of course not always sufficient to only look at price and where price is only one criterion among several, the purchaser needs to decide the most economically advantageous tender (MEAT) or the best value for money. This means that the tendered prices are only a starting point in the evaluation. To determine MEAT, it is necessary to establish the total cost of ownership or whole-life cost (TCO or WLC).

Factors affecting the immediate cost of acquisition are as follows:
- initial price
- cost of financing
- terms of payment
- performance and technical guarantees
- liquidated damages
- conformance with programme

Medium-term WLC considerations:
- build costs
- running costs
- costs of spares
- operation and maintenance costs
- after-sales service/support

Long-term WLC considerations:
- component replacement life
- retro-fitting costs
- dismantling costs
- disposal costs

The result of the MEAT assessment is to rank tenders received either by price, or in accordance with assessment criteria specified in the invitation to tender documents. This establishes the lowest assessed tender, which is then recommended for the award of contract.

Comparison of tenders is a relatively straightforward exercise but complications can arise when tenderers offer alternatives and options. The financial evaluation of options is carried out in accordance with the same basic principles, but prior to this a decision must be made as to whether the alternative is to be considered. For example, a novel item of plant may be offered on the basis of improved performance and cost saving but this may involve extra costs in redesigning and fitting associated plant. In these instances total acquisition cost (TAC) and total cost of ownership (TCO) can be helpful. Then analysis of acquisition costs, operating costs and disposal will all be considered. It may also be valuable to identify where cost and value are added through the supply chain processes, for example, in the production of the product where a key requirement will be having reliable and fixed/known lead times.

Post-tender negotiation (PTN)

This involves negotiations with tenderers. If undertaken, then it is important that it is carried out in a structured and controlled way to avoid second bidding opportunities at a 'Dutch auction'. Any post-tender negotiation must be carried out on the basis of a recorded plan and strategy, setting out the negotiation objectives and giving the same treatment to all tenderers. Indeed, some have a view that PTN is unethical (as negotiations will often only take place with a "selected few") and PTN is not allowed or practiced formally by some companies and organisations because of this.

Disadvantages of tenders

Tendering may not always give the intended open competition and fairness; major reasons for its use. Indeed tendering may be merely "going through the motions" as tendering processes can be influenced by those who have power and influence over the eventual selection process. Tenders may also be selectively issued and suppliers' responses can be influenced. Additionally I am also reminded of a procurement manager who once said to me, "we are always able to pre-cook the tender board."

The private sector will usually disregard tendering completely and moves straight to negotiating, as they see the following disadvantages of the tendering process:
- Sometimes it is necessary to clarify technical points.
- The supplier may wish to give better alternatives that can only be found when negotiating
- Tendering is slow and expensive to administrate and is also expensive for suppliers.
- Tendering is of no use in a "monopoly"
- Tendering conflicts with "newer" collaboration approaches and working more closely together with suppliers
- Tendering prevents post-tender negotiations

Supplier Appraisal

The supplier appraisal will be governed by the strategic significance of the product or material being sourced. The results will be based on criteria established by the purchaser in liaison with the user or customer and the purchaser's knowledge. Once a list of potential suppliers has been created, it will be necessary to identify which of them is capable of supplying the materials or products to the required standard. This appraisal may of course be undertaken during any tender evaluation process. There is a range of different appraisals that can be carried out and the appropriate option would be chosen by considering the use and the strategic importance of the purchase. The range of appraisals includes the following:

- No appraisal; where the value of the purchase is low and there is no risk in the market place
- Elemental appraisal questionnaire; where the value of the purchase is low but of a significant value which merits further analysis, or where, there is an element of risk in the market place (an example of an elemental questionnaire; "weighting factors-method one" will follow soon)
- Comprehensive appraisal questionnaire with visits to suppliers, where the value or risks are extremely high

Assessment aspects

There are many aspects that can be assessed on a supplier's ability, attitude, organisation, finance, structure, products and production methods. We will look now at all of these:

1) Assessment of Supplier Ability
Suppliers may be assessed for their capabilities to supply, for example:
- Capacity
- The number and quality of their workforce
- The number, age and quality of equipment
- The size, layout and location of premises
- Quality policies
- Environmental policies
- Lead time reliability records

2) Assessment of Supplier Attitude
Suppliers may be assessed for their interpretation of the market and especially in long-term relationships.
Their attitude will depend on:
- Shared goals
- Organisational strategy
- Client management
- Future prospects

3) Assessment of Supplier Organisation
Suppliers may be evaluated on the type of organisation, for example:
- Organisational culture
- Lines of communication
- Levels of trust and delegation
- Levels of integration
- Internal and external relationships
- Management style

4) Assessment of Suppliers Financial Data
From information given by the supplier or collated from other sources, the financial information needs to be evaluated to determine:

- Profitability. This measures the performance of the supplier to exceed costs and make a profit
- Gearing. This looks at the long-term loans that the company uses for funding where high gearing suggests the company is open to financial instability
- Liquidity. This identifies the cash flow position of the supplier
- Stock Turn. This identifies how expedient the company is at rotating goods through the company. It is based on financial turnover divided by the value of the stock on hand; it is not a measure of the actual physical goods stock turn

5) Assessment of Suppliers Organisational Structure

From the information gathered, it will be possible to identify the strengths and weaknesses in the suppliers' structure and culture, for example:

- Hierarchical structures may be cumbersome, bureaucratic and may restrict communication and extend lead times due to their inherent "silo" functional process structure.
- Flatter structures offer quicker response times for decision making and communication, for example where supply chain management is adopted as a philosophy and will result in a cross functional management structure

6) Assessment of Supplier Product Data

By research into the price structure, the required specifications and the quality standards, it will be possible to identify those suppliers can produce the product to the needed requirements. Related products on offer from the supplier may create opportunities for the purchaser to multi-source and reduce their supplier base.

7) Assessment of Supplier Production Process

When applicable, with information on capacities and production facilities, it should be possible for the purchaser to identify the strengths and weaknesses in the supplier's ability to provide the product. The internal supply chain of the potential supplier can be usefully analysed to identify possible cost savings. Production equipment and procedures can also be analysed to ensure they are up to date and appropriate to the standard required.

Weighting Factors; method one

With so much information available from the appraisal system it will be necessary to identify the criteria which are most important in identifying the preferred source. Weighting can therefore be applied to the attributes related to the critically and can be determined by the procurement department and the user/customer.

For example with long-term relationships, organisational strategy would be allocated a high weighting to reflect its importance. The following is an example of an elemental questionnaire/ weighting where from questions asked of the supplier, an initial identification is made of the ability to meet the requirements of quality, quantity, time, place and price can be established. Next, the purchaser can nominate a grade for each area, scoring from one, as unacceptable to five, as meeting all requirements.

Area	1	2	3	4	5	Comments
Quality: Procedures Manual Audits Testing Policy						
Quantity: Capacity Flexibility Bulk Individual Discount						
Time: Admin Production Collation Despatch Priority						
Place: Group Address Individual Optional Referral Notification						
Price: Bulk Discount Cost Breakdown Warranties Flexibility Improvement						

Weighting Factors; method two
Another example of applying a weighting factor follows (overleaf):

Area	Max Points	Score
Quality	40	
Quantity	30	
Time	10	
Place	10	
Price	10	

The above example emphasises that a high importance has been given to the quality of the product delivered, along with ensuring the right quantity is delivered. This suggests that the item is essential to production and that the price paid is not as important. A lower rating is applied to price, place and time as these factors are seen as not having as great an impact on the operations as the others. Clearly the purchaser will compile the details of each area with justification for the scoring being given.

Negotiating

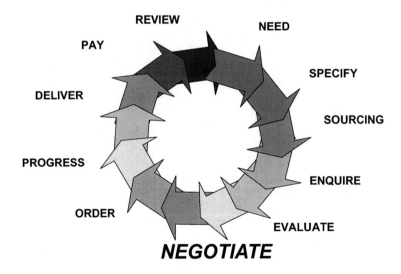

Use of negotiations

We have earlier noted that the private sector will generally move straight to negotiating with suppliers and not be involved in tendering. However in the public sector, direct negotiations

may also occur, when the following conditions are found:
- Single tender action has been approved
- Suspected "cartel" amongst suppliers
- Prices are over "known" levels
- Consistent award, historically, to the same supplier
- To test/evaluate the market
- Need for more than one supplier

Public sector negotiation will usually be regulated by Governmental directives, which requires adherence to strict rules to ensure the equality of treatment of suppliers; negotiations generally will not be open or transparent.

What is Negotiation?

Negotiation can be defined as "the resolution of conflict through the exchange of concessions." This will mean trading concessions, not donating them, and is only undertaken with people, who have the power to vary the terms, are able to vary these, and can give you something in return.

One of the key activities of procurement is therefore to negotiate acceptable agreements with suppliers and when negotiating, it is important that the purchaser follows the correct process and clarifies all areas of concern, before implementing any agreements.

Advantages of negotiations can be seen as follows:
- Relatively expedient
- Value for money when single sourcing
- Unclear requirements can be clarified
- Inexpensive
- Flexible and not prescriptive
- Confidential

Disadvantages of negotiations are seen as below:
- No transparency
- No clear audit trail
- Requires skill and competence
- Seen as a competition with winners and losers
- Can need a lot of preparation

When to negotiate

The total negotiation process can be either comprehensively actioned, or only parts of the process may be used.

Comprehensive negotiations should take place when the value and risk involved in the contract represents considerable commitment from the buying organisation.
Full negotiations should not take place for low value and low risk Kraljic routine materials.

Here the negotiation process should only be followed to an absolute minimum as the onus is on the buyer to bargain with a wide supplier base. Buyers should be easily able to get the best deal centred on quality, quantity and lowest price.

What to negotiate

Negotiations will be conducted from the three perspectives of the customer, the buyer, and the supplier. The customer's need must be met, the buyer must guard against risk and obtain value for money and the suppliers must be respected as a business entity in their own right and entitled to an acceptable profit margin. Looking at each of these three perspectives means:

- Customers may wish to influence the supplier selection, quality and time of delivery. The customer may also carry more authority and may also be a specialist in the product being purchased
- Suppliers may influence the price, quantity and delivery of materials. There may be only a few suppliers, or they may hold patents or other rights to materials and products
- The buyer must decide what criteria have priority within the negotiation and use their skills to achieve the best possible deal, which achieves these objectives

It will be seen therefore that what is generally being negotiated will come under the five "rights" headings:

- Quality, this will include quality of the product as well as quality of systems, procedures and personnel
- Quantity, this will include delivered quantity as well as capacity to supply and store.
- Price, this will include the total cost price analysis (TAC/TCO) taking into account the cost of materials, overheads and profit, but it may also be advantageous to negotiate improvement in prices paid by the supplier to their suppliers. Not many supply chain initiatives in fact do go back to the suppliers' supplier; indeed most initiatives stop at the first level supplier and therefore restrict the available opportunities
- Place, this will include where the products are sourced from and where they are delivered
- Time, this will include time of delivery as well as total lead-time including the reliability/consistency of the agreed lead times

Planning the negotiation

Information should be gathered on:
- Customer requirements including specifications and timings. Where appropriate the buyer should internally negotiate with the customer to broaden specifications, and in so doing, create a larger supplier base to negotiate with
- The marketplace, including the number of suppliers, alternatives/substitutes, technological advancements, market restrictions, market incentives and what other buying organisations are doing
- Supplier ability, including financial stability, capacity, resources and reputation. Where

the negotiation involves a long-term agreement the supplier's motivation and environment should also be analysed. From this information can be identified key criteria from the information, including cost models and options, which can be then bargained/negotiated for.

Objectives for the negotiation

There are other negotiation options available other than price, such as delivery, payment terms, people, extras, contracts, terms, documents, follow up, service, timing, schedules, urgency, guarantees, conditions, place etc. Therefore, it will be possible to move the negotiation forward to an outcome that still gives cost reduction and value add and it will help to:
- Set objectives and targets based on information gathered and customer requirements.
- Be prepared to move and inter relate these to reach agreement
- Create timed agendas to ensure the negotiation is efficient. Ensure the agenda allocates most time to the areas you wish to discuss, and which carry most value (or risk) to you

Preparation for the negotiation

The following guidelines can be used

1) Set clear objectives
- Be clear what you want
- Have a firm opinion of what the party wants
- State your objectives in terms of needs of the other party.
- Identify the others needs, these may have been revealed earlier. For example; what are the key needs; what are the financial needs; what problems do they have; what priorities do they have; what alternatives are there; what do you know about peoples nature; how will decisions be made; how will all of this relate to what you intend?

2) Identify negotiation elements
- Look for the variables
- List them and divide them into: quantifiable, unquantifiable
- Consider which are essential, attractive extras, relatively unimportant
- Think about the importance, you and the other party will give to these (do not assume you will think the same)
- For each element ask: what is my best guess of the likely point of agreements; what is lowest I can accept; how will the other party see this?

3) Decide on concession and value
- What are you/they prepared to trade? (e.g. reduce payment terms by x)
- What will you give?
- What will they want?
- What do you think they may concede?

4) Calculate overall effect of the package
- Add up what you may have to trade

- If total is too high, reconsider individual elements
- You should have a range: the ideal to minimum acceptable

5) Prepare your stances; get the see-saw ready
- Look at the total and think where they may start
- Make the opposite point, your starting point
- Consider each individual item in turn
- Estimate for each one where they will start
- Determine where you want to start by: looking at the individual points of balance; the overall package; the different emphasis to give to each elements; the fall black position

6) Prepare for the meeting
- Remember you are trading values rather than costs
- Prepare what you can give
- Prepare what likely to be offered
- Prepare where you can devalues
- Prepare where you can increase the value

7) Rehearse
- In front of a mirror
- Use a tape recorder
- Try it with a friend
- Role play

Conducting the negotiation

- Ensure the agenda covers all the areas you want to discuss. Write down and confirm any areas that are agreed.
- Use elements of behavioural persuasion: logic, emotion, threat and body language, to secure the outcome you want. Show enthusiasm for the agreement and use statistics and figures to justify your argument.
- Ask relevant questions and ensure you get comprehensive and acceptable answers. Open questions (who, what, where, when, why, how) can be used to gain information and understanding. Whilst closed questions (yes/no) can gain confirmation or identify areas of dispute.
- Gain movement by trading the concessions or options you have organised prior to the meeting. The following guidelines may help:
  - Do not give, trade reluctantly; e.g. "if, then"
  - "Build up" what you want to give; e.g. stress the cost: "Well If I could do, it would involve a lot more work", e.g. exaggerate credibly: "Well I could do that but look at how much it involves", e.g. what it can solve: "Well if I do this, then it will remove for you" e.g. imply it is exceptional: "I never normally do this, but"; e.g. imply it is beyond the call of duty: "I am not sure what the boss will say"
  - Maximise the perceived value of everything you offer

- "Put down" their concessions; e.g. depreciate: "I suppose that is a very small step"; e.g. amortise: "well that saves only £x per week"; e.g. devalue: "I have that already"; e.g. accept, but doing a favour: "I do not really need it, but if it helps you"; e.g. deny any value: "That really does not help"

- Use tactics and ploys to reach objectives.
  - Tactics are skilful manoeuvres employed to reach objectives. When discussing with people, there are often delays. This is often because the other people are searching for meaning and looking for reasons behind your questions. It can make sense therefore to be clear why you are doing things so that what they may see as hidden is made clearer. If come over as being more "devious" than you really are, it will not help.
  - Ploys can help you to be clearer, they can however be seen as cunning manoeuvres, and therefore may be seen as being unethical. The following are examples of ploys:

Flagging	"May I ask", "Perhaps I can suggest" = prompts thought and discussion
Summarising	Test progress ;lets you restate; = helps you stay on top
Psychology	Playing for time; coercion; pretending; creating physical discomfort; keeping you waiting etc. etc.
Defend/attack	Usually warning give which allows time to counter attack. Option is to go straight in without any warning
Countering	Focus on the possibility of agreement rather than agree/disagree spirals where finally will even fail to agree to disagree!
Rituals	Never make the first offer; do not make unacceptable conditions; allow adequate time; use the whole process and do not shortcut those who want the "ritual"
Future	End on a pleasant note as an ongoing relationship often will be involved. Remember negotiation is adversarial and can get acrimonious at times, however, hard bargains have to be driven so plan a pleasant ending
Listening	Active listening is needed, a brand new skills for many (see separate checklist)
Questioning	Use open ones and phrase them carefully. Want a dialogue not a monologue
Body language	Again a whole new skill for many , (see separate checklist)

Controlling the negotiation

- Concessions and agreements should be clearly recorded and verified. The buyer should do this to ensure the outcome relates to their terms and conditions.
- Implementation plans can be used to identify milestones. Regular meetings should form part of this plan to discuss progress against targets.
- A vendor rating system can be implemented to monitor performance against contract.

Behaviour and negotiation styles

Negotiation involves people dealing with people, therefore behaviour (what people do and say), is involved. Four types of negotiator behaviour can be found overleaf:

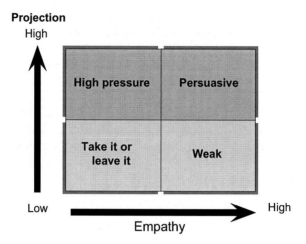

These four positions or styles can be described as follows:

- High pressure negotiators are aggressive, insensitive, want to win but are self defeating; they fail to see the others point of view, e.g. "the used-car salesman" who is pushy, causing many people to walk away.
- "Take it or leave it" negotiators; these have little interest in anything apart from their own position, e.g. unhelpful customer service people who say there is nothing more they can do.
- Weak negotiators are those who "mean well" and are over sensitive to the other person and with no means of persuasion, e.g. the procrastinator.
- Persuasive negotiators have a creative understanding of the other party, are well informed and get both agreement and commitment to the satisfaction of all sides; this is the ideal and balanced overall approach.

Behaviour in negotiations is also shown by the following evaluation of sales and buyers evaluating each other. Traits of a good buyer as seen by salespeople are as follows:

- Does not act aloof towards the seller
- Does not try to get a lower price to be used as leverage against the existing current supplier
- Assists in contacting appropriate people in their company when they find they lack knowledge or authority. They also explain the buying process in their company
- Allows adequate time for a presentation
- Has a working knowledge of their company's products
- Maintains good credit standing and pays invoices promptly
- Have good relations with their company's top management
- Follows ethical procurement practices

Traits of a good salesperson from the buyer's perspective are seen as follows:

- Offers a thorough presentation and a good follow through
- Has a good working knowledge of their product line
- Is willing to go "into bat" for the buyer within the suppliers company
- Shows knowledge of the market and a willingness to keep the buyer informed

- Has a good working knowledge of the buyer's product lines
- Uses imagination in applying their products to the buyer's needs
- Uses diplomacy in dealing with operating departments
- Follows ethical sales procurement practices
- Prepares well

Models of negotiations

The following Positional and Partnership Model negotiation are illustrative and "ideal-typical." It will be seen that these represent extremes, in reality, negotiations/negotiators may well use all three positioning at various times.

Hard positioning bargaining	Partnership negotiation	Soft positioning bargaining
Adversary participation	Problem solving participants	Friendly participants
Goal is victory	Wise outcome is reached, amicably and efficiently	Goal is agreement
Demand concessions	Separate the people from the problem	Make concessions
Hard on people and the problem	Be soft on the people but hard on the problem	Soft on people and the problem
Distrust	Independent of trust	Trust others
Dig in and maintain position	Focus in interests not positions	Change position easily
Make threats	Explore interests	Make offers
Mislead what the bottom line is	Avoid having a bottom line	Disclose the bottom line
Demand one sided gains	Invent options for mutual gain	Accept one sided losses to reach agreement
Insist on your position	Develop mutual options and decide later	Insist on agreement
Try to win a contest of will	Insist on objective criteria	Try to avoid a contest of will
Apply pressure	Reason and be open to reasons, yield to principle not pressure	Yield to pressure

The choices of the style (win/win; win/lose) will often be more intricate than those presented by the above model. Behavioural and cultural understanding is increasingly important, because others do not behave as we might do ourselves; after all, perception is reality.

Building trust, respect and integrity is vital for a sustainable deal, but knowing how to achieve this without being seen as weak and without being used is not always going to be easy or straight forward.

Action time: A general model of negotiation

The "Big Red Orange" bargaining game requires that individuals be paired into bargain groups.

One person in each bargain group plays the role of Dr. Smith. He needs the juice from 2,000 big red oranges. Unless Dr. Smith can obtain this juice, many lives will be lost to a rare disease, for which Big Red Orange juice is the cure.

The other person plays the role of Dr. Jones who needs the rinds from 2,000 big red oranges to cure another fatal disease.

Neither party knows the other's role description.

Each is also told that they have £250,000 to buy big red oranges.

The problem is that only 3,000 big red oranges are available for sale from Mr. Big (the game coordinator).

Dr. Smith and Dr. Jones are told either to agree on an offer to Mr. Big or to submit competitive bids. If bidding is undertaken, it is "winner takes all."

A coin flip determines the "winner" if equal bids are submitted.

After five minutes of discussion, the two parties are to agree on one a negotiation solution.

Task
What do you think will happen?

Discussion: A general model of negotiation

If the parties submit **competitive bids**, they are forcing a solution. One person will be totally successful (at preventing deaths); the other will be a total failure.

Competitive bidding is common because the parties typically do not communicate the juice versus rind issue to one another. Both parties think in terms of obtaining 2,000 oranges and tend to treat each other as adversaries trying to obtain a scarce resource.

However, if the parties communicate and engage in joint problem solving, they may reach a **win-win collaborative** solution in which one party uses the juice from 2,000 oranges and the other party uses the rind from the same 2,000 oranges. In this way, both parties can meet their objectives.

If the parties fail to collaborate or force a solution, other techniques are possible. Each party may agree to share the "loss" and **compromise** by buying 1,500 oranges apiece. Some sacrifice is required, but the parties will be making equal sacrifices and each party will be saving some lives.

Another possible solution occurs if **one party accommodates the other**. For example, if Dr. Smith takes 1,000 oranges and Dr. Jones gets the remaining 2,000 oranges, then Dr. Jones reaches his goal because Dr. Smith sacrifices his interest. This resolution is surprisingly common.

Finally, both parties can conceivably "walk out" and **fail to submit any resolution** to Mr. Big. This indicates total avoidance of the problem and results in the direst consequences – no cures are possible. Note that the non-collaborative options all indicate some degree of failure, given the potential win-win solution to the exercise.

When playing the game for "real", then non-collaborative solutions occur about 75% of the time, usually because both parties approach the interaction with mutual suspicions. Collaborative solutions will involve changing from:
- one-off relations to longer term relations
- being seen as opponents to colleagues
- "buy/sell" trading to working together for mutual benefit
- mistrust, bluff and suspicion in negotiations to honesty, fairness and openness
- "squeeze" on price to working together to find solutions that reduce costs
- "opposite side of the table" to sitting at the same side of the table

Checklist: Negotiations Summary

- Regard each other as equals
- Abide by the rules of discussion
- Put cards on the table on the major issues
- Patience is needed
- Empathy is vital
- State clear objectives
- Avoid confrontation
- Position disagreements carefully
- Deal with concessions progressively
- Do not reach for something that is out of reach
- Be open, but maybe you need to keep back your motivations/priorities
- Stick to your objectives
- Keep up your guard
- Remain professional
- Never underestimate people
- End positively

Negotiations: Six questions to ask

1) What are your objectives?

2) What are the other party's likely objectives?

3) What are the likely points of differences?

4) What options and bargaining power have you?

5) What is the other parties bargaining power?

6) What are the possible trade-offs or concessions?

Action Time: Delta Ltd.

Delta Ltd. is a large manufacturing company of electric washing machines. It has a turnover of over £10 million per annum. Recently it has designed and developed a new generation of high-tech washing machines, which employs the latest technology and the unique selling proposition of being able to wash clothes using only 30 percent of the energy consumed by traditional models; it also has a unique control system to reduce the amount of detergent needed to achieve excellent results.

Jane Tilly, Director of Marketing, feels Delta has a winning product, providing it can establish itself in the market-place, gaining the acceptance of sceptical customers and the trade. Reliability and cost are the vital elements.

The Director of Procurement is Susan French, who recently joined the business from a rival company in Italy. Susan has an MBA from a famous UK business school and is a professionally qualified buyer. She thinks the company must improve its approach to sourcing. Her experience working in Italy has convinced her that any improvements in quality, design and total acquisition costs can be greatly improved by more innovative and professional strategic sourcing.

Delta has a large procurement department, run on very traditional lines. Contracts are awarded on the principle of lowest price and are carefully constructed in an effort to eliminate any chance of the suppliers avoiding their responsibilities, as some have tried to do in the past. There are three main procurement divisions. Head of Equipment Procurement, Jim Peterson, began in the engineering department and steadily worked up to senior management. He likes telling new members of his team: "I got where I am today by not making mistakes". One of the key elements of any washing machine is the electric motor. The sourcing of this item is fundamental to the success of the product. As the managing director of the company has said in a memo to the production manager, the future of the company is staked on the new product.

Traditionally, the motors used in Delta's machines have been from the UK market, in particular Omega Ltd. Jim Peterson has already suggested that the contract for the new machines be placed with Omega, a locally-based manufacturing company employing about 100 people. Unemployment in the area is quite high and the current recession has hit the company hard: in recent years Omega has reduced its R&D expenditure and cut back on several major investment programmes. Delta has a corporate strategy, part of which is to support local industry and the local community.

Omega has suffered from quality problems in the past and has had to employ inspectors and checkers to reduce the number of faulty motors leaving the factory. Jim Peterson feels sure that with an extra tight contract and improved inspection and checking procedures at Delta's end, he will be able to ensure the consistency of quality. And of course Omega is very competitive on price (up to 10 percent cheaper than its new rival, SKS), a vital factor in the traditional procurement decision. Susan French, on the other hand, takes a different view. In recent times the improved quality and competitive price of several South Korean suppliers has called the traditional sourcing decision into question. One supplier in particular, the SKS Corporation, has recently established a sales office in London and seems to have a good reputation.

Jim and Susan have crossed swords on several occasions regarding sourcing decisions. Jim thinks that Susan does not understand the realities of the situation; Omega is a well-known company which has worked closely with Delta. Susan feels that Jim is too conservative and that a more pro-active approach would reap great quality and price rewards. She is determined to use SKS.

At a recent meeting to discuss the issue, the Managing Director had to step in to restore order as Susan and Jim got into a heated debate. Jane Tilly brought them back to earth by pointing out: "The key issue is not whether Omega or SKS are acceptable to us; it's whether they are acceptable to our customers."

The sourcing decision is vital to Delta's future. It must be made in the light of that and take into account the cost of having to go through the process again should the decision be less than optimal.

Tasks

1. As Managing Director, what factors would you consider need to be taken into account before supporting either Jim's or Susan's sourcing and ordering decision?

2. What further information would you like before making a final decision?

Action Time: Global Oil Co. (GOC)

You have recently been appointed as contract manager at GOC and since taking up the post you have been made well aware about the dissatisfaction with the level of service your customers are receiving from contractors. The complaints appear to be legitimate. Fortunately you now have the opportunity to build creditability with your customers as a new servicing contract is due for award soon. You will have to secure supply and satisfy your internal customers with a higher service level at less cost to GOC.

A company called Service Contracts Limited (SCL) has been successful in winning the contract for the past five years. They were not the best on price but the contract was awarded on the basis that they ware known and are the sole agent for the original equipment manufacturer in the region. This equipment is essential for the GOC operations.

SCL's service record has been poor on call-outs, repairs, efficiency and response times with the SCL staff also occasionally showing poor attitudes and sometimes they appeared rude to the GOC staff. Others matters were:

- related to SCL's invoicing which did not give adequate data in terms of what parts were used during the routine or emergency maintenance
- regular breakdowns were common and cost GOC a lot of money
- Long lead-time on spares was used as the excuse for delays by SCL.

Task
Assuming that the contract is up for renewal shortly, please give a detailed account of what you need to do on the agreement and contract, so as to remedy matters.

Action Time: Automotive Supplies Ltd. (AS Ltd.)

AS Ltd. is a multinational supplier to automotive original equipment manufacturers (OEMs) and operates from three sites.

They make 35 plastic component products that are supplied to the OEM customers in 15 kilo bags. For raw material, AS Ltd. purchases large volumes of various plastics from various suppliers.

Recently one OEM customer implemented just in time processes causing changes for AS Ltd. of reduced customer order lead times, reduced order sizes and increased order frequency. This all contributed to higher costs for AS Ltd.

Studies of AS Ltd. processes were therefore undertaken and this initially revealed that costs could be reduced on the inbound supply chain by increasing the order size to suppliers and by switching to receive plastic materials in bulk at one site.

Task
1) As an expert in supply, what information would you require to enable a decision to be taken?

2) What do you think should be done? Please justify your response.

3.0. The procurement cycle: the order and post-contract steps

In this part of the book, we examine implementing of contracts and managing supplier agreements. The legal aspects of contracts are explored including an overview of EU influences on contracting.

We continue with the handling of contracts and partnerships and the replenishment differences for dependant and independent demand. Finally, progressing and delivery are examined along with payment and reviewing; this latter part covering key performance indicators.

Implementing Contracts

It is essential in the implementation of a contract, that all parties involved are aware of their roles and responsibilities. The supplier must be conscious of their responsibilities regarding the delivery of the products or services in line with their contractual obligations. The purchaser must ensure that the contract is managed in accordance with company policy, and ensure that the customer is kept aware of any developments.

The user/customer must keep procurement informed of any changes to the process or design that may affect the supplier contract. If a sales department represents the customer, then precise forecast information must be maintained. If marketing is involved, any promotions or discontinuations must be communicated within an adequate timescale.

Orders, contracts and supply agreements

The contractual arrangements must be structured to match the particular requirement. Requirements vary and this section will look at these; it therefore represents an overview of the procurement order and contract practices.

Examples of different types of arrangements are as follows:
*   spot orders are placed as and when required
*   one-off purchase orders
*   framework agreement is for a fixed term for a specified supply, but with no initial commitment to buy
*   call off agreement, for example, fixed price contracts for a specified supply, therefore there is an agreement to buy
*   contract with varied rates, dependant on certain criteria, for example, on volume quantity order, on early payment etc.

These may have been set up through a bidding process, by competitive tendering or by negotiation.

Procurement is responsible for ensuring that the best-fit commercial conditions are applied to the particular purchase. In applying these, procurement must take account of any relevant legislative requirements. For example, chemicals are subject to the COSHH (Care of Substances Hazardous to Health) regulations, the waste electrical and electronic equipment (WEEE) Directive, while the Health and Safety at Work Act (HASAWA) applies to the majority of purchases.

Low-value purchases can be satisfied by the invitation of bids from a small number of suppliers, without the formalities and costs of tendering. The bids must be provided in a form allowing comparison, so that the best can be selected. These types of requirements are normally covered by a simple purchase order with standard terms of trading printed on the back.

Managing supplier agreements

The type of agreement made and used, will in part be dependant on the process and procedures used by a company and set processes will ensure that suppliers are being dealt with fairly. Having the right type of agreement ensures the company is trading on a sound legal basis and we will examine legal aspects shortly. The type and form of contract can be standardised, but be also capable of adapting to suit varying situations.

A contract plan may also be used to identify the work to be completed and the resources required. If this is being used, it will require a concerted effort by the buyer and customer prior to the sourcing.

The size of the contract, in terms of resources, will need to be established. Internally, this involves the staff hours and systems resources involved, and if a product is involved, then an analysis of production and costs will be useful.

Contracts may also be subject to Government directions. UK public sector procurement for example, recognises the fact that the contract award is not the end of procurements involvement and that continual improvement and value for money will be a part of the contract life-cycle. Confirmation of budget availability or 'phasing' will need to be established where applicable, with cost centres. These will effectively form the authoritative level by which the contract will be based.

Procurement should be involved to ensure the procurement decision meets the needs of the customer. Long-term agreements will need to be closely managed, as the basis for these agreements is often cost reduction and value-add to the benefit of both parties. Due to the time and resources invested in such relationships, it is in the buyer's interest to commit an adequate amount of time to managing these contracts.

Contract award

Following the previously discussed tendering or the negotiation process, the contract will have been formally awarded and the eventual 'contract' that has resulted from the tendering or negotiation process, will comprise of the following:

- the original enquiry document
- the selected tender
- any subsequent relevant correspondence between the tenderer and the purchaser, particularly that arising from the tender assessment (e.g. questionnaires) and post-tender negotiations
- the letter of contract award

It is only necessary for the purchaser to confirm acceptance of the contractor's bid and, for simpler contracts, the contract generally comprises a contract letter that refers to the enquiry, tender and questionnaire and any other relevant correspondence or minutes. For some very large contracts, contracts staff might produce an agreed contract document, comprising a comprehensive consolidated version of all the agreed provisions of the enquiry, bid and questionnaire. This represents the total and final agreement between the parties. If any post-tender negotiations have led to significant changes to the original bid submitted, the contractor might be asked to submit a revised tender incorporating all agreed changes.

The letter of contract award must set out clearly the basis of the contract and stipulate any conditions precedent to the award (i.e. any conditions with which the tenderer must comply before the contract is regarded as firm).

It is the responsibility of procurement to ensure that:
- the appropriate terms and conditions are specified
- there is a definition of when offer and acceptance takes place
- there is an approved digital signature or equivalent
- all legal principles have been followed

Legal Aspects of contracts

English law

These notes are based on the requirements of English law. Scottish law differs from English law and the law that relates to England and Wales derives from four main sources:
- Common law
- Equity
- Statute law
- European Community law.

The common law is the very centre of English law. It is the body of law and precedents built up over many years based on judges' and the courts' decisions on cases heard and the customs of the various courts of the land. Equity is another form of law derived from the results of cases decided by the courts. Both common law and equity differ from statute law in that the latter is laid down by parliament in the form of published Acts of Parliament, maybe following EC law.

It is common law that provides us with the following definition of a contract:
"A contract is an agreement between two or more parties which is intended to be enforceable by the law."

There are various statutes directly relevant to contracting – the main ones are the Sale of Goods Act 1979 (SOGA), amended by the Supply of Goods and Services Act 1994 (SGSA) and the Unfair Contract Terms Act. To make an enforceable contract, three essential elements must be present and correct:
- capacity (the power or authority) to act
- intention to create legal relations
- agreement (follows from offer-acceptance)

We look at each of these below:

Capacity
This means that both parties must have the legal authority and ability to enter into a contract. In simple terms, the parties should usually be 18 or over and of sound mind. If one or other of the persons entering into a contract does not have the necessary power, the contract may be void (unenforceable) or voidable (the innocent party has the option to set the contract aside, i.e. the contract may operate as a valid contract until one of the parties takes steps to avoid it).

There are certain groups who do not have 'capacity' and so cannot enter into contracts:
- minors (though exceptions exist)
- those with a mental disorder
- those under the influence of alcohol
- corporations (which require agents to form contracts on their behalf)

Companies are usually registered under the Companies Acts and their power to act depends on their constitution and the nature of their business. A company's constitution consists of two major documents: the Memorandum of Association and the Articles of Association. The importance here is that if a company enters a contract to do something that it has no contractual power to do, then the other party to the contract may not be able to enforce it. In other words, the company may escape its liabilities under the contract.

Because it is impossible to state exactly all the powers necessary to do everything a company may need to do; there are also implied powers. This means that the courts will take it for granted, even if it is not specifically stated in the company's constitution, that a company's powers include taking normal steps incidental to running a business (e.g. employing staff, buying materials) and powers appropriate to the particular type of business. Usually anything which is a natural or reasonable extension of permitted activity will provide adequate capacity and, therefore, a valid contract.

Intention to create legal relations
Both parties must intend that their relationship will have a legal effect. This is taken for granted in commercial or business transactions but not in social or domestic arrangements. However, even a social or domestic arrangement may be contractually binding if both parties have made it clear, expressly or by conduct, that such was their intention.

Offer – Acceptance – Agreement
An agreement arises when an offer is made, followed by, an acceptance of the offer.

The **offer** may be express or implied:
- Very often a contract is formed after an express offer. For example, John offers to sell his second-hand car to Jim for £1,000.
- Implied offers are also common. For example, a customer at a petrol station, serving himself with petrol, is making an implied offer to buy the petrol.

An offer may be made to a definite person, as in the case of John and Jim above; this is the normal situation. However, an offer may also be made to the world at large; for example, this can happen where a person offers a reward to anyone who may help to find a stolen valuable item.

An offer does not take effect unless and until it is communicated to the offeree. An offer, once made, does not remain open forever. It may be terminated in various ways. It may therefore:
- Be withdrawn by the offeror, unless it has already been accepted (However, withdrawal is not effective until it is communicated to the offeree)
- Be rejected by the offeree
- Lapse if the offeree fails to accept it within a reasonable time
- In addition, the death of either offeror or offeree terminates the offer

Meanwhile, **acceptance** is defined as: "An unconditional assent to all the terms of an offer." It must be absolute and unqualified. A qualified acceptance is not acceptance and is instead a counter offer (or cross-offer). For example, if Jim says to John 'Yes, I'll take your car, but only for £900", then this is not an acceptance. In fact it ranks as a new offer (a counter-offer): Jim is offering to buy John's car for £900. This offer may or may not be accepted by John. Unless and until John accepts, there is no contract.

Acceptance must be communicated to the person making the offer (either directly or through a reliable third party). Acceptance is only effective when it is received by the offeror (and not when despatched by the offeree). The contract only exists from this time.

The term 'battle of the forms' occurs in a situation of 'offer' and 'counter-offer'. It describes the common situation when a seller and a buyer are each trying to deal on their own standard contractual terms and conditions. Where there is a discrepancy between the conditions offered and those accepted, it may not be clear whether the buyer's or the seller's terms and conditions apply.

Electronic contracts

The increasing use of e-business means that contracts are now being formed by electronic communication, so there are now various pieces of legislation to govern e-business transactions; these include the Electronic Communications Act 2000. The European Union's E-commerce Directive 2000/31/EC set out to remove barriers to the availability of information society services within the EU. The Directive states that provision must be made for the drawing up and conclusion of contracts electronically. The UK Electronic Communications Act 2000 therefore ensures the legal validity of e-contracts and The International Chamber of Commerce's uniform rules on e-trade settlement state that an electronic offer and/or acceptance becomes effective when it enters the information system of the recipient in a form that the system can process.

Legal principles of consideration

Consideration is the bargain or exchange aspect of the agreement; it is a promise on one part for an act on the other or can be a promise for a promise, i.e. quid pro quo. Without consideration there is usually no contract (though there are limited exceptions to this rule).

There are certain rules applying to consideration:
- Consideration must be valuable, but, need not be adequate. This means that what is offered by one party to the contract must have a monetary value, but that value need not be equal to what is offered by the other party. In such a case, one party will have got a bad bargain, but the courts do not concern themselves with that: provided the consideration has some monetary value, however small, it is sufficient to make the contract valid.
- Consideration must not be based on the past. In other words, you cannot force someone to do something for you on the strength of something you did for them in the past.
- Consideration must be given by both parties.
- In commercial contracts, consideration is normally money, but it need not be. For example, some contracts are on the basis of barter.
- A framework agreement with no specific commitment is not a 'contract' because there is no consideration, so consideration is sometimes injected by making a nominal payment (e.g. £5).

Contractual terms and conditions

It is the responsibility of the buyer to ensure that the company is protected legally. "Caveat Emptor" – let the buyer beware, being the rule here.

Procurement must consider and decide which are the right commercial terms and conditions to apply. These could be bespoke to the organisation or might be based on available international or national standard forms. Examples of these are as follows:
- IMechE/IEE (Institutes of Mechanical Engineers and Electrical Engineers respectively), Model Form General Conditions of Contract; MF/2 for Supply of Electrical, Electronic or Mechanical Plant; and MF/3 for Supply of Electrical and Mechanical Goods
- CIPS (Chartered Institute of Purchasing and Supply) Model Form of Conditions of Contract, available to members on www.cips.org.uk

Model forms of contract will allow for basic terms and conditions to form the main frame of all company contracts and with specific clauses being added according to the nature of the product or service being purchased. Unless made explicit through specific (express) terms in the agreement, terms will be implied, according to the local legislation that has been developed to deal with commercial disputes in the business environment.

Conditions and warranties will form the basis of the terms, accentuating the importance attached to each of the obligations, which form the agreement. Clauses can be used to secure against risk, but also as a bargaining tool. The buyer can agree the inclusion or deletion of clauses for small concessions.

The terms and conditions of sale or of contract do set out the obligations and liabilities of the parties; they are a statement of risks. The key risk areas to be dealt with are as follows:
- price
- payment
- defects
- completion and delays
- standard of care and workmanship liabilities and indemnities

Essentials of a valid contract

The essential ingredients of a contract are as follows:
- **Agreement**: This is formed when one party has accepted the offer of another
- **Consideration**: Without consideration there is usually no contract (though there are limited exceptions to this rule). Consideration was more fully covered above, but is simply, where each side has promised to do or to give something to the other
- **Intention**. The parties must intend their agreement to have legal consequences
- **Form**: In some cases, certain formalities (in writing) need to be observed
- **Capacity**: The parties must be legally capable of entering into a contract
- **Genuineness**: The agreement has to be entered into freely and involve a "meeting of minds"
- **Legality**: The purpose of the agreement must not be illegal or contrary to public policy

Where a contact has all these requirements, then it is said to be valid. If one party does not live up to the promises then the other party may sue for a breach of contract. Meanwhile, if essential elements are missing, then the contract will be void, voidable or unenforceable:
- Void means the whole contact is null and that at no time has a contract existed.
- Voidable covers contracts founded on misrepresentation and some agreements made by minors. The contract may operate as a valid contract unless and until one of the parties takes steps to avoid it.
- Unenforceable means it is a valid contract but it cannot be enforced in the courts as one party refuses to carry out its terms.

The conditions of the contract will form the main body of a contract and breaching these terms and conditions, allows the claimant, the right to disown the contact or assert their right to damages. Warranties are terms but carry less influence, as whilst a breach of warranty allows the claimant rights to claim damages, they cannot disown the contract.

Usually, express terms are formulated to limit responsibility, the amount of damages that may be incurred and any changes in price.

Specific Clauses

There are many specific clauses that may form part of a contract and these can include:
- **Addresses:** communications must be sent to the address stated
- **Arbitration:** how disputes will be settled
- **Assignment:** controlling who the work is contracted to
- **Default:** non-delivery
- **Entirety:** what is not in the contract does not exist
- *Force Majeure:* mitigating events out of your control
- **Law:** deciding which countries law is used in foreign contracts
- **Liability and Indemnity:** protecting against the risk of consequential or indirect loss
- **Notices:** what means of communication will be used to pass information
- **Payment:** when and how payment is made
- **Sub-contracting:** restrictions on sub-contracting
- **Unenforceable:** Protecting the whole contract from individual terms, which cannot be enforced
- **Variations:** how variations to the contract are approved

The terms on which a contract is concluded may include more than just the terms expressly laid out in the contract. For example, additional terms can be implied:
- by fact (an implication that is obvious to both parties),
- by statute (legislation)
- by the courts (with precedent set in cases)
- by custom (for example, the trade acceptance that one case of a product, contains one dozen items)

Privity of contract

The doctrine of privity means that a contract cannot, as a general rule, confer rights or impose obligations arising under it on any person, except the parties to it. Common law has reasoned that only a promisee may enforce the promise, meaning that if the third party is not a promisee, then they are not privy to the contract; therefore only a person who is a party to a contract can sue on it.

However, if the doctrine of privity was inflexibly applied it would cause considerable injustice and inconvenience; accordingly many exceptions to it have been developed, the main ones being as follows:
- **Collateral contracts:** A contract between two parties may be accompanied by a collateral contract between one of them and a third person relating to the same subject-matter. There must, however, be an intention to create a collateral contract before that contract can be formed.
- **Agency:** The concept of agency is an exception to the doctrine of privity in that an agent may contract, on behalf of his principal, with a third party and form a binding contract between the principal and third party.
- **Statutes:** Certain exceptions to the doctrine of privity have been created by statute, including price maintenance agreements; and certain contracts of insurance

enforceable in favour of third parties. For example, under the Road Traffic Act 1972, an injured party may recover compensation from an insurance company once he has obtained judgment against the insured person.

Meanwhile, The Contracts (Rights of Third Parties) Act 1999 reformed the common law rule of privity of contract. Section 1 provides that a third party may in their own right enforce a term of a contract if:

(a) The contract expressly provides that they may do so

(b) The term purports to confer a benefit on them (except where on a proper construction of the contract it appears that the parties did not intend the term to be enforceable by the third party)

The relationship between a buyer, a supplier and the supplier's supplier can have critical impacts; consider the following case study:

Case Study: Upstream Suppliers in the Supply Chain Alpha Co.

Alpha Co. is an assembler of high volume branded electronic consumer goods. Alpha Co. integrates technologies, defines products, designs finished goods, prototypes and assembles the core product. All accessories, packaging materials and component production are outsourced.

Plastic Parts Ltd.

PPL is a first tier supplier of mouldings and uses three sub-contractors to supply components — Gloss Paint Ltd., Special Coatings Ltd. and Liquid Gaskets Ltd. Originally it had been anticipated that materials would be pulled through the supply chain based on monthly demand forecasts and weekly delivery requirements. In theory, PPL would sell moulded parts to Gloss Paint Ltd. who painted the parts and scrapped a percentage due to their process yield.

The painter sold on the remainder either back to PPL or on to Special Paints for metallic coating. Special Paints would add their value then sell the parts onto Liquid Gaskets. It was expected that the suppliers would order, from the next lower tier supplier, the volumes required by the next Company in the chain plus their anticipated or actual yield rate loss.

Start up

Difficulties became apparent as none of the companies had anticipated Forrester effects or quality, defect liability issues. A lack of production synchronisation resulted in Alpha Co. purchasing involvement on a daily basis to expedite parts between moulding and the factory. This was done on an ad-hoc basis by telephone and weekly visits. Other key issues identified were a lack of co-ordination between the independent companies, low process yields and missing batches of parts. Feedback on quality began to be received from the distribution centre that products had too many imperfections. When checking it was found that Gloss Paint Ltd. had a lack of employees that were skilled to the required level; additionally the managing director of Gloss Paint insisted on working shifts in the hand-finishing booth to achieve the yield and volumes required.

An intermediate solution
This relied on Plastic Parts inspecting the components after each supplier had added its value. Plastic Parts had to act as guarantor for the receiving contractor that the inbound components were of the appropriate quality. Any defects then created would be, at least in theory, the responsibility of the receiving contractor as a result of damage during its value adding operations. The main contractor returned damaged or otherwise rejected parts to the previous contractor for credit note purposes. Plastic Parts was then in a position to determine the amount of money owed to each company. This solution allowed the inbound logistics chain to supply the assembly plant with at least some of the part sets required.

Gross volumes of the product were planned to be in excess of three hundred thousand units. During the production run, less than ninety-one thousand units were produced due to inadequate supply, damaged parts, and late delivery. To avoid this occurring on higher volume product runs for other regions, generic design changes were implemented, based on the use of alternative technology solutions that allowed for a simplified supply chain to be developed.

The delayed ramp-up and the inability to deliver sufficient volume of acceptable component sets reduced the total number of products produced by more than 69.8%. This created a net financial loss for both production and the product creation programme. The relationship with the principle customer of Alpha Co. was also negatively affected as a result of failing to deliver almost stay batches on time.

Statute

The terms implied by statute are particularly relevant in contracts for the sale of goods. A contract for the sale of goods is an agreement where the seller transfers or agrees to transfer the property in goods to the buyer for a money consideration (the price).

The Sale of Goods Act 1979, amended by the Sale and Supply of Goods Act 1994, implies certain terms into contracts for the sale of goods, for example:
- Goods must be as described, of satisfactory quality, and fit for any purpose that the consumer makes known to the seller
- Goods are of satisfactory quality if they reach the standard that a reasonable person would regard as satisfactory, taking into account the price and any description
- Aspects of quality include fitness for purpose, freedom from minor defects, appearance and finish, durability and safety
- It is the seller, not the manufacturer, who is responsible under the Act

If goods are not of satisfactory quality the buyer is entitled, if they act within a reasonable time to reject the goods and get their money back.

The Supply of Goods and Services Act 1982 extend the provisions of the Sale of Goods Act to contracts which are not just purely for goods. This Act implies into contracts for the supply of a service the terms that:
- the service will be carried out with reasonable care and skill,
- within a reasonable time, and
- where no price has been agreed, for a reasonable charge

These terms apply unless they have been excluded and there are strict limits on the circumstances in which an exclusion or variation will be effective. Any material used must be of satisfactory quality. The law treats the failure to meet these obligations as a breach of contract and the consumer is entitled to seek redress.

The use and application of exclusion clauses is subject to the provisions of the Unfair Contract Terms Act 1977. This Act regulates the use of exclusion clauses and severely limits the concept of freedom of contract. In non-consumer sales (where a business is selling to another business) any exclusion clause can only be valid if it passes the test of 'reasonableness'.

The Act lists a number of guidelines to determine whether a term is reasonable. Of these, the strength of the bargaining positions of the parties is the most relevant. In commercial relationships, the courts will deem most businesses to have equal strength and, therefore, most exclusion clauses will be regarded as valid. Therefore, the implied terms of the Sale of Goods and Supply of Goods and Services Acts can be excluded.

Intellectual Property Rights (IPR)

When products and services are purchased, the supplier has certain rights under law on the creativity and innovation in the same way as if they owned physical property. The owner of the IP can therefore control and be rewarded for the use so that this will encourage further innovation and creativity for the benefit of all.

In some cases IP gives rise to protection for ideas but in other areas there will need to be more elaboration of ideas before protection can arise. It will often be not possible to gain IPR unless they have been granted, however some IPR, like copyright, arises automatically without any registration.

The main types of IPR are as follows:
- Patents cover inventions, those new and improved products and processes that are capable of an industrial application
- Trademarks for brand identity of goods and services, this is to allow for differentiation between different traders
- Designs for product appearance that cover the whole or part of product resulting from the features like lines, contours, colours, shapes, texture or materials of the product itself

- Copyright for material such as literary, artistic, music, films, sound recording and broadcasts, including software and multimedia

However, IPR also covers broader aspects like trade secrets and plant varieties; additionally more than one type of IP may apply to the same creation IP, for example the glass Coca Cola bottle is covered by trademark on the name and also on the design of the bottle.

Legislation on copyright is covered by the Copyright, Designs and Patents Act 1988, and full details of this (and all the other legislation covered in this section), can be found on: www.legislation.hmso.gov.uk/legislation/uk.htm.

From a procurement aspect it may be useful to negotiate with the supplier on the IPR, so as to be able to use or acquire for example, tooling, designs and materials to manufacture items in the case if any supplier defaults. From a supplier point of view, IPR is one of the sources of competitive advantage and marketplace differentiation. Accordingly when this applies, buyers will ensure, IPR a part of their normal evaluation and assessment process.

EU Influences on contracts

Consider the following:
- A businessman is negotiating a contract with a company in another State of the European Union, but neither party wishes to apply the law of the other country.
- A lawyer is advising parties to a contract involving parties in different States.
- An arbitrator has to decide a dispute under a contract "to be governed by internationally accepted principles of law".

All these need to know the principles of contract law shared by the legal systems of the Member States and to have a concise, comprehensive and workable statement of them.
The Principles of European Contract Law Parts I, II and III provide this and have been drawn up by an independent body of experts from each Member State of the European Union under a project supported by the European Commission and many other organisations.

The principles are stated in the form of articles with a detailed commentary explaining the purpose and operation of each article. In the comments there are illustrations, ultra short cases which show how the rules are to operate in practice. Each article also has comparative notes surveying the national laws and other international provisions on the topic. The Principles of European Contract Law Parts I and II cover the core rules of contract, formation, authority of agents, validity, interpretation, contents, performance, non-performance (breach) and remedies. Part III covers plurality of parties, assignment of claims, substitution of new debt, transfer of contract, set-off, prescription, illegality, conditions and capitalisation of interest.

The Commission on European Contract Law

A common law does not to exist in the European Union. The above Principles have therefore been established by a more radical process and no single legal system is used as their basis. The rules of the legal systems outside of the Communities have also been considered and the existing conventions, such as The United Nations Convention on Contracts for the International Sales of Goods, 1980 (CISG). In short, the Commission tries to establish those principles which it believed to be best under the existing economic and social conditions in Europe.

The Commission has made an effort to deal with those issues in contract which face business life of today and which may advance trade, especially international trade. However, the Principles do not intend to apply exclusively to international transactions. The European Parliament has proposed the enactment of a binding European Contract Law by 2010 as the ultimate goal after careful studies and preparations. It remains to be seen what happens in the political arena involved, especially when many consider that the different member states contract laws present no real barriers and that there are more important barriers to trade such as fiscal taxation and the lack of coordination on EU directives. Meanwhile the Consolidated Procurement Directive 2004 for the Public Sector and the New Directive for the Utility Sector has been agreed and changes the way that these regulated sectors have to contract for goods, services and works.

This emphasizes the changing nature of legislation and demonstrates the requirement for Procurement professionals to maintain "a watching brief." Such legislation knowledge would also be required for the "normal" health and safety legislation, environmental legislation and the waste electrical and electronic equipment (WEEE) Directive.

Checklist: Contracts with Customers and Suppliers

Although in law a simple telephone call can constitute a contract, and therefore would be binding, if would be foolish to rely on unrecorded and unsigned agreements, even to vary the terms of a standard contract. A written contract not only enables you to record what is done for a customer, it also gives the opportunity to state how important matters, will be handled. But a contract can be a millstone if it contravenes one of the many laws on 'unfair' contract terms. Professional advice should therefore always be sought.

Meanwhile the following questions may help:
- Do you have a contract or written terms of business?
- Do you confirm in writing all telephone agreements or changes over the phone to written terms?
- Are you relying on a copy of somebody else's terms? (These may be defective, inappropriate or illegal)
- Do you know who you are really making the agreement with?
- Do you record the registered company number of the customer or supplier on your agreements?
- Does your contract exclude liabilities for, say, your own negligence?
- Do you know that you and your customers have rights concerning the acceptance and rejection of bought goods?
- Do you always read your suppliers terms of business, including the small, hard to read grey print on the back of their invoices?

- Do you always check out business references?
- Do your terms of business make it unambiguous what you will do, when it will be done, how you will he paid, and what will happen if there is a dispute?
- It you are buying or selling overseas, have you settled which countries legal system will apply?

Handling Contracts and Partnerships

A contract register can be used to monitor progress and spend. This will also identify those suppliers who are being used and when. This also allows the buyer to identify opportunities to extend short-term relationships and review long-term relationships.

Levels of authority will be set to control spend, such as with basic requisitions and orders. It is assumed that with longer term, high-risk and high spend contracts, that the authority levels will be authorised by senior management. The following is one example of this.

Example of spend limits/order/tender procedures in a Government-owned oil exploration and production company:
- Spend up to £1000: phone order allowed
- £1000 to 10000: RFQ/PO is needed
- £10000 to 50000: RFQ/PO with sign off up to £20000 by a Manager, £20000 to 50000 sign off by the General Manager
- Spend of over £50000: ITT via Tender Committee who operate at three levels:
  - Internal Tender Committee (ITC); Spend over £50000 to £2 Million. Sign-offs are dependant on managerial grades with break points of up to £500K, up to 1 million and up to £2 million.
  - Higher Tender Committee (HTC); £2 to 10 million. Sign off by committee made up of managing directors of government owned companies
  - Central Tender Committee (CTC); over £10 million. Chaired by Government and signed off by the Oil Minister.

The level of buyer involvement in managing contracts must be established and this may take the form of any or all of the following:
- Support and advice; for example, the decision on which source to use may be with the budget holder/end user or, if the product has not been sourced before, then there may be an opportunity to develop a supplier
- Contract negotiation; here it will be the direct responsibility of the buyer to negotiate terms and conditions on behalf of the customer
- Contract management; here it is the buyers' responsibility to manage the total procurement process from identifying the need, agreeing specifications, identifying potential suppliers, supplier appraisal, contract negotiations and contract implementation including performance measurement

Collaborative partnerships may be established for strategic items of high value and critical materials and products. These will aim to reduce costs and improve performance for both the buyer's organisation and the supplier. To be a collaborative partnership, it will need to be based on trust and cooperation and without this, plus shared information and shared goals, then the partnership merely become a long-term contract. We examine further such collaborative arrangements later.

Handling orders

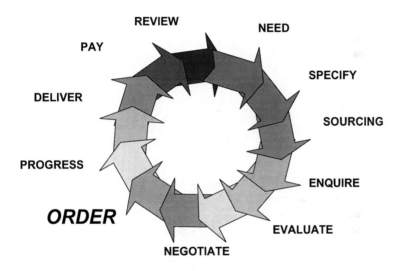

General purchase orders for low risk/low spend items can be handled at local or administrative levels. These orders need to be checked for details before being dealt with. Alternatively, in some cases, procurement cards can be used where the customer will buy direct and their spending budget will simply be charged accordingly.

Blanket orders may have been established for items that have a recurrent usage as this will result in reducing the order costs. Another advantage here is that a variety of items can be controlled and distributed via a single source who is left to self manage stock levels; perhaps using a Kanban system for items such as stationery, electrical components or small engineering fittings.

Replenishment

In deciding when and how much to order (the time and the quantity), we can find that demand comes in two distinctive types. Each has a different replenishment method for deciding when and how much to order:
*   Independent or random demand; this is independent of all other products; e.g. a tyre manufacturer for tyre puncture repairs. It is end consumer driven and random,

and therefore has more uncertainty and uses reorder point/level systems (ROP/ROL) for inventory replenishment/management

- Dependant or predictive demand; this is due to demand elsewhere; e.g. tyre manufacturer for new cars. It is more driven by the derived demand of supplier/customer ordering and therefore enables more anticipation and more certainty than is found with end product consumer buying. Dependant demand uses manufacturing requirement/resource planning systems (MRP/MRPII)

Replenishment for Independent demand

The "When to Order" decision will be simply; "when stocks at a level that is able to satisfy demand, until the replenishment order is available."

This in turn requires the following questions to be asked:
- How much demand is expected during the supply lead time?
- How long will replenishment (the supply lead time) take?

There are two reorder methods that can be used to check to see if an order should be placed (it should be noted that these two methods are often confused in the literature, and discussed then as if they were the same):

1) At a specific time period (the ROP i.e. the reorder point in time).
- This is called periodic review but it is also called the periodic inventory time based method, the order up-to-level system and the fixed order interval method. This has a fixed order time period (FOT) e.g. at a time "trigger" of every Wednesday.

2) At a specified level of stock remaining (the ROL i.e. the reorder level).
- This is called continuous review and is also called the perpetual inventory action level method and the fixed order quantity method. This has a variable order time period (VOT) e.g. when at the ROL where the "trigger" is the quantity level in stock.

When making replenishment decisions, then the following must be considered:
- Supply LT (SLT). This is the time that follows from determining the need, placing an order, up to the time the order is available for issue. Accuracy of data is needed and the SLT includes many different steps such as the external suppliers lead times, plus, all of the internal steps of the requesting/ordering between customer/user and the receiving/available for the issuing lead times.

- Supply LT Variability (SLTV) if applicable. Variability can arise from many steps in the SLT, for example (a) from Suppliers who quote a 10 to 12 week delivery, thus giving a vague and unclear starting point (b) from Internal tendering procedures where tender boards miss out a planned session, or, they did not complete all the tenders to be reviewed and then do not met for another week. SLTs must therefore be measured on a continual basis to identify any variability and it must be then examined and controlled. To effectively control inventory, companies must know objectively what their SLTs are. Unfortunately, many companies do not (as is more fully explored in "Excellence in Inventory Management; how to minimise costs and maximise service", (2007), by Emmett and Granville)

- Average demand (Av.D), or the forecasted demand, during the supply lead time. This is sometimes called the lead time demand, which, more correctly, is the demand during the supply lead time
- Demand variability (DV) if applicable. This is the difference between the average demand and the actual demand, over time and it is measured by the standard deviation
- Setting a required Service Level (S/L). This is needed to ensure the correct stock level is held and will be available to meet the service requirements. It is to cover against any supply and or demand uncertainty/variability

Where demand and supply lead times are certain, predictable and known then the calculations are easier; known and fixed supply lead times with known and fixed demand create for simpler decisions. For example:

Fixed demand   **50 units per week**
Fixed supply LT   **2 weeks**

Then one order option is 100 units ordered every two weeks. Here we will just have cycle stock; that stock that is held to cover the predictable supply/demand balance.
The keys to having such predictability are found for example:
- Where the historic demand and supply lead time are good proxies for the future
- With long mature product life-cycles
- There is no promotional product activity

However for most companies, such certainty is not the real world and conditions of uncertainty are normal. For example, a marketplace that works against certainty as it has demand volatility and increased product variety by introducing new products and creating competition.

Reduced and shorter product life-cycles limit the value of historic data and additionally, with wider global supply bases, this may cause complications for supply lead times. All of the variabilities on demand and supply lead times mean greater stock covers are required; this is called safety stock. The following will illustrate the calculations needed to cover against the "probability" that we will be dealing with uncertainty:

1.0.	Average demand	50 units per week
	SLT	2 weeks
	Demand variability	12 units
	Service level	95% (i.e. 1.64 standard deviations)

2.0.	Then 50 * 2	=	100 (cycle stock)
	12 * 1.64 * $\sqrt{2}$	=	<u>28</u> (safety stock)
		ROL	<u>128</u>

So the overall formula is:
Av.D * SLT; for the cycle stock/demand lead time, plus
DV * S/L * √SLT; for the safety stock:

3.0. To illustrate the concept of variability again, if we get SLT variability of plus 1 week:

Then 50 * 3 ___ = 150 (100 cycle + 50 safety stock)
12 * 1.64 * √3 = 34 (safety stock)
ROL 184

Here the "extra" for the variability is 50 + 34

Some important conclusions are possible from this example:
* The longer the lead-time, the more safety stock
* SLTV is critical

The "How Much to Order" decision

So looking first at the fixed/constant order quantity (FOQ)/continuous review-variable order time (VOT) interval options first, we find that:

* Each time there is an issue/withdrawal from stock, the stock position is reviewed to see if a replenishment order is needed
* The same quantity is ordered each time, but it is ordered and delivered at varied times, e.g. 10 tonnes week 1, 3, 4. Suppliers are therefore expected to deliver when needed with any quantity required
* The quantity to be ordered uses the economic order quantity (EOQ, see below), less the free stock (also see below). EOQ finds the optimum order quantity, at the balance between the cost of placing and the cost of holding, an order
* The decision on whether to order is triggered by the ROL. This is calculated from the demand lead time (average of demand * Supply lead time), plus the safety stock calculation (DV* S/L * √SLT)

With the Variable order quantity (VOQ)/period review-fixed/constant order cycle time (FOT) interval, we find that:
* The stock position is reviewed at a fixed time to see if a replenishment order is needed. As this is at a fixed time, this can then facilitate more regular deliveries from suppliers as they know when to expect an order
* A variable quantity (VOQ) for each order which is placed at the same time. E.g., 3, 5, tonnes ordered every Friday to "top up" back to the targeted maximum inventory level required
* The time period (FOT) setting is influenced by EOQ, with the high annual usage items being ordered more frequently (for example, annual demand quantity, divided by the EOQ, gives the number of orders per annum)
* The maximum level of stock is determined by the EOQ for the more stable demand/ SLT. For more uncertain demand/SLT, the maximum level is determined by the

average of demand * Supply lead time, plus the safety stock (DV* S/L * √SLT), plus, the additional allowance of average demand * review period (for demand before the next review period)

- The quantity ordered (VOQ), i.e. the "up to level," is the maximum stock level, less the free stock

There are some other simplified variations for inventory replenishment with independent demand; the minimum – maximum and the two bin methods:

The **Two bin** method starts with the holding of two identical quantities of maximum stock, the maximum stock being that needed to cover the supply lead time. One "bin" lot is then used to satisfy demand and when this bin is empty (the ROP); the second bin is then used and on order placed to replenish the empty bin.

The order quantity is therefore fixed at one bin (FOQ) and is placed at a variable time (VOT) as the usage will vary before reaching the ROP/ROL. The two bin method is useful for low cost, high demand items that have large order quantities. So if a new order has a SLT of two weeks and the usage is 10 items per day per full week, then 140 items is the ROL and ROP at the start.

Minimum-Maximum has a maximum level set, for example, set at the EOQ plus the ROL. The minimum level becomes the ROL and this is set by the average demand, the supply lead time and safety stock. When the ROL is reached (at a VOT), then orders are placed at the required quantity to return back to the maximum level, therefore giving a variable orders quantity (VOQ).

Similar to the basic EOQ model, min-max has more varied order amounts. It is analogous to the thermostat on a heating system where when the temperature gets below the minimum, then the boiler is turned on and supplies heat at a rate dependant on how much the temperature has fallen, and how much heat is being consumed during the lead time required to restore the room temperature to the required level.

Economic order quantity (EOQ)

This is a simple way to determine the order quantity and the size of an order. It is found at the balance between the cost of placing and the cost of holding, an order. EOQ makes assumptions that there will be no stock-outs, zero lead times and that we can "safely" order when at zero stocks. This is really not realistic when faced with uncertain demand, the need for variable order quantities and supply lead times with variability. However, where repetitive ordering occurs, EOQ should be considered, for example, make to order, purchase for stock holding (such as wholesalers) and stable maintenance, repair and overhaul (MRO) items. As essentially an accounting formula, EOQ requires much data, which may not be readily available, such as the holding and order costs, the different line items, the demand and the product unit costs. EOQ will not therefore apply in every situation, it does however give indications for reorder levels and points; it also emphasises the importance of calculating order costs.

EOQ Model:

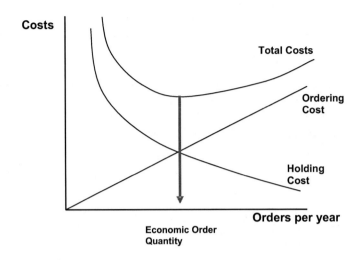

The order costs rise with the number of orders per year, whereas the holding (or carrying) costs fall with the number of orders as the volume stock turn is greater.

The formula is as follows:

$$EOQ = \sqrt{\frac{2RS}{CI}}$$

R	=	Annual demand	say 3000
S	=	Order Cost	say £20
C	=	Product Unit Cost	say £12
I	=	Holding Cost	say 25% of C

$$EOQ = \sqrt{\frac{2 * 3000 * 20}{12 * 0.25}} = 200 \text{ units}$$

The above figures used are for illustration only. Each company will, need to verify its own figures. Benchmark figures in literature can be dangerous, for example the writer has seen quoted figures of £5-£15 at the lower end and £50-£75 at the higher end: quite a variation for alleged standard benchmark figures!

Exaggerated costs are the common mistakes when using EOQ whereas in reality small variations will generally have little effect. Critical costs must however be always calculated by each company and be re-evaluated at least once a year. The critical costs are the order cost and the holding cost. It may not always be appropriate for example, to include all the costs incurred in procurement/ordering and warehousing/holding, as shown opposite.

For **order costs**, if repetitive and regular ordering is undertaken; then the fixed order costs are lower than found with a long tendering process (for, say, capital equipment). For procurement from external suppliers, then the order costs would include the cost to enter orders, any procurement process approvals and also the processing after goods receipt, such as quality checking, invoice checking and payment.

With internal ordering, such as requisitions from stores, then the order costs represents the time to make the work order, time with selection/picking/issuing and any inspections. To calculate the costs, it can be more effective to determine the percentage of time spent performing the specific activities and multiply this by the total labour costs for a time period, typically a month, and then dividing this by the units processed in this time period. Order costs are mainly therefore the cost of people in processing orders, but it may also include communication costs.

On the **holding or carrying costs**, this represents the cost of having inventory on hand; such as the storage costs and the investment costs. The investment cost is calculated by the value * interest rate and the insurance charge (which is related to the value of inventory). Storage costs are frequently mistaken, as these should be the variable costs based on storing stock/inventory and are not all of the fixed and variable costs of running the warehouse. The deciding factor is; are the costs directly affected by the inventory levels? If yes, then include the costs. The cost per pallet stored is a useful here, but then care is still needed as average values can be misleading as one pallet could contain £100,000 or £100 value of product. As the costs are applied in the formula as a percentage of the inventory value, then inventory needs to be classified based on the ratio of the storage space to the value. For example, the pallets of high valued product are allowed for separately from the pallets of low valued products.

Meanwhile, the conclusion from purely an EOQ point of view is to order the high annually used items often, and the low annual used items are ordered more infrequently. When being used to determine a specific order quantity, EOQ is useful for minor stock items of low values with known steady prices, demands and supply lead times. Where there is demand variability, such as seasonality, EOQ can still be calculated but using shorter time periods; ensuring that the usage and holding/carrying costs are also based on the same time period. EOQ is not really appropriate where there is random erratic demand with price fluctuations and variable supply lead times.

Replenishment, free stock and current stock balance

The above discussion has considered when an order point trigger can be calculated. Of course it is more than likely that stock is on hand and this must therefore be allowed for.

The current stock balance will be recorded that allows for issues, receipts, orders placed etc. What is needed however is the measurement against the order point trigger, the so called "Free Stock" position. This is an adjustment to the current balance that allows for any of the following conditions:
- Addition of stock already ordered
- Addition of stock in transit (if not recorded in the stock already ordered)

- Subtraction of stock already allocated to customers from the current stock balance
- Subtraction of stock on hand being retained for any special purposes.

Comparisons: Continuous and Periodic Review

The following comparison between the continuous and periodic review replenishments methods illustrates the main differences:

Parameter	Continuous Review(CR) FOQ	Periodic Review(PR) FOT
How much to order, plus, need to allow for the Free Stock position: The stock on hand, plus any stock expected, less, any stock allocated or being kept for special use.	A fixed order quantity (FOQ) when at the ROL. Typically the EOQ is ordered.	A variable order quantity(VOQ) , (as dependant upon what has been used since the last fixed time check and what is now needed, if any, to bring back to the "up to level"). Allow for Av.D * SLT plus, Av.D * Review Period plus, the Safety Stock calculation
When to order	When at the ROL therefore a variable order time (VOT). The ROL is calculated by the Av.D * SLT plus, the Safety Stock calculation	Fixed order cycle (FOT), as there is a predetermined time when to order. The time is influenced by the EOQ (annual demand quantity, divided by the EOQ, giving the number of orders per annum)
EOQ	Amount to consider ordering when at ROL	Helps in setting the review period frequency of when to order
Assumes/Prefers	Certainty with constant demand, lead times and prices throughout a period.

Suppliers have to deliver at any time (as it is a VOT) | Can deal better with uncertainty.

Suppliers can make regular planned deliveries (as it is a FOT) |
Stable demand	Lower safety stocks	Higher safety stocks as protecting over a longer time period
Seasonal/variable demand	Higher stocks due to big demand swings	Lower stocks
Control	Needs continual / perpetual monitoring of inventory levels, therefore is more responsive	Checked at the review period only
Usage	Most common for low value items and infrequently ordered "C" items. Used by industrial manufacturers.	Most common for high valued and critical "A" items. Used by FMCG industry as gives a rhythm for checking whether to place and order or not.

Replenishment for Dependant demand

It will be recalled that dependant demand is due to demand elsewhere; e.g. a tyre manufacturer supplying tyres for new cars (known as original equipment/OE). This is a more direct customer driven decision and therefore enables more anticipation and more certainty. Materials requirement planning systems (MRP) are commonly used. These are integrated computer systems planning tools used in production/manufacturing to determine the following:

- What input materials are required?
- How many?
- When needed?

Also used is manufacturing resource planning (MRPII) which follows on from MRP but adds in production capacity calculations. MRP is also one of the parts of ERP (enterprise resource planning) systems such as SAP.

The basics of an MRP system are below:

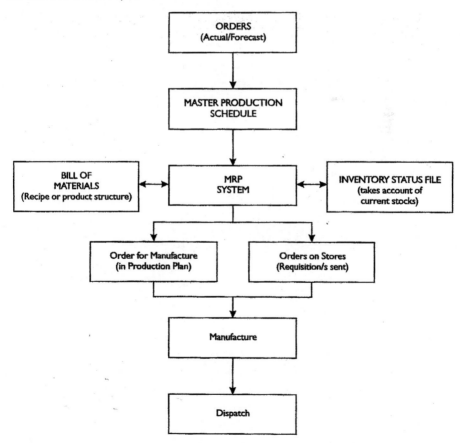

MRP has the following basic principles:

- Demand information goes into the master production schedule (MPS) which covers a specific time period and allocates the demand for each product into time buckets of days or weeks
- The component structure for each product is held in the bills of materials file (BOM) which is the menu of parts and sub-assemblies item by item
- MRP calculates from the top level of the BOM the gross requirements needed. It then accounts for quantities in stock or already on order and then calculates the net requirements for the item. If there are any batching needs, such as a minimum order of 100 items, these are allowed for. Finally the MRP logic calculates against the lead times for supply and brings forward order dates accordingly. It then goes on to the next level of items until the lowest level of the BOM is reached
- The output from MRP is a set of time purchased materials requirements showing how much and when each item should be purchased

To be effective MRP needs accurate forecasting and well defined product structures in the bills of materials files (BOM), along with known and reliable supply lead times. A common error found by some users of MRP is (again) the reality of unreliable supply lead times and also that the original default settings are not reviewed.

In theory, MRP systems will give the stores/users, known and predictable receiving times for stocks that will also be in stock for only a short/minimal time. As mentioned earlier, inventory is given a wider consideration in the book, "Excellence in Inventory Management; how to minimise costs and maximise service" (2007) by Emmett and Granville.

Progressing and delivery

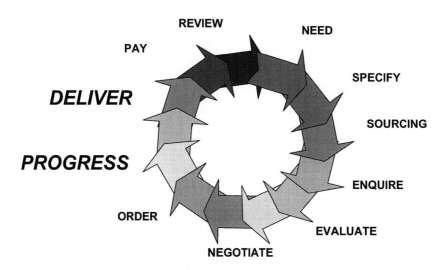

If all appropriate agreements have been made, including firm and agreed supplier lead times, then providing the buyer/customer has fulfilled their part of the bargain, then it can be reasonably accepted that the supplier will also complete their part of the contract.

Accordingly, it should not be necessary to spend time progressing and expediting orders. Indeed with collaborative supply chain thinking coupled with appropriate supplier monitoring and performance reviews, then expediting can be seen as being an admission of defeat. It is also largely superfluous with Incoterms Ex-Works buying; an option available for example, when global sourcing where track/trace visibility is then proactively a part of the process. (Both collaboration and global sourcing are explored further in part 4.0 of this book).

However, for one-off purchases where there is no history or record of supplier performance, then some progressing and checking maybe required to ensure suppliers meet their contractual agreements. It can also be widely used for critical items required for example, in oil and gas production and also, for where there are no proper arrangements or collaborative supply thinking.

When expediting it is necessary to determine:
*   which orders to expedite
*   the date(s) to check
*   the checking actions needed, for example, writing/e-mail, personnel contacting, telephone contact (on B items), supplier visit (on A items)
*   the system for record keeping

After delivery, on receipt into warehousing/stores, then the following activities are involved:
*   Establish which unloading area is to be used; ensuring it is safe and suitable for the operation
*   Record the arrival of the vehicle and note the transport security locking systems, for example, container seal(s)number(s)
*   Break the security locking system with the driver present
*   Check the order documentation and record each item against the consignment note
*   Ensure the vehicle is safe before unloading
*   Unload the vehicle
*   Assemble the goods in the goods receipt area
*   Check the goods for quantity (use blind checking?) condition and possible damage
*   Carry out any required quality checks
*   Report any discrepancies and condition/quality at once
*   Record/notify the system of receipt
*   Move the goods out of goods receipt area as soon as possible to the appropriate destination:
    -        location in the warehouse where goods are to be stored
    -        the staging/holding area they are to be held in (such as quarantine)
    -        direct to the user

Clearly the time taken to do this will impact of the overall supply lead time and this receiving lead time up to the time available to issue, may need careful management, especially in those operations where procedures require inspection by internal end users before goods are accepted. It has been known for goods to take some weeks for this process to be undertaken and for goods, meanwhile, not to be entered into a stock management system. Where replenishment is being done remotely and away from the stores environment, we also have known new orders being placed, because of this "system gap" in the practical visibility.

Meanwhile, more on stores and warehouse operations is available in "Excellence in Warehouse Management" by Stuart Emmett (2005).

Payment and reviewing

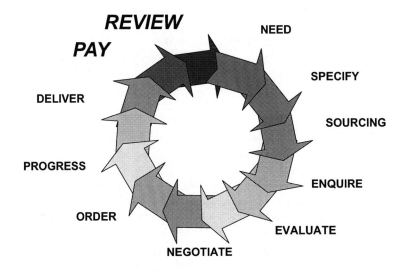

Payment

Clearly before reviewing, on an individual order basis, the payment to suppliers needs to be completed. This will be in accordance with agreements in contracts from earlier negotiations. Payment terms are often a major aspect of the supplier appraising and evaluation steps.

If however the agreements and terms were for pre-payment, for example, on overseas procurement by letter of credit terms that involve payment on presentation of shipping documents at the country of shipment, then payment has already taken place earlier in the procurement cycle.

Late payments are a source of friction between suppliers/customers and can also be in breach of contract terms. The handling of any payment complaints from suppliers must also involve the procurement department; it is really not acceptable for procurement people to blindly direct such supplier queries to finance department. Supplier performance is important, and not being paid on time in accordance with agreements will be a major source of discontent and can ultimately lead to changes in suppliers' performance. Procurement, therefore, must be aware of all payment problems and issues with suppliers.

Reviewing

It will be recalled that the market in which an organisation competes and the products it provides, will be part of the business strategy. This will define what goods will need to be sourced to satisfy market demand; this will in turn provide the basis for the procurement strategy. The sources to be used are then identified by procurement in order to meet these strategic decisions.

The amount of reviewing, monitoring and control allocated to an agreement will depend upon the importance of the product or service being procured, in relation to the business strategy.

Reviewing price

The cost of the material or product can be measured from two angles:
* Cost of acquisition
* Cost of the product

Traditionally, purchase price was the only measure used; however modern procurement methods recognise the long-term benefits of managing the total cost of ownership (TCO), as we looked at earlier.

Product material costs are made up of different cost elements and these costs will include acquisition costs, cost of operation and cost of disposal. The costs involved in procurement of materials or products, will include the direct material and labour costs of production including expenses, production, overheads, administration, sales and distribution.

A cost model, if available, will identify the total costs including the profit.

We will examine supplier's methods of pricing later in part 4.0., meanwhile an example of a cost breakdown for a product sourced from China to being "on sale" in UK Retailer follows:

Breakpoint	Cost in pence	Comments
Raw Materials	15.5	
Wages and profit	6.5	Profit is a few pence
Total FOB	22.0	
DDP	32.0	
Sell Wholesale	45.0	Profit is 13 pence
VAT	7.3	
Retail Sell	99.0	Profit is 36.7 pence, less the distribution/retail costs

Source: Sunday Times 18 February 2007

The type of contract pricing agreement, will contribute to the make up of the cost elements. Fixed price agreements will be simple to calculate. Longer-term contracts will need to take into account fluctuations in raw material prices and other cost factors.

Reviewing Procurement Costs

Procurement costs must be monitored to ensure the buying process is cost effective. The buyer should be aware of the costs involved in raising an order and this will involve all the direct and indirect costs, including salaries, expenses, departmental suppliers, heating, lighting, communications etc.

Ratios can be used to identify costs and indicate trends. These can include:

$$\frac{\text{Department costs}}{\text{Total value of orders}} \times 100 = \% \text{ Procurement efficiency by total spend}$$

$$\frac{\text{Department costs}}{\text{No of orders placed}} \times 100 = \% \text{ Average cost of orders}$$

Reviewing Total Organisation Spend

Total spend of any organisation can be defined as the suppliers agreed price, plus, the procurement costs. Information regarding spend should be readily available from the finance department, or from any procurement systems.

An ABC analysis of all agreements will identify the high priority contracts, which require closer control and monitoring. ABC analysis should be reviewed regularly to account for changes in market conditions.

Organisation budgetary control

Financial budgets are used throughout organisations. A budget is a plan and a forecast in financial terms, covering a specified period of time. Budgetary control involves the setting of objectives, in monetary terms, and enables managers to plan and control the resources they are responsible for.

When regular comparisons are made between what was planned and what actually occurred, any variance can be remedied or the plans can be revised. Budgets as a management tool are therefore very important.

There is no perfect budgetary control system. If it is to be effective, though, it should be tailored as closely as possible to the needs of the company. An effective budgetary system will be possible if the following points are adhered to:
- There must be a system in place for the efficient collection and processing of accounting data.
- All of the management team must be committed to and involved in the budgetary process.
- The will to act on budgetary information quickly and positively, must be encouraged.
- Managers must be trained in budgetary control and interpretation techniques.
- Good lines of communication must exist within the organisation.

Constructing a Budget

Two of the most popular methods of setting budgets are as follows:
1) Zero-Based
This way to establish budgets is to take a view that all forecasts are developed from a zero assumption basis about what costs or revenues might be for future periods. The budget is built

up without any reference to previous periods. It is based upon what is likely to occur, derived from the forecasts.

2) Historical Costs
In this type of budgeting, previous knowledge of costs is used as a basis on which to formulate the forthcoming period's budget. For example, if postage and stationery costs equalled £20,000 last year, and the inflation rate is 5%, the budget for the forthcoming year would be set at £21,000. This system can be fraught with difficulties, however, if those responsible do not take into account the many factors that affect revenues and costs over a year.

After making the above choice then the following process can be used to construct a budget:
* Determine the assumptions, for example, the sales forecasts, the future unit cost estimations etc.
* Specify the demand; for example, the daily number of orders to be placed
* Analyse the process and resources needed; for example, if 100 orders are to be placed a day and the known operative rate is 2 orders per hour, then 50 labour hours are needed
* Apply the financial factors, for example with order placing, 50 labour hours at a labour cost of £x per hour, gives the labour cost per day for order placing
* Evaluate; to see if the plan looks realistic and conforms to expectations from others in the organisation. This may mean iteration is then required
* Finalise the budget/forecast plan

Variance Analysis

After the implementation of the budget forecast plan, eventually the forecasted levels will become actual levels. The actual and the expected or the forecast plan are compared and thereby enable the financial performance to be assessed. On receipt of these figures, the next task is to explain the variance. These will be due to changes from the time when the budget was planned and the current time. Budgets are after all, a forecast and will rarely be 100% accurate in the months when the "actual time" later has come.
Changes may have been caused by one or a combination of the following:
* **Volume**
  For example, order throughput was forecast at "x" orders, the actual was plus/minus "x"

* **Mix**
  For example, spend was forecast at 80% low value and 20% high value, however the actual was 60%/40%

* **Performance**
  For example, order placing rate was forecast at 2 order per person hour, actual was 1.6; therefore more labour hours (and cost) were incurred.

The impact of the variance can then be assessed and adjustments, where appropriate, can be made; for example, to the physical activity/operations/KPIs and to the financial budget.

A budget therefore, enables performance to be monitored and controlled on a period basis; provided of course, the system for collection and allocation of the relevant data is an efficient one.

Advantages/disadvantages of budget control

The use of budgetary control systems has advantages as follows:
- Resources are controlled efficiently.
- Motivation of those involved can increase if they are included in the budgeting process.
- Decisions can be based on the examination of problems and corrective action.
- Plans can be reviewed regularly.
- The activities of the various functions, in the company, can be coordinated effectively.

Meanwhile the most common criticisms of using budgets are:
- Budget setting and monitoring are time consuming and can prevent people performing their jobs.
- As mentioned above, planning is an inexact science and the results can be totally different from what was anticipated.
- Some managers may be happy to achieve only the budget targets and not push beyond this.
- The setting of budgets can de-motivate, if targets are imposed or set at levels that are felt to be unrealistic.
- Some budgets can actually constrain managers and prevent them from taking opportunities which may arise.

Reviewing costs and risk factors

Procurement has a direct responsibility, both externally and internally, to check and see that all risk factors are accounted for. External risk factors will include the number of suppliers, length of lead-time and other considerations affecting price and security of supply. Where there are several suppliers, risk associated with security of supply may be low, however, continuity of supply may still carry risk where the quality offered by the available suppliers is of a low standard.

Internal risk factors will include loss of production and loss of sales. These will have to be estimated on the basis of non-delivery. Failure to deliver goods to the marketplace may ultimately result in lost market share. Lost sales can be measured as follows:

Days not available * sales price
Average day's sale

Poor procurement performance will be reflected in the extras costs of:
- Reordering
- Re-handling and re-storing the replaced items
- Returning the non required items

- Loss of revenue or, delayed revenue creation
- Effects on reputation and goodwill
- Re-evaluation of performance and subsequent improvement/re-alignment costs

Key performance indicators

Supplier performance must be monitored in a positive manner to motivate better results. Long-term relationships will only succeed where both parties are committed to continuous improvement. Key performance indicators (KPIs) can be used to ensure control of all procurement activity and highlight any deviation from the standards expected.

The actual KPIs used will depend on the product or service being purchased and they can then be monitored to ensure supplier interest is maintained in the contract and also to build historical data for reference.

Defining key performance indicators

In general terms, the KPIs will cover those quality, quantity, price, place and time aspects, related to the goods being purchased and also to the relationship with the supplier. Examples follow:

Quality includes:
- Rework
- Rejects
- Warranties
- Procedures
- Complaints
- Control

Quantity includes:
- Full or Part order receipts
- Discounts
- Minimum order levels

Price includes:
- Consumables
- Tooling
- Overtime
- Rework
- Materials
- Labour
- Downtime
- Absenteeism

Place includes:
- Accuracy of delivery to location
- Tracking availability whilst in transit

Time includes:
- Lead times
- Emergency response
- Setup

Relationship issues include:
- Service levels
- Skill levels
- Response times to requests

KPIs are measurable and therefore are objective criteria. Subjective criteria can also be involved based on the buyer's perception, for example to commitment, attitudes and mannerisms including:
- Motivation toward individual contract commitments, future business etc.
- Response to constructive criticism, problem solving etc.
- Input into problem solving, innovation etc.

Additionally, surveys can be used to collate subjective opinions; for example the supplier survey mentioned below.

Performance Benchmarking

It can be useful to compare an organisations own operations activities with other organisations; the benchmarking process.

Benchmarking is measuring performance against that of best in class companies so that the best practices are revealed. This information is then used to improve performance. Benchmarking is commonly miss-understood. At a basic level it includes comparisons of performance with that of others. But benchmarking is much more than this. The measures may tell you who is doing well, but statistics do not give you any useful information that you can use to improve performance.

Benchmarking is therefore all about sharing information on practices for continuous improvement. It includes the sharing of quantitative and qualitative metrics as well as the processes.

Best practices are those actions necessary to achieve the best productivity, at the lowest possible cost. But not everything about a best practice works well in every situation. The best practice procurement being performed in a mine in South Africa may not be the same best practice as in a mine in Poland. We must keep the context in mind.

Undertaking benchmarking

Benchmarking can be undertaken inside a large organisation, or against external companies or through benchmarking "clubs". The selection of partners for benchmarking is therefore as important as the measures and the practices themselves. There are four general categories of benchmarking partners that should be considered:

- **Internal:** These are operations within the same company or group. There is an existing relationship, and it is easy to establish a baseline and criteria for comparability. The gains achieved, however, are limited to the best that your own company is already doing.

- **Competitors:** Direct competitors can provide very useful priorities for improvements. Most companies are interested in the results, but don't want to provide their data in case it reduces their competitive advantage; it is extremely unlikely that they will show a competitor how they run their operation;

- **Industry:** Comparison with other companies in industry provides useful trend information. Opportunities for improvement are very good, but are limited to the best that the industry is presently achieving. Industry trade associations are useful to contact here.

- **Best in class:** This is benchmarking at its best as it is determining who has the best practice in a particular process, such as annual plant shutdown planning or procurement practice, regardless of industry sector. Business process and practices information can provide broad new perspectives and the best opportunity to find "break through" ideas and innovations.

Procurement KPI benchmarks

The following indicators can be useful to make such comparison's to enable learning and improvement.
- Total procurement expenditure as a percentage of sales revenue
- Procurement operating expenses as a percentage of total procurement spend
- Number of procurement staff as a percentage of the companies total staff
- Sales revenue per procurement employee
- Total procurement spend per procurement employee
- Number of active suppliers per procurement employee
- Procurement spend per active supplier
- Cost of operating the procurement function per active supplier
- Percentage of active suppliers for 50%, 75% and 90% of procurement spend
- Percentage change in number of active suppliers in a reporting period
- Percentage of total spend with any "deemed" sensitive suppliers e.g. local suppliers, small companies etc.
- Percentage of total company purchases handled by the procurement department

Supply chain KPIs

The entire supply chain performance can also be measured and the following KPIs can be used.

Description	Measurement tool	Definition	Units
Customer orders fulfilment	On time/in Full rate (OTIF) Lead time	% orders OTIF Receipt of order to despatched/delivered	% Hours/Days
Customer satisfaction	Customer Survey	A sampling survey to ask for customers experiences, for example: -Support available -Product availability -Flexibility -Reliability -Consistency -Comparison to the competition	% satisfied
Supply management	On time/in full (OTIF).	As above	%
	Supplier Survey.	A sampling survey to ask for suppliers experiences, for example: as in the above customer survey	% satisfied
	Effectiveness.	Year over year improvements	%
	Lead Time	Time placed order- time available for use	Hours/Days
Inventory (measure for each holding place of raw materials, work in progress and finished goods)	Forecast accuracy.	Actual/Forecast sales per SKU.	%
	Availability.	Ordered / Delivered Per SKU.	%
	On hand.	Value on hand/daily delivered value.	Days
Cash flow	Cash to cash.	Time from paying suppliers, to time paid by customers	Days
Quality	Quality.	Non conformances, as appropriate	Per 100 or 1000 or million
Operations	Utilisations.	Used/Available.	} Units
	Productivity.	Actual/Standard.	} Hours
	Costs.	Actual/Standard.	} Costs
	Lead times.	Time start/time completed per operation.	Hours or Days
People Relationships	Internal.	Absence rates	%
	External.	Sampling Survey, as customers / suppliers above.	% satisfied
Costs	Total supply chain or per operation cost.	Cost per time period/ Units.	£ per unit

Applying key performance indicators

The process for applying KPIs and the gathering of data must be agreed with all interested parties, along with the format in which the results will be produced. This could be a basic spreadsheet or a more visual group of data using graphs or gauges. The levels of acceptance need to be set and the procedure for remedial action agreed by the establishing the reporting structure and the levels of authority, along with direct contacts and substitutes. The level to which the KPIs are "drilled down" will need to be established, for example with Quality KPIs:

Quality KPIs

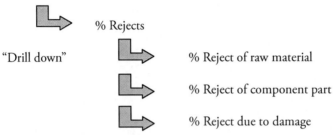

"Drill down"

% Rejects

% Reject of raw material

% Reject of component part

% Reject due to damage

Using Weightings

A weighting system, like used in evaluation, can also be applied to prioritise the most important criteria. For example:

Quality	30
Delivery	25
Quantity	20
Price	15
Communication	10

This system can be simplistic (as shown here), but for complex and expensive projects it can be highly comprehensive.

KPIs' reporting structures

The reporting structure should ensure that deviations from the KPIs are clearly and easily communicated both in a cost efficient manner and as acceptable time frame. The reporting structure should link the supplier, buyer and customer in a horizontal visible frame. meanwhile, the operational, tactical and strategic levels should be linked in the vertical hierarchy.

Software can meet this need whilst a simple visual system can give adequate information in an appropriate format. For example, the 'Traffic High Light System' uses colour codes to report performance:

Green = Acceptable
Amber = Cautionary
Red = Unacceptable

This simple system can be implemented quickly and easily as a basis for more comprehensive performance measurement:

Supplier A

	Jan	Feb	March	April	May	June
Quality	Green	Green	Amber	Green	Green	Green
Delivery	Red	Amber	Red	Green	Green	Green
Quantity	Green	Green	Green	Green	Amber	Green
Price	Green	Amber	Green	Green	Green	Green
Communication	Green	Amber	Red	Green	Amber	Green

KPIs and Suppliers

Once key performance indicators (KPIs) have been established and a system created, the relevant parties will need to adhere to the process. If a significant change is involved, this should include a timed plan for the introduction and induction of individuals with identified responsibilities within the process. Responsibility levels, lines of communication and reporting should also be included.

The supplier will need to commit to the programme and to recognise its advantages, for example, the performance measurements should also be of benefit to them. The customer and any other interested parties must provide the required information expediently and recognise the benefits they will gain in terms of improved performance, reduced costs and greater cooperation. Without the cooperation of the customer and the other links in the supply chain, it can be impossible to collect the necessary data.

Supplier rating schemes, also rely on the participation of the supplier and the buyer's internal activities, which both include goods-in and despatch, along with the customer.

KPIs' Effects on Suppliers

Suppliers must be given a thorough introduction to the supplier rating programme and understand their role. They must be encouraged to ask questions and be given thorough answers, so that, they can implement the process with little or no delays/errors. The buyer in turn will need to understand the supplier's strategies and objectives in order to apply the performance measurements and improvements effectively; of course, this information may have already been learnt when sourcing the supplier. The supplier must be able to trust the buyer where the cost of commitment is substantial. For small to medium enterprises, the amount of effort and resources required for monitoring and maintaining performance measurement might be overwhelming; buyers should take this into account.

KPIs' Effects on Customers

Customers/users must also understand the value of performance measurement and recognise their role. Customers and other activities must interact with procurement as part of the responsibilities of an internally integrative supply chain.

Customers will need to be shown the benefits and cost savings and added value should be demonstrated. Equally the customer should be made aware that poor supplier performance that is not reported; would result in continued poor service.

The buyer can prioritise the customer's needs in order to maximise the benefits for them. Therefore in addition to understanding the suppliers' viewpoint, they will have to understand the customer.

Monitoring Supplier Performance

Supplier performance should be measured over a period that is sufficient to capture any trends or fluctuations, such as seasonality. This however may not be necessary for projects to be completed within a specific time frame.

Performance monitoring must be a set objective, for which individual buyers must take responsibility. Each buyer can be given the responsibility of monitoring individual agreements or suppliers. Alternatively, the responsibility for monitoring, as an activity, may be given to an individual or specialist team.

Information must be gathered, stored and distributed in an acceptable format. It should be available to management and suppliers on a regular basis. Quantitative information on time and costs must be distributed to both suppliers and customers. This information should also take into account the quality expected from the supplier in terms of commitment and attitude. Measurement should be made against historical data and projected improvements. The supplier should be driven toward continuous improvement to remain competitive; they should not be driven towards bankruptcy by making increasing and unrealistic demands.

Comparisons can be made against similar suppliers to create a league table of performance, this information being controlled for confidentiality reasons.

Downgrading Supplier Ratings

Suppliers who fail to keep within the set tolerances must be notified within an agreed timescale. They should be given details of the non-compliance including dates and times. The supplier must also be informed of their reviewed grade and the records updated. This can be used to trigger a closer analysis of the supplier's performance to ensure the situation does not deteriorate. The supplier needs to be given the opportunity to explain why they have failed to perform and where the deviation is severe, a meeting should be arranged to resolve the problem. The buyer should give the supplier guidance on how to achieve the required standard; this could include advice, cooperation, and the sharing of knowledge.

Where the supplier has to improve then a timescale should be set; additionally regular meetings may be necessary until the problem has been corrected, and the supplier can assure adherence to the expected performance requirements. Contingency plans may need to be drawn up in case of any recurrence.

Upgrading Supplier Ratings

Suppliers who have maintained or improved their performance should always be informed and thanked, for example:

'A' class suppliers should be commended.
'B' class suppliers should be upgraded.
'C' class suppliers should be upgraded.

Good suppliers can be encouraged to sustain their efforts and similar suppliers gauged against the improvements attained by others. This information can be discussed with these improved suppliers to try to identify improvement opportunities. This important concept of supplier development is considered in greater detail in section 4.0.

Increased performance should be rewarded and rewards used as an incentive for suppliers to maintain and exceed the performance expected. Acknowledging suppliers' efforts is important in building relationships. The rewards may be intrinsic in value such as, a certificate of achievement or other publicity. Buying companies can create promotional contests to highlight the importance of performance improvement.

Substantial improvements or innovations may justify longer contracts, or other business opportunities. The buyer should always be looking for suppliers who can compete in tomorrow's market place. This will assist the buyer's organisation in staying ahead of the competition.

Longer term contracts and repeat business reflects the aims of modern procurement practice, such as reducing the supplier base for critical items and forge closer working relationships where both the supplier and buyer are committed to continuous improvement.

Reviewing Supplier Performance

Supplier performance measurement methods should be regularly reviewed, to ensure that it is still in line with organisational strategy and company policy. Review meetings should be agreed with suppliers and customers/users and form part of the contract. For critical items regular reviews will be necessary.

The performance information collated will create a "performance profile" which will be invaluable to the buyer when analysing potential and existing buyers and for determining standards. The suppliers' opinion of their own performance, as well as that of the buyers' organisation, should be taken into account. Where suppliers are undertaking identical measurement themselves, then the comparisons should present no surprises, thus removing any conflicts of the "you did/I did not" nature. This can assist the buyer in making improvements to their internal supply chain, so also demonstrating a good working relationship with suppliers and assisting in the promotion of their organisation to other suppliers, as a quality client.

Having clear and agreed KPIs can help to prevent problems, consider how this might has assisted to prevent at least some, of the following "kaleidoscope" of problems

Case Study: Jones Limited

Jones Limited produces a range of fast moving consumer products that are sold to retailers. They have traditionally enjoyed a strong position in this marketplace for many years. However, the market has recently become increasingly competitive with two companies who previously were producing for the wholesale sector. They are now able to produce on a marginal cost basis to the retail sector and therefore these new entrants have very low costs, and are also highly efficient.

Jones Limited now needs to become a leaner and lower cost producer and therefore the business needs to concentrate on:
• Making their standard products cheaper
• Keeping lower levels of raw material inventory
• Having customer demand driven production

There was widespread discussion and disagreement about the best way forward. Some of the board members were interested in the raw materials supplies side of the organisation and the contribution that it may make to increased efficiency and profitability.

However, the Production Director (that the buying department reported to), said that in his opinion, most of the suppliers were a law unto themselves. The Sales Director observed that Jones Limited was themselves suppliers to their retail customers and that Jones Limited had to worked closely with them; indeed the Sales Director was sure that they would be able to obtain demand information from the retailers so the Production could be more demand driven and that in turn, would perhaps mean having more responsive suppliers. After much discussion, the Managing Director decided a new procurement manager was to be employed to move forward the buying department. This was made a Procurement Director designate position and would therefore report direct to the Managing Director.

As the newly recruited Procurement manager, you are well aware of the challenges of sourcing and managing suppliers. However you are concerned that there is a general lack of awareness of these problems within Jones Limited and you appreciate that you have an interesting few months ahead.

You have undertaken an initial survey of the procurement function and this has revealed the following:

- Suppliers were being selected on the basis of a technical specification
- All purchases seem to be all treated in the same manner regardless of value or type
- Suppliers are generally selected on a lowest price basis
- There are two suppliers for the most of the products purchased; you were told that this was so that Jones Limited could play one supplier off against the other in price negotiations; indeed you heard the expression "squeezing suppliers" many times.
- No effective supplier KPIs exist

As if these general problems were not enough, you also learnt that specifically, two major suppliers of important raw materials were causing immediate problems:

- Packright Limited was demanding a 12.3 % price increase to cover for increase in fuel/energy prices due to the last escalations in the world oil market prices. They have said that as they have now been talking to Jones Limited for over 7 weeks but have got no satisfactory answer, consequently if this increase was not forthcoming, then Packright have said that all deliveries would be suspended.
- Enzyme PLC were becoming unreliable by increasingly showing poor delivery/late arrival performance, coupled with product damage as a result of poor packing or, in-transit damage.

It was also clear to you, that relationships with suppliers tended to be short term and adversarial. You have observed some heated discussions taking place with Enzyme PLC over a late delivery. You were however unable to determine what the performance levels were supposed to be, as you were told that there were no supplier performance criteria available. You are aware that you will need to engage with suppliers and therefore see that supplier management and relationships will need to be improved and whilst, you will be unable to develop and maintain deep relationships with every one of the suppliers, you are confident that something must be done.

You decided to have a discussion with some of your staff about the reality of working differently with suppliers so that they could see that the old methods were not always the best. Some of the comments you had were as follows:

"I do not believe that suppliers can be a positive partner as they also deal with our competitors. They cannot therefore be trusted and we therefore have to be secretive with them on many things."

"We do not have the time to work together. This will take up too much time; and we only have time have to focus on what is likely to be happening next week".

"We are low cost driven, so anything else is secondary. It is them and us. They are our opponents!"

"My job is to focus on crunching numbers, creating purchase orders and chasing up suppliers; it is not my job to be nice with suppliers."

Clearly, in the real world of personalities and professional relationships that exist at Jones Limited, there are some obstacles to be climbed.

Loss and Disputes

Where there has been a poor supplier performance or it has been determined that there has been some loss and a dispute ensures, then legal considerations are needed.

Direct loss

In law, there is no clear definition of direct loss. This is due to the fact that when the courts consider damages, they will consider each case upon its own facts. What the parties have agreed in the contract and the circumstances of breach, this will then the court to award damages. However it does not necessarily follow that when consequential loss is excluded, economic loss or loss of profits cannot be recovered.

Where, for example, likely losses are loss of business, loss of profit and the increased cost of finding a replacement service, it can be argued that such would be direct losses. Examples of what constituted direct loss are losses that flowed directly and actually, in the ordinary course of events, from breach of contract; particularly loss of profit, expenses thrown away and money spent as a result of the breaches, might all be recoverable as damages.

Direct loss has been defined as that which flows naturally from the breach without other intervening causes, and that which is independent of special circumstances.

Indirect loss

This is the opposite of direct loss and it has been held that the words "indirect or consequential" did not exclude liability for damages which are the direct and natural result of the breach.

In a recent case on what constitutes direct and indirect loss, the judge defined "consequential" as "such loss as the claimants may prove over and above that which arose as a direct result of such breaches the claimants may prove, in accordance with the rules laid down in the first limb of the rule in Hadley v Baxendale".

Where consequential or indirect loss is excluded in the contract, this does not necessarily mean that economic loss or loss of profits cannot be recovered. The increased cost for a claimant of, for example, finding a replacement service is likely to be considered as direct loss. However, damages for loss of business and therefore loss of profit will only be recoverable if they are closely related to any breach by the defendant.

Disputes and resolution

Clearly where these can not be settled, then courts of law become involved. This can be expensive and is also public, plus also the cost of delay, cost to reputations etc.

Alternative Dispute Resolution (ADR) is an alternative to litigation and arbitration provides an opportunity even when direct negotiations have failed for parties to control the outcome of their dispute. Alternative Dispute Resolution (ADR) is the collective term for the ways that parties can settle civil disputes, with the help of an independent third party and without the need for a formal court hearing. The term originated in America in a drive to find alternatives to the traditional legal system which was felt to be adversarial, costly, unpredictable, rigid, too professionalised, damaging to relationships and limited to narrow rights based remedies compared to creative problem solving.

The acceptance of ADR grew as the preferred term in business and civil litigation worlds as its popularity is based on the following facts:
- Quicker than litigation
- Relatively cheaper
- Can help to resolve disputes without damaging commercial relations

Methods of ADR

There are some very different characteristics and some of the methods of ADR are well known: the use of Ombudsmen such as the Parliamentary Ombudsman, and the various Regulators like the Energy Regulator, OFGEN and the Rail Regulator.

Mediation is also used successfully to resolve a wide range of disputes, whether or not they involve money, including cases involving problems with child residence and contact; neighbour and land disputes, clinical negligence and personal injury cases as well as in business and commercial areas. Mediation gives the party or parties in dispute, the opportunity to reach a settlement without a court hearing and with the help of an independent third party, a mediator.

The mediator's job is not to make a decision; instead they will help the parties to explore the strengths and weaknesses of their cases and to identify possible solutions helping them to reach a solution between themselves. Agreeing to use mediation does not prevent the parties from being able to eventually continue with court proceedings, if they cannot come to an agreement. Mediation is a flexible process and, with experience, a Mediator can exploit that flexibility. Mediation is a voluntary, non-binding, private dispute resolution process in which a neutral person helps the parties tries to reach a negotiated settlement.

Essentially, the following framework provides safe foundations on which to build.

Mediation procedures
1) Preliminary contact between the Parties and the Mediator to:
- Agree to mediation
- Agree terms of mediation including date/s, duration, location, representation, legal framework, costs and documentation.

2) Limited, brief written summaries of the case are submitted by Parties in advance to:
- Inform the Mediator
- Focus Parties on the real issues.

3) Initial joint meeting at which:
* The Mediator clarifies the position and establishes ground rules
* The Parties present a summary of their case to each other
* Issues are clarified.

4) Private, confidential meetings between the Mediator and each Party separately to:
* Examine the important issues and needs of each Party
* Encourage openness about weaknesses as well as strengths
* Discuss options for settlement.

5) Joint meetings as appropriate throughout the mediation at which Parties may:
* Negotiate directly
* Discuss differences, particularly in understanding of fact or expert opinion or likely legal outcome
* Set the settlement down in writing or agree further action.

The Mediator brings negotiating, problem-solving and communication skills to the process, deployed from a position of independence and neutrality, making progress possible where direct negotiations may have stalled.
During the mediation process the mediator fulfils several important roles:

* A manager of the process, providing firm but sensitive control conveying confidence that it is all worthwhile and giving momentum and a sense of purpose and progress
* A facilitator, helping the parties to overcome deadlock and to find a way of working cooperatively towards a settlement that is mutually acceptable
* An information-gatherer, absorbing and organising data and identifying common ground shared goals and zones of agreement
* A reality-tester, helping parties take a private realistic view of the dispute rather than public posturing and muscle flexing
* A problem-solver, bringing a clear head and creative mind to help the parties construct an outcome that best meets their needs when compared with the alternatives of non agreement or an imposed decision by an arbitrator judge or jury.
* A sponge, which soaks up the parties' feelings and frustrations and helps them to channel their energies into positive approaches to the issues
* A scribe, who writes or assists in the writing of the agreement, checking that all issues are covered and that all terms of the agreement are clear
* A settlement-supervisor, checking that settlement agreements are working and being available if problems occur this is occasionally requested
* A settlement-prompter, who, if no agreement is reached at the mediation, will help parties to keep the momentum towards settlement

The essence of mediation and the reason for its success is that it introduces a powerful structure and dynamic into any negotiation or dispute discussion. The mediator acts as a catalyst being an independent neutral who is committed to helping the parties to settle, but who does not have a stake in the dispute either as a party or as an advocate or representative.

Less well known ADR methods include the following:
- Neutral Evaluation where a neutral third party provides a non-binding assessment of the merits of the case
- Conciliation which is similar to mediation but the third party (conciliator) takes a more interventionist role
- Expert Determination where an independent expert is used to decide the issue
- Neutral Fact Finding is used in cases involving complex technical issues where a neutral expert investigates the facts of the case and produces a non binding evaluation of the merits
- Med/Arb (a mixture of mediation and arbitration) is where parties agree to mediate but refer the dispute to arbitration if the mediation is unsuccessful.

The relationship between ADR and the Courts

For some time it has been Government policy that disputes should be resolved at a proportionate level, and that the courts should be the dispute resolution method of last resort. Although ADR is independent of the court system, a judge can recommend that parties involved in litigation enter into it. The court may also impose cost sanctions if it decides that one or more of the parties has been unreasonable in refusing to attempt ADR. The courts will also take into account behaviour during the pre-litigation period including whether or not an attempt has been made to use ADR.

For some types of dispute, specific pre-action Protocols exist to set out the steps parties are expected to take before issuing court proceeding. For all other types of disputes parties are expected to follow the Practice Direction for Protocols. These details are available on: www.dca.gov.uk/civil/procrules_fin/contents/practice_directions/pd_protocol.htm

Monitoring strategy and performance

No single business or procurement strategy will ever sustain in the long run due to the ever changing dynamic market and external demands. Procurement and supply chain strategies will need to be constantly worked on. The following diagram shows one way to monitor the strategy; the iterative nature of the monitoring process will be seen.

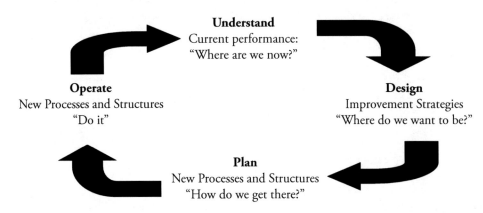

Understand
Current performance:
"Where are we now?"

Operate
New Processes and Structures
"Do it"

Design
Improvement Strategies
"Where do we want to be?"

Plan
New Processes and Structures
"How do we get there?"

On understanding the current performance, the aim is to describe the current supply chain performance. On the design improvement strategies, the aim here is to design improvement strategies and challenge every detail in the current supply chain. Here the requirement is to consider the changes needed to make the improvements to take you towards the vision/future situation required. After this, the remaining stages of Plan and Operate the new processes and structures will easily follows.

This whole process is more fully covered as a Model for Supply Chain Improvement in "Excellence in Supply Chain Management - How to understand and improve supply chains" by Stuart Emmett (2008).

Supply Chain analysis

To monitor the total supply chain the following questions can be asked:
- When were all the lead times last examined?
- When were all the supply chain processes mapped?
- Were value added and non-value added activities clearly identified?
- What barriers are there to increasing service and reducing costs?
- Are there multi functional teams working on improving materials and information flow?
- Have manufacturing and supply lead times been reduced in the last three years?
- Have lot sizes and set-up times been reduced in the last three years?
- Have all inventories been reduced in the last three years?
- Are inventory buffers in existence to protect against quality problems?
- Are there agreements with suppliers and mutually agreed goals for continuous improvement?
- Are suppliers certified to "no inspection" required?
- Are communications "fit for purpose" and are both electronic and also face/face?
- Is lead-time precisely known for both supply replenishment and for customer deliveries?
- Is little time spent on expediting?
- Are performance measures weighted towards short lead times and quick response with minimal inventory levels?

The following case study looks at procurement in NHS Supplies and describes the situation seen by its author back in the late 1990s. It does illustrate the need for a central role of supply chain management in procurement.

Case Study: NHS Supplies

The traditional trading patterns of the past decades are changing rapidly in almost every sector and the NHS is no exception. The main drivers for this change are technological developments, an expanding trade and a dramatic increase in customer expectations .In order to exploit these opportunities, supply chain management, and purchasing in particular, is being put under the spotlight.

In my experience as a consultant, standards of purchasing vary tremendously within the NHS. There are some excellent departments with high-calibre individuals who are imaginative and skilled in a wide range of modern purchasing techniques. But there are also some buyers, who are less imaginative, having lower skill levels and are often more interested in filing than doing a good deal.

In one trust I examined recently, a 17-strong department was responsible for using just 40 percent or so of its £60 million total spend. All of the expenditure on pharmaceuticals, and most of that on the estate, was outside the involvement of the department. Even in areas where purchasing was involved, such as IT consumables and food, the rest of the organisation's view of purchasing staff was that "their job is to order what we tell them to". Some problems were evident: there were too many petty controls, for example, far too much emphasis on paper pushing and very little real added value. There was also a severe lack of useful information with which to make sensible decisions. For example, if a buyer wanted to know how much was spent with a particular supplier in the previous year, what else was bought from them, how they had been performing recently or how their prices had moved, it was difficult and time consuming to access the data.

If they wanted to ask more fundamental questions, such as by how much a supplier's performance was improving or declining, whether any of its main competitors were also supplying the trust, or how many different users in the trust had dealt with that supplier, it was virtually impossible to find the answers. Yet, access to information like this is the first step in a purchasing improvement programme. One reason for the problems was the culture of suspicion and blame in which the function operated. And this kind of stultifying environment brings its own problems. Good staffs with imagination and intelligence either leave through frustration, or gradually become disenchanted. In some organisations, keeping your head down and blaming others when something goes wrong is the only way to survive.

What trusts like this need is a three-fold programme.
- First they must change the structure of the purchasing department, promote the best staff and encourage new employees to adopt modern ideas and gain experience of up-to-date buying techniques.
- Second, they must improve their purchasing systems, so that administration is more streamlined and information is more accessible.
- Third, and perhaps most importantly, they must embark on a scheme of attitude and culture change, so that everyone with supplier contact - not just those in purchasing - understands the main implications of their behaviour and how their actions affect the way their suppliers respond and behave towards them.

These staff needs to be given new ideas and the enthusiasm to act on them. If they can grasp the nettle and make these changes, then really dramatic improvements should be forthcoming. Ineffective departments add cost, not value. They miss the chance to save money by not taking a more commercial approach to agreeing and awarding contracts. They miss opportunities to encourage suppliers to improve their quality of service, product, and delivery. They also miss opportunities to drive down internal costs through efficient processing, and to drive down external costs through managing and removing the "extras", which so often creep in and can sometimes add as much as 25 percent to a price.

Besides this, service levels can be substandard. While there could be a high level of stock available, for example, it could take up to seven days to get that stock to the ward, or office, that needs it. World-class organisations get stock items delivered in minutes, rather than days.

Taking a professional approach to purchasing is crucial. Not only does it add value - through the achievement of bought-in cost savings, better supplier relationships and quality improvements - it also helps organisations to minimise most of the commercial and legal risks that can accompany the sourcing process. It is vital that NHS Trusts' purchasing staff are well resourced, trained, and supported. There must be the procedural arid organisational backing in place to allow departments to operate effectively and really add value.

One technique that is currently being adopted in many industries is supply chain integration. True integration provides the ability to balance long-term future capacity and forecasted demand throughout the supply chain. It also helps to identify potential bottlenecks arid constraints, and to find solutions with partners. If applied throughout a trust, it would offer substantial benefits. It would mean that all processes were properly aligned, operating relationships were streamlined, and trouble free and key suppliers were seen as part of the overall process of service delivery.

Supply Chain Integration is an emerging and powerful method of purchasing that uses e-commerce and a range of other management tools to integrate and streamline the whole supply chain to produce significant, sustained advantage. It has recently been described as "an alignment of the end-to-end supply chain and the creation of an integrated and high-performance entity that will deliver superior end-customer value". Examples of organisations exploiting SCI in the consumer electronics and automotive industries show leading firms offering customised products, while achieving significant savings and efficiencies. This involves breaking down barriers and building trust and collaborative relationships with users and suppliers.

It is clear that purchasing in the NHS is under scrutiny and unlikely to remain unchanged. The new Purchasing and Supply Agency has a mission to save money and make buying in the NHS more efficient. The changing market place and the demands facing the health service will force a re-evaluation of the whole supply chain. Only by integrating the supply chain can the full benefits be realised. I only hope that purchasers grasp these with both hands.

Source: Supply Management 15 June 2000.

To emphasise the continual need for reviewing strategy, the following case studies illustrate how supply strategies have changed in recent years.

Case Study: A UK Car Assemblers Supply strategy

The company has a focused product supply strategy that is integrally linked to the philosophy of the 'extended enterprise' where the destinies of suppliers, dealers and workers at every level of the business are inseparable. This is reinforced through promotional and marketing messages which stress the responsibility the company owes to its dealer network. The former chairman had previously and publicly threw down the gauntlet to component suppliers, in a bid to make them understand that the company was not a meal ticket. Nowadays, threats are replaced by promises. The following statement for the MD explains their current position:

"Our relationship with the supply community today is very pervasive. It is not just about price and output any more, nor has it been for a long time; but it is about culture, management style and about whether the right things are happening within the framework of the business for a particular partner to be someone in whom we can invest a long term, life time partnership relationship. You have to handle it with care."

The company now recognizes that a supplier can be a positive partner and a loyal companion while serving different customers, and that having different dialogues can be healthy. "We have to share the benefits, to understand that you cannot have a lifetime relationship unless the partner is financially healthy, but that achieving this does not introduce a price and cost structure that is uncompetitive to the end product," the MD says. "At one time, people would say, 'if we do this, it will benefit X, Y and Z as well, but we take the view that you waste a lot of time in that narrow mind-set. It is more productive to think about the fact that by both of you being involved there is a benefit of shared knowledge and experience which benefits everyone, in particular your customers. We have recognized that just because you happen to be the biggest link in the chain which comprises the extended enterprise, this does not imply superiority. You need to use your facilities, resources and even your philosophical capability to extend processes in all directions, both internally and externally."

Reflection questions:
1.   What brought about the change in relationships?
2.   What are the key aspects now involved?

Case Study: Supplies practices in Japan

These are characterised by suppliers being given clear specifications and blanket orders with predictable end customer schedules. They use fewer and local suppliers with the following requirements being common.
•   Fast response to customers requirements

- Frequent JIT deliveries of small batches
- Short supply lead times
- Quality circles team approach
- Zero defects with elimination of inspection on receipt
- Zero defects production with quick process changeovers

The consequences of such practices are:
- High quality at lower cost
- Increased productivity
- Early identification of scrap and defects
- Low inventory carry costs
- Minimum paperwork controls

Reflection questions:
1. What are the key aspects involved here?
2. What type of relationship exists here?

Finally, in comparing procurement activity, say annually, the following strategic measures can be used:

- Total procurement expenditure as a percentage of sales revenue
- Procurement operating expenses as a percentage of total procurement spend
- Number of procurement staff as a percentage of the companies total staff
- Sales revenue per procurement employee
- Total procurement spend per procurement employee
- Number of active suppliers per procurement employee
- Procurement spend per active supplier
- Cost of operating the procurement function per active supplier
- Percentage of active suppliers for 50%, 75% and 90% of procurement spend
- Percentage change in number of active suppliers in a reporting period
- Percentage of total spend with any "deemed" sensitive suppliers e.g. local suppliers, small companies etc.
- Percentage of total company purchases handled by the procurement department

Action Time: MNC Global Chemicals

MNC Global Chemicals are a multi national chemical manufacturer with a strong manufacturing presence in Europe, Far East & USA.

The Global Head of Procurement (GHOP) believes the function could perform better and that improvement opportunities are being missed.

At a recent meeting with the Global Head of Finance (GHOF), it was clear that as far as the budgets were concerned, that procurement was well on target. Indeed the GHOF said that the GHOP had nothing really to be concerned about.

However the GHOP remained concerned by the reported dissatisfaction from customers and what further concerned the GHOP greatly, was the belief in the business, that procurement added no value.

Task
What that needs to be done to demonstrate the performance of procurement?

4.0. Procurement best practice, tools and techniques

In this final part of the book we look at a variety of aspects that reveal best practice and indicate some useful tools and techniques.

We start with suppliers pricing and price analysis and then take a wider look at the role of using relationship based approaches.

Global sourcing is then looked at followed by outsourcing. Next we examine the role of information communication technology and E-business with a wide discussion on E-procurement. We continue with Corporate Social Responsibility including the environmental "green" aspects and conclude with our views on the importance of Supplier Development.

Suppliers' Pricing

Price is the value of a product or service measured by money. It is the consideration to be paid or given, for an article, goods, service or something that desired, offered and purchased. It involves cost with the total sum involved including the price, plus, all that is associated with owning or using a product or a service.

In procurement, comparing prices enables evaluation and appraisal of the relative values offered by different suppliers.

Economists view supply and demand as balanced by the influence of price, and the point where equilibrium is found, is the point where supply and demand are equal. Therefore slight changes in price may cause substantial changes in demand; here the demand is said to be elastic, and for example, suppliers will consider reducing prices as a lower price will result in enhanced revenue.

An example here is the growth of cheap air line travel.

Where however substantial price changes have little effects to the demand, then the demand is said to be inelastic. This will happen where:
- There are few substitutes or competitors
- Buyers are slow to change habits and practices and do not search for alternatives
- Buyers do not challenge high prices

An example here is the price of oil.

The theory on elasticity of demand applies in times of "perfect" competition where the market sets the price. Perfect competition may also apply in commodity markets, for example cocoa beans for confectionery manufacture, however some buying has to operate in "imperfect" competition and here the most common forms are:

Type	Number of Suppliers	Supplier Market Entry
Monopoly	One	None
Oligopoly	Few e.g. oil production	Limited
Monopolistic competition	Many	Competition between suppliers

Pricing strategy

Price negotiation is an important aspect in procurement. In terms of the supplier and the buyer, then the following are the considerations on pricing.

Suppliers will consider:
- The market position occupied ranging from a monopoly position with the seller setting the price (subject to legislative controls), to pure competition where the market sets the price
- The nature of demand; elastic or inelastic
- What the buyer will pay, charging what the market will bear
- Competitors prices
- Suppliers need for the business
- Perceived long term value for the supplier, for example, payments, continuity of orders
- Supply of standard "commodity" products or specialised "bespoke" products
- Product life-cycle stage, for example, declining products may be price discounted
- Order volumes
- Pricing options, see below
- Pricing for market penetration purposes by pricing low to win a larger share

In turn, purchasers will consider the following on pricing:
- The risk attached to the purchase and the method of pricing, from firm price to cost pricing
- The position in the market; for example, a monopoly supplier
- The number of suppliers in the market and the possibility to source from another supplier
- Prices paid by other buyers
- The relationship of price with value
- Payment terms
- Price analysis to determine what is "reasonable"
- Order volumes

Price analysis

Price analysis is the breaking down of a quoted price into its constituent elements for the purpose of determining the reasonableness, or otherwise, of the proposed charge. The cost knowledge and information the buyer needs will come from past experience, from internal costing estimates or, from the suppliers provided cost information.

Additionally, other management accounting practices such as life-cycle costing, target costing etc. are helpful. No procurement manager can be effective without a good knowledge of costing.

Price variation

Prices can vary at different times due to many reasons, for example:
- Quality, for example, use of brand name from a non brand name
- Quantity, for example, incentives in placing larger orders
- Time, for example, in buying in quiet periods
- Cost, for example, early payment incentives
- Place, for example, changing to ex works terms for import purchases

Price indexing

This involves reviewing price increases, with, market price increases and makes a comparison with published price indices, for example:

- UK's Consumer Prices Index allows comparison of the inflation rate in the UK against that in the rest of Europe.
- UK's Retail Price Index; this is an average measure of change in the prices of goods and services. Once published, it is never revised.
- UK's CIPS Price Indexes covering basic commodities
- USA's Bureau of Labour Studies; Producer Price Index

The usage of such indices can be extended beyond simple comparisons, for example, your prices have risen last year by 4% but you expected a reduction of 3%. However the external indexing shows an increase of 7%, therefore in effect then your prices have remained static.

Price and value

Price and value are not the same, with value often being viewed what comes over the whole life of a product or service. Alternatively value is often seen as being what the customer perceives it to be and is something they are prepared to pay for. By conducting analysis on existing materials and products in liaison with other departments, cost savings can be made throughout the supply chain.

Value analysis is often carried out as a team project with input from the user, research and development, procurement, warehousing, production, distribution and finance. As part of a team, procurement will collate data on products and materials from the marketplace. Existing and potential suppliers can be involved in making suggestions to reduce costs and add value as well as looking for opportunities to reduce costs in product components and materials, packaging, storage and distribution, with also opportunities to add value to existing product design. Procurement may for example, suggest alterations to existing products within the early or mature stage of their life-cycle.

Price Options

All the above factors will influence the final decision and, in practice, the agreements between sellers and buyers will be of two types, firm price agreements and cost price agreements.

Firm price agreements are often said to be more advantageous to buyers for the following reasons:
•   Suppliers bear all the price risk changes, meanwhile the buyer knows what is to be paid
•   Suppliers have the maximum incentive to produce efficiently and on time, as the supplier has to pay for all cost increases, but will keep all cost savings
•   A minimum of administration is needed

With cost price agreements, the supplier adds a fixed percentage to costs or agrees a fixed management fee, for their profit, and the buyer pays for all costs. This can be seen as being disadvantageous for the buyer as:
•   Buyers bear all the financial risks
•   Sellers have no incentive to be more efficient or effective as their costs are being paid "anyway"
•   Administration can be difficult as buyers need to have all the appropriate knowledge of the sellers processing practices and cost structures

Cost-plus agreements are however very common in the supply of services such as distribution. Here the purchaser, who has recently outsourced the service, will still have "in-house" knowledge of all the cost structures. Of course this knowledge will need to be updated over time.

Cost-plus is also becoming increasingly common in projects and contracting. At the construction of T5 London Heathrow Airport there is also cost sharing of any savings or overruns; other aspects of the T5 contract are as follows:

The T5 Contract

The T5 Agreement is central to everything that's good about Terminal 5.
It is BAA's response to a project whose sheer size and complexity defy traditional construction management techniques. Legally binding, in essence it's a contract in reverse. Instead of specifying what redress can be taken in the event of things going wrong, it aims to stop problems happening in the first place. This is done by fostering constructive behaviour and a recrimination-free environment. Key features include:

Ownership of risk
In contrast to most so-called partnership deals, risk is not shared between client and contractors. BAA carries it all, allowing contractors to concentrate on delivering results. The focus is on managing out the cause of problems, not their effects if they do happen.

Complexity management
The task of building T5 is split into 16 main projects, plus 147 sub-projects of between £30 million and £150 million each. The agreement binds BAA and its 60 key first-tier' suppliers only, these suppliers are themselves responsible for the appointment and management of second- and third-tier suppliers, who must also work within the spirit of the agreement.

Close supplier involvement
To avoid the traditional and potentially damaging demarcation between design and build, key suppliers were brought on board at a much earlier stage in the planning process than is usual. This enabled potential hitches to be spotted before designs were finalised and construction began.

Integrated teamwork
Both within and across teams, the concentration has been on proactive problem-solving rather than the avoidance of litigation.

Shared values
Common induction programmes and regular communication initiatives help to ensure that all of the 6,000 workers from 400 supplier companies who can be involved at any given time share the same values and objectives, which include being proud of working on T5 and delivering the project on time, on budget, to quality and safely.

Source: Human Resources November 2004.

Clearly T5 represents more than just cost plus, but continues into a whole different collaborative relationship with suppliers; a theme we examine next.

Relationship-based approaches

Simply, the following supplier relationships can be noted:

Relationship	Examples of Procurement methods used
Transactional	Competitive tendering and spot buying
Cooperative	Negotiation and preferred suppliers with framework agreements
Collaborative	Open book and joint working towards continuous improvements

The change from more arms length transactional relationships to closer working collaborative relationships can also reflect a move towards more adaptive and effective supply chains. It will also involve different levels of trust, shown overleaf as levels one to three.

Level one trust	Level two trust	Level three trust
Boundary trust	Reliable trust	Goodwill trust
Contractual	Competence	Commitment
Explicit promises	Known standards	Anything that is required to foster the relationship
Standard performance	Satisfactory performance	Success beyond expectation
Mistakes bring enforcement	$\Longrightarrow$	Mistakes give shared learning for advantage
Exchange data for transactions	Cooperate on information for mutual access	Cognitive connections and joint decision making
Animal brain	$\Longrightarrow$	Human brain
Symbonic	Share	Swap
Time bound (as far as the contract says)	$\Longrightarrow$	Open-ended, ongoing and leaving a legacy

These levels of trust also make for an interesting comparison between transactional and collaborative relationships and an "ideal-typical" comparison follows.

Transactional relationships	Collaborative relationships
Price/Risk Price orientation Price dominates One way Customer demands sensitive data Customer keeps all cost savings All risk with supplier, the buyer risks little "What is in it for me" Short term	Total cost of ownership Shared destiny dominates Two way exchanges Exchanges of sensitive data Mutual efforts to reduce costs, times and waste Shared risk and benefits "What is in it for us" Long term
Negotiations Strong use of ploys in negotiations Power based Win/lose "One off" deals Walk in and out of, change is easy Easy to set up Adversarial and maybe inefficient for one party "Partnershaft"	Mutual gains "rule" discussions Equality based Win/win "For ever" together Difficult to break, change is difficult Difficult to set up Challenging to implement and continue with Partnership

(continued opposite)

Interpersonal Relationships	
No personal relationships	Strong personal relationship
Separated/arms length	Close/alliance
Low contact/closed	Shared vision/open
Predatory power based	Proactive and more people based
Hierarchical /superior subordinate	Equality
Blame culture	Problem solving "gain" culture
Alienated employees	Motivated employees
Trust	
Trust is based on what the contract says (contractual trust)	Trust is based on goodwill, commitment and cooperation
Little ongoing trust	Continual trust plus risk/benefits sharing
Power based "spin"	Pragmatic "tough" trust
Controls	
Strong on tactical/ departmental controls	Strong on marketing strategy and supply chain alignment
High formal controls	Self controlled
Rigid contracts	Flexible contracts
Technical performance and the specifications "rule"	Work beyond just "one" technical view
Resource and capacity capabilities	Mutual long term capabilities
Measure by non compliance	Both measure and agree remedial action

Changing from more transactional methods to collaborative approaches goes far beyond the technical issues, of say ICT connectivity, and fully embraces the soft skills. The view and belief here from sponsors of collaborative approaches is that if all players would work well together that a lot more would get done more efficiently and more effectively. It is seen that the evidence for this from relationship principles is overwhelming.

However many people will not subscribe to such a mutually sharing collaborative supply chain management approach. A major reason for not doing this is that procurement is founded on power and therefore two way collaboration sits here as an uneasy concept. We look at power in procurement below.

Another major reason however is that soft skills are the hard skills for many people in business. Indeed, supply chain management collaboration between companies is unlikely to succeed, without appropriate recognition that soft skill development is required.

Power

As mentioned earlier in part 2.0. and also above, relationships in procurement between buyers and sellers will vary; power is not always equally distributed.
For example buyers have power when:
- They have a high spend
- They are a large company with a good reputation that sellers desire to be associated with

- They are a growing developing company with future potential
- They have a large market share and influence
- The supplier market is very competitive

Meanwhile sellers have power where:

- There are barriers to entry for other suppliers into their market, for example, requirements for specialised research and development
- They have "unique" products. For example, OEM spare parts
- They are monopoly or oligopoly; the association of power to monopoly or competition markets is shown further below:

Feature	Monopoly	Oligopoly	"Perfect" competition
Supply & Demand Control	Statutory	Fewer companies, with the possibility of market collusions	No controls, all open
Barriers to entry	Retained and look to maintain "status quo"	High costs to enter the market for "new" suppliers	Few to no barriers and low costs to enter
Market view	Focus and concentrate.	Large and valuable markets. Possible cartels	Customers can easily "switch." Continual search for providing what is required and needed.
Customers view	No really considered as the customer has no choice	Sometimes	Customer "rules"
Prices	Can charge "What the market will bear"	Stable and related to costs and desired profits. Possible price fixing.	Demand driven, possible cost plus provision.
Examples	Some oil companies	UK Supermarkets	UK Car assembly

The relative power dominance, between buyers and suppliers, can be further seen as follows:

With the buyer dominant:

- Then there is often a small number of big buyers who buy a large percentage of a sellers output
- It is easy for buyer to switch as there are many sources of supply
- Low transaction costs
- "Take it or leave it" approach

With seller dominant:

- There is often a small number of big sellers who supply to many buyers
- It is difficult for buyers to switch as there are few sources of supply
- High transaction costs
- They can "enforce"

With such relative levels of dominance, then this leads to unequal power distributions; these can be seen as a foundation for the forming of adversarial relationships.

Sharp eyed and experienced readers will also see the connection to the Kraljic portfolio where for example, the buyer's behaviour may be as follows:

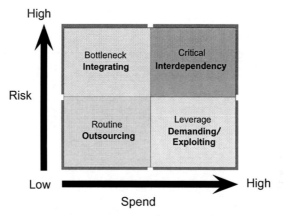

In turn; the link to more collaborative approaches maybe seen:

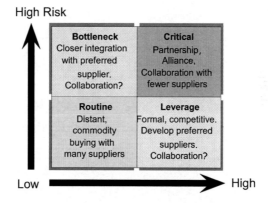

In turn, related to risks, then we can see a strategic and tactical approach to procurement forming, as follows:

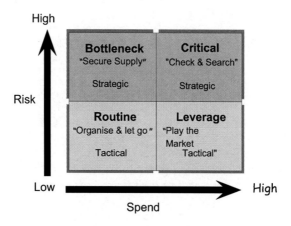

From this we can then see that there are actually varied levels of trust, openness and information exchange that results in varied types of relationships involved:

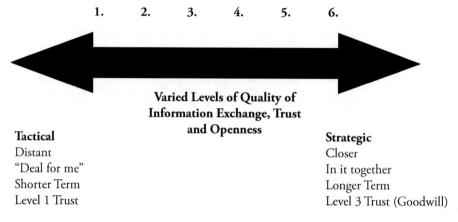

| 1. | 2. | 3. | 4. | 5. | 6. |

Varied Levels of Quality of Information Exchange, Trust and Openness

Tactical	**Strategic**
Distant	Closer
"Deal for me"	In it together
Shorter Term	Longer Term
Level 1 Trust	Level 3 Trust (Goodwill)

We can expand this further where:

Tactical procurement uses the new trainee and junior buyers and has the following types of relationships:

1. Adversary relationships; "Take it or leave it"
2. Transactional relationships; Normal ordering
3. Single Source relationships; Exclusive agreements usually at fixed price for a specific time

Strategic procurement uses the more senior buyers with the following types of relationships:

4. Strategic alliance relationships; Working together for a specific purpose
5. Collaborative relationships; Commitment with shared risks/benefits
6. Co-destiny relationships; Interdependency

Relating this back to Kraljic, then the following gives us an ideal typical perspective:

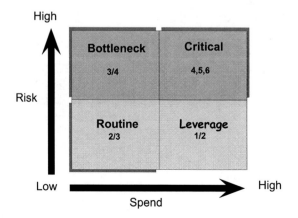

Keeping in our ideal typical view, then we can recap on the following stereotypes between transactional and collaborative approaches.

Transactional relationships have the following characteristics:
- Short term
- Separated/arms length
- Wiifm ("What's in it for me?")
- "One off"
- Low contact/closed
- Little trust
- Price dominates
- "One night stand"
- Power based
- Win/loose
- One way (customer demands sensitive data)
- Customer keeps all cost savings
- All risk with supplier, customer risks zero
- Power based "spin"
- Adversarial and inefficient
- Hierarchical/superior subordinate
- Blame culture
- High formal controls
- Rigid contracts
- Alienated employees
- Predatory
- Technical Performance specifications "rule"

Whereas **Collaborative relationships** are typified by the following:
- Long term
- Close/alliance
- Wiifu (us)
- "For ever"
- Shared vision/open
- Trust/risk/benefits
- Shared destiny
- "Marriage"
- Equality based
- Win/win
- Two way exchange of sensitive data
- Mutual to reduce costs, times and waste
- Shared risk and benefits
- Pragmatic trust
- Challenging to implement and continue with
- Equality
- Problem solving culture
- Self-controlled

- Flexible contracts
- Motivated employees
- Proactive
- Work beyond just "one" technical view

These differences are shown very clearly in the following case study on contracting:

Case Study: Contracting: Adversary or Collaboration?

The £757 million UK's Wembley National Stadium is one of the largest, most costly and complex construction schemes in the UK. Like all mega-projects, it poses enormous technical and logistical challenges. How a project is procured has a huge bearing on whether problems arise, and whether disputes break out between different parts of the construction team.

The stadium, was due to open on 13 May 2006, is being built under a design-and-build contract. This is a modern procurement method under which the main contractor (Multiplex at Wembley) in effect becomes the agent for the client, as well as being responsible for building the job.

This is a departure from the norm as traditionally; clients would deal independently with a designer, quantity surveyor and main contractor. Under design-and-build, however, the main contractor becomes the client's single point of contact, managing all other contractual relationships and the associated construction risks. The contract was also let on a fixed-price, lump-sum basis, shifting project risk to the contractor.

Dumping risk

Simon Murray, chairman of contractor Geoffrey Osborne and former director of major projects at Railtrack, says that in principle, "having a single party who you deal with and who takes responsibility is good, but it shouldn't be absolute. It's naive to put all risk onto the team doing the project. And if you are doing something of national significance, the idea that you can dump risk is absurd."

Risk dumping happens when companies pass responsibility for danger or problems that may occur during construction to firms they hire to do work for them.

"Main contractors' relationships with the supply chain are very patchy," Murray says. "There are some who want to get the lowest possible price and dump risk on the people they hire to do the work. Yet those who really know how to do things are the suppliers and specialist contractors." He contends that lowest price generally offers a false economy, since it forces suppliers to compromise on the quality of their technical solution.

Graham Edgell, group procurement director at contractor Morgan Sindall, agrees: "A lot of clients are after a quick process — they just want the job done, without any added-value. Because we make such a stupendous effort for such small reward, and our guys are under such pressure to deliver for the sum agreed, there's no opportunity of letting your guard down. You've tied yourself to a price and then you've got to go out and do it."

Despite the UK construction industry tradition of firms "buying work" — taking on projects at cost, simply to keep its people and plant active — British firms walked away from Wembley. Multiplex, however, claimed it could deliver the job for the price offered, and told its shareholders it would turn in a profit.

Adversary relationships

Wembley's great technical challenge was the structural design, construction and erection of its signature arch. Multiplex awarded steelwork firm Cleveland Bridge a lump-sum, fixed- price subcontract to fabricate, supply, deliver and erect the arch and roof.

However, this deal has encountered problems. In a claim against Multiplex for non-payment, Cleveland Bridge alleges that "by spring of 2003 there were serious problems arising from late and incomplete design by the civil and structural engineer, and delays in providing design information. The design changes and late information caused substantial costs increases, and delays and disruption to the subcontract works." Though Cleveland Bridge and Multiplex agreed a plan for accelerating work, plus compensation for the resulting change in the subcontract terms, a legal row then broke out, over alleged non-payment and contract breaches.

Despite the integration that should have been achieved by using a design-and-build contract, "Wembley is a graphic example of old-style adversarial contracting," according to Bob White, chief executive of Constructing Excellence, who have the task of improving performance in the construction industry. Despite the problems construction consultant Frank Griffiths says, "Wembley thought that a fixed-price, lump-sum contract could be the solution to all its problems. But that is only fine if the contractor has all the resources, time and money required for the project."

For such a contract to work, he adds, there has to be a rigorous work programme in place, and the client also needs to understand how the work is going to be subcontracted. "Through using a design and build contract, Wembley thought it had off-loaded risk to Multiplex, but it hadn't."

BAA and Collaborative approach

Other such mega-projects have taken a different approach. British Airports Authority (BAA), which is building Heathrow's Terminal 5 and they have enormous in-house procurement and project management teams, which supervise and reduce risk at all stages of design and construction.

"BAA has spent a fortune on ensuring they're informed," says Gil Howarth, founder of project management company Howarth Associates. Both have elected to work in partnership with their contractors, using the same offices, sharing information and resources, and, crucially, any savings or overruns.

BAA ditched conventional, reactive contracts, in which one party claims against another for delays or extra costs, in favour of creating incentives for proactive behaviour that would pre-empt problems. This tactic was guided by study of other major construction schemes, which revealed that, as a client, pushing risk to arm's length offered no real protection. "The client is always accountable in the end, on cost, time and health and safety — everything," says Riley. If the project were to go wrong, its failings would have an impact on BAA's reputation in the industry and on its standing in the City."

BAA took the radical step of accepting all risk, and took out £4 billion worth of insurance. "By doing that you take away negativity, allow space for innovation and create the opportunity for people to perform at levels they haven't been allowed to before," explains Riley. A special contract, the Terminal 5 Agreement, was produced for the project, requiring totally integrated teams, including principal subcontractors up through main contractors and designers to BAA itself and British Airways, Terminal S's end user. Contractors are paid on a cost- reimbursable basis, with performance encouraged by offering bonuses for beating target costs and completion dates; conversely, they share some of BAA's "pain" when schedules and costs overran. The agreement engaged all the key players early on to identify risks well before they come into the construction programme, leading to highly evolved risk-management strategies.

Cost efficiencies

The style of collaborative project management practised by BAA grew out of the North Sea oil and gas industry 30 years ago, and was being adapted for the construction sector by BAA and other clients more than a decade ago. But partnering only grabbed attention following the publication of two government-sponsored reports in 1994 and 1998 respectively, "Constructing the Team", authored by Sir Michael Latham, and "Rethinking Construction", by Sir John Egan.

Egan calculated the UK's £58 billion a year construction sector could achieve cost efficiencies of 30 percent, reduce defects by 20 percent and increase profitability from 2 percent to 5 percent by developing better leadership and greater focus on customer needs, by integrating processes and teams, and by adopting an agenda driven by quality rather than cost. For clients, this meant releasing large volumes of work in a steady stream to give contractors more continuity, and adopting them as preferred suppliers. For contractors, it meant breaking the practice of paying subcontractors late and of casually hiring and firing labour. Egan urged: "Industry must replace competitive tendering with long-term relationships based on clear measurement of performance and sustained improvements in quality and efficiency."

Source: Extracts from "A Game of Two Halves" in Supply Management 6 October 2005 by Andrew Mylius (the features editor of New Civil Engineer).

Changing procurement

This move towards more collaborative relationships will completely change procurement in some organisations, as the following indicates:

Old Procurement	New Procurement
Select lowest cost	Select on best value
Late involvement of key suppliers	Early supplier involvement
Defensive and confrontational contracts	Collaborate, cooperate, trust, honesty and sharing
Costly risk transfers leading to low profit margins	Open allocation of risks with auditable decisions and improved profits
High costs due to duplications, delays, disputes and defects (all are waste)	Time and cost savings without compromising quality
Poor H&S record	Improved H&S
Low rates of production/construction	Shorter lead-in times speeds production/construction
"Silo" working practices	Cooperation and longer term views foster training schemes and shared learning
No whole life costing	Focus on Asset management
Every contract is a steep new learning curve	Learning transferred from project to project and continuous improvements
Dissatisfied users/customers/tenants	Increased satisfaction and wider community benefits

Source: After "Partnering Works" The Housing Forum Report (2003)

Indeed the UK oil and gas sector has its Supply Chain Code of Practice (source: www.pilottaskforce.co.uk) that has changed the ways procurement operates. This Code outlines a set of best practice guidelines that will:
- Improve performance
- Eliminate unnecessary costs
- Add value and boost competitiveness

First adopted by the industry in 2002, signatories undertake to work towards full compliance. They include major purchasers (Oil and Gas operators and principal contractors) and suppliers (companies providing goods or services). As will be seen below, this builds on the above collaboration principles and applies them practically. The use of an external third party (FPAL) who collates information and shares it amongst members, whilst retaining the commercial confidentiality of individual sources, is also interesting.

The Code applies to three key stages within the procurement and commercial process:

1. Plan
Transparent planning of contracting activity by major purchasers to improve supply chain capability:

Major purchasers
- Communicate forward plans to the industry including areas and types of activity, expected contract value and timing.

- Support the annual industry Share Fair where major purchasers communicate future plans and internal contacts to the Supply Chain.
- Publicise a list of internal contacts to facilitate discussion around future plans with the contracting community. Maintain up-to-date First Point Assessment Limited (FPAL) Purchaser Profile including "how to do business with us" guidance, a contacts list and information on forward plans.

Suppliers
- Review Purchaser plans, FPAL Purchaser Profiles and attend Industry Share Fairs to understand future requirements.

2. Contract
Streamline pre-qualification, tendering and negotiation processes to reduce bidding costs, eliminate waste, add value and increase competitiveness:

Major Purchasers
- Where pre-qualification data is required only invite bids from suppliers registered with FPAL with an up-to-date capability assessment.
- Eliminate supplier data duplication by utilising FPAL throughout the tender process.
- Use industry standard ITT Models where appropriate. These embody fair contracting principles, encourage participation, invite bidders to demonstrate where they can add value, define value-based award criteria, outline timeframes and avoid data duplication.
- Provide appropriate de-briefing for all bids.
- Use industry standard contract forms where available (LOGIC type or company-specific global contracts), minimising amendments or additional terms and conditions.
- Include payment terms of 30 days in all contracts.

Suppliers
- Keep FPAL records valid and up-to-date, with Capability
- Assessments where required by purchasers.
- Refer purchasers to FPAL if duplicate information is requested.
- Participate in the Industry Mutual Hold Harmless as appropriate to company activity.
- Use standard industry contracts (LOGIC type or company-specific global contracts) minimising amendments or additional terms and conditions.

3. Perform and Pay
Increase feedback dialogue and shorten payment cycles to improve performance:

Major Purchasers
- Include performance indicators in all significant contracts with an appropriate review programme for the life of the contract.
- Give FPAL performance feedback at appropriate stages during the contract to improve mutual performance, minimise waste, learn from mistakes and best practice, and report on the extent of Code compliance achieved by both parties.

- Pay all valid invoices within 30 days.

Suppliers
- Track and discuss key contract performance indicators
- Request and participate in FPAL performance feedback, including assessment of Purchasers' performance.
- Submit complete and valid invoices with supporting documentation in a timely manner.
- Adopt a prompt payment policy for own suppliers.

Making the change

What fundamentally will have to be changed when following a collaborative approach? Well this topic has been more fully covered in "The Relationship Driven Supply Chain" (2006) by Emmett & Crocker, but to briefly note here: people first, and also the following:
- Contracts to simple flexible approaches
- Intensive management involvement
- Periodic performance monitoring
- Internal controls for confidential information
- Problem solving procedures
- Supplier is seen as a customer = "reverse customer service" as what suppliers do affects what happens to the customer
- Cross functional supplier/customer teams
- Hub (supply chain managers) and spoke (suppliers/customer) organisations?

It is people that change a company and it is the people who make the relationships in and between companies. In the changing of a company culture ("what is down around here"), then this will need to pass through the following "ideal-typical" stages:

Aspect	"Stormy/Blame" Culture	"Steady/Sane" Culture	"Sunny/Gain" Culture
Goals	Announced	Communicated	Agreed
Information	Status symbol and power based	Traded	Abundant
Motivation	Manipulative	Focused on staff needs	A clear goal
Decisions	From above	Partly delegated	Staff take them
Mistakes	Are only made by staff	Responsibility is taken	Are allowed as learning lessons
Conflicts	Are unwelcome and "put down"	Are mastered	Source of new innovation
Control	From above	Partly delegated	Fully delegated
Management Style	Authoritarian/ aggressive	Cooperative	Participative/ Assertive
Authority	Requires obedience	Requires cooperation	Requires collaboration
Manager	Absolute ruler and feels superior	Problem solver and decision maker	Change strategist and self confident

Once the culture has been defined, this will need the examination of all internal and external relationships. Trust will often remain a major barrier; however, without trust, there will be no relationship.

Case Study: Effective partnership working

The UK Audit Commission (1998) use the term 'partnership' to describe a joint working arrangement where the partners:
- are otherwise independent bodies;
- agree to co to achieve a common goat;
- create a new organisational structure or process to achieve this goal, separate from their own organisations;
- a plan and implement a jointly agreed programme, of-ten with joint staff or resources;
- a share relevant information; and
- pool risks and rewards

The key points are:

Deciding to go into partnership
1. Does this organisation have clear and sound reasons for being involved in its current partnerships?

2. Where new partnerships must be set up to meet national requirements, what groundwork is being done locally to maximise their chances of success?

3. Are changes in behaviour or in decision-making processes needed to avoid setting up partnerships with only limited chances of success?

Getting started
4. Have all the partnerships in which the organisation is involved been reviewed to evaluate whether the form of the partnership is appropriate to its functions and objectives?

5. Do all the partnerships have an appropriately structured board or other decision-making forum?

6. When setting up a new partnership, how are prospective partners identified?

Operating efficiently and effectively
7. Do partners share the same main objectives for the partnership?

8. Are the partnership's objectives consistent with those of the partnership organisation?

9. If an outsider watched a partnership operate, would they be able to identify the partnership's main objectives?

10. Do the partners know where the boundaries between the activities of the partnership and of their own organisations lie?

11. Do the members of partnership steering groups have sufficient authority to commit their organisations to decisions?

12. Are partnerships prepared to delegate responsibility for parts of their work to particular partners?

13. Do large partnerships have an executive group that all the partners trust to make decisions on their behalf?

14. Are project-planning techniques used to ensure the separate agreement of all the partners to a course of action in good time, when necessary?

15. Do the partnership's decisions get implemented effectively?

16. Are partnership staff selected for their technical competence and for their ability to operate both inside and outside a conventional public sector framework?

17. What actions are taken to build and maintain trust between partners?

18. If members have dropped out of a partnership, what lessons have been learnt about how to maintain involvement in the future?

Reviewing success

19. Does each partnership have a shared understanding of the outcomes that it expects to achieve, both in the short and longer term?

20. What means have been identified for measuring the partnership's progress towards expected outcomes and the health of the partnership itself?

21. Has the partnership identified its own performance indicators and set jointly agreed targets for these?

22. Are the costs of the partnership known, including indirect and opportunity costs?

23. Are these costs actively monitored and weighed against the benefits that the partnership delivers?

24. What steps have been taken to make sure that partnerships are accountable to the individual partners, external stakeholders, service users and the public at large?

25. Are some or all of the partnership's meetings open to the public?

26. Is information about the partnership's spending, activities and results available to the public?

27. Does the partnership review its corporate governance arrangements?

28. Has the partnership considered when its work is likely to be complete, and how it will end/handover its work when this point is reached?

Source: The Audit Commission: A Fruitful Partnership: effective partnership working, 1998

Global Sourcing

This is reality for many companies, especially as we advance towards living "in a global village", the expression popularised, if not originated by, the former US President, Ronald Regan. The following diagram, adapted from Monczka and Trent, shows how global sourcing has developed.

REACTIVE TO PROACTIVE

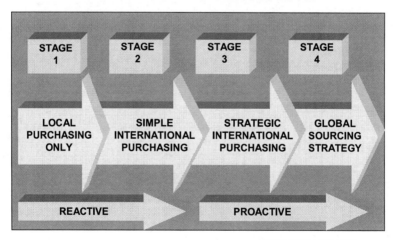

MONCZKA & TRENT

In considering global sourcing, the following questions need answering:
• Do we have the freight and import knowledge?
• Have we the necessary expertise?
• Should we source direct or use an agent?
• Will we get reliable supplier lead times?
• Will we need to "cushion" for longer supply lead times?
• What is the country's infrastructure?

- What is the country's political stability?
- What are the country's business methods?
- Will we be able to specify clearly what we want?
- What about fluctuating currency?
- What payments terms will be used?
- What Incoterms should be used?
- What are the impacts of varied landed costs?
- Can we fully implement our preferred supply chain management methods with suppliers?
- Are there any local import requirements that apply, such as licences, quotas?
- Do we have the knowledge of culture, business differences?

In this latter regards, the following is a guide to cultures. This simplification indicates the potentially complex area.

Cultural Aspects	More Western	More Eastern
Culture generally	Diverse	Homogenous
Preferences	- Fight for beliefs and "positions" - Clear cut - Specific - The Facts	- Need harmony - Ambiguous - General - Unspoken agreements
"I"/ "We" balance	Individualistic	Group is more important
Emotions	Displayed in public	Held back in public
Orientation	Towards results	Process orientation
Communication	Verbal	Non verbal
In Lectures	What is spoken	Who is speaking
View of Time	Follow times strictly	More relaxed view
Objectives	Outcome orientated	Relationship and process orientated
Business/ Respect and face	Business on hand and the details. Manners mildly important. Direct criticism can be acceptable.	Look for respect to be shown. Good manners are important, never make them look foolish. Use "positives" e.g. if might work better if...."
Seniority	Age and rank of less importance	Counts a lot; age, rank and years of service
Personal space	Some find closeness embarrassing.	Will often "sit close." Mirror the body language.
Hospitality	Often not involved.	Do not refuse refreshments. Can expect to be taken out.

Controlling Import Supply Chains

A substantial amount of goods are now imported and as more UK companies have outsourced manufacturing, then importing is a growing trend. Large scale volume importing is already the norm for many companies, especially those involved in handling fast moving consumer goods and many types of industrial products.

Importing involves a more distant supplier with extended transit lead times. As lead times are one of the calculation components in deciding how much to order from suppliers, then knowledge and control of lead times is critical.

However, what often happens is that a decision is taken to import using the Incoterms of Cost, Insurance and Freight (CIF) or Cost and Freight (C&F) and therefore here, procurement has left the organisation of the transit with the suppliers. Effectively therefore the associated lead time and its management and control is also externalised. Importing companies then find that often they have to spend time expediting and checking just where the goods are and when they will arrive.

Delays in transit times can also cause potential product shortages, with impacts to customer service levels and to not satisfying requirements. When there are regular repeat orders, then delayed transit times or a regular performance of unreliable delivery, will inevitably add to increasing stock holdings. This is because the buying company will need to hold more stocks to protect against the uncertainty of the suppliers lead time.

Benefits of changing to EXW/FOB terms

It is however possible to better control the imports by switching to Incoterms Ex-Works (EXW) or Free on Board (FOB) terms. By doing this the following potential benefits will be realised:
- Control and knowledge of exactly what is happening. Management needs to recall here that the management cycle not only involves planning, organising, directing but also, controlling
- Visibility and knowledge of exactly where the products are during the transit. Now, the transit it is your direct reasonability and is now in your full control
- Cheaper freight costs; as you are now, directly, paying them. Importers and buyers need to realise that suppliers will more than likely have a margin on the freight costs they have paid

A useful place to start making such a change is to understand some of the aspects of total supply chain management, for example:
- What are your costs of holding inventory?
- What supply lead time is required?
- What part of the supply lead time, is the transit lead time?
- What are the benefits of reliable and consistent on time in full receipts?
- How does this compare to the current situation?

Answers to these questions will always be revealing and often shows that the internal company structure is fragmented and unorganised to undertake effective global sourcing. Answers will also provide the basis for accessing the benefits of changing and assuming a decision is made to investigate a change, then the next steps are as follows:
- Ask for the suppliers EXW price
- Negotiate freight terms, possibly by going out to tender for a freight forwarder on a global or regional basis

- Check on the track/trace system to be used. This can be a simple key stage point reporting with spreadsheet recording, or, an instant on demand access to a freight carriers existing tracking system
- Assess the risk of changing, for example, possibly extra management costs, insurance covers and freight variation rate exposure. It is important to ensure a like for like comparison with the current methods as many of the current costs may well be hidden, for example, the insurance and freight increase costs are currently being paid for in the existing CIF terms
- Compare and contrast
- If deciding to change, and effectively changing the buying strategy, then it will often be necessary to ensure that the internal organisational structure supports the changes

There is much evidence to support that the changes detailed above are worthwhile, as shown in the following case studies.

Case Study: A major food retailer changes import procedures

Spending of £1200 million on imports via third party wholesalers and £500 million on direct imports; for example, home and leisure products were ordered through UK agents who arranged everything to Delivered domicile duty paid (DDP). Meanwhile, beers, wines and spirits were bought EXW works or FOB with freight arranged through various forwarders.

A change in management identified that they had:
- no systems
- no cost visibility
- no economy of scale
- poor product availability
- an internal fragmented structure; for example, Trading on product selection, negotiations, selection of suppliers, and ordering; Finance on letters of credit, payments; Logistics on order quantity and phasing into supply chain

The company tendered and then outsourced to one forwarder but maintained and determined carrier selection when appropriate. The results were:
- Freight costs fell by 8 percent
- Duty charges reduced by 10 percent
- Fuller visibility of supply chain
- Reduced stock levels
- Centralised the previous fragmented internal control as a new structure followed the new strategy

Case Study: A major clothes retailer changes import procedures

Nearly 200 stores with 70% of products imported, mainly from Far East. They identified that they had the following problems:
- No accurate data therefore no visibility
- Orders arrive "unexpectedly"
- 40% time spent of phoning/checking
- Paid high demurrage/rent port costs
- Restricted on buying currency forward
- Poor QC

The solution was to:
- Change from C&F to FOB and use one UK forwarder
- Set up a simple database tracking on the transfer points of PO, confirmed, tariff heading, cargo booked, authorise shipment, confirm shipment, documents banked, documents received, arrival time, clearance time, arrival at DC., QC checked, released/available.
- Integrated all their internal systems

The benefits reported were:
- Lower demurrage costs
- Improved warehouse efficiency due to scheduled arrival's
- Improved finance due to forward currency buying
- Quicker customs clearances
- Better product visibility and availability

Case Study: Move to EXW created success

A supplier of cleaning products who supplies branded products to major retailers and cash and carries, along with own-label products to a number of the leading retailers, found that cost-cutting initiatives had become a way of life in the face of major supply chain challenges.

The company's supply chain manager noted that: "In the past four or five years we have had to work hard at controlling our costs at a time when there have been no price increases from our customers". The operation therefore changed to buying products ex-works. The challenge of importing consignments cost-effectively was made more difficult by the low-value nature of the products, many of which are very light and use up large quantities of space.

The companies' success was seen as being directly related to its freight cost management and arrangements.

For those interested in Incoterms and international transport, the book "Logistics Freight Transport-national and international" by Stuart Emmett (2005) maybe be useful.

As seen in the case studies, global sourcing will involve the use of outsourcing; a subject covered next.

Outsourcing

"Virtual" companies give testimony to the fact that just about everything can be outsourced. In the supply chain, common candidates for outsourcing are distribution, production and as shown below, increasingly procurement.

Procurement outsourcing

The following summarises what one company says about outsourcing this specific function:

What is involved?
- The transfer of selected services/activities to a third party, not the transfer of control
- Enables concentration on core business
- Normally multi-year agreements
- Contractually linked to targets, such as minus cost, plus service etc.
- Geared to set/step performance improvements

Levels of outsourcing
1. Migration of infrastructure (people, technology, systems, supplier management)
2. Assume responsibility for some process
3. Offers added value functions such as strategic sourcing, supplier relationships
4. Formulation of strategy

Why outsource procurement?
- For same reasons as would outsource anything
- Enables core concentration by the business
- Increase efficiency due to economies of scale of people, systems etc.
- Reduces, commonly, costs by up to 15%
- To drive change and to introduce new technologies more easily
- Connect to a larger supplier base

How does it work?
- Aggregate spend by pooling requirements
- Access higher levels of expertise
- Tap economical labour sources in transactional processing by "offshoring"
- Operations after the transition are more "self-service"
- Adjustments needed to now being more automation intensive
- More centralised purchasing contact
- More use of operating performance matrices
- More formal service level agreements (SLAs)

153

Going forward
- Needs a careful consideration of current circumstances. it may not suit everyone
- Executive team decision is due to: need for change, merger activity, urgency for cost reduction, ability to change, reducing fixed costs
- Scope for savings/need for capital/prioritisation/sharing of benefits
- Future vision/capability/investment needed/strategic nature

Companies who outsource will have taken the basic decision of "Buy in" rather than "DIY". Many aspects of outsourcing are common ones and this section will therefore look at these common elements of outsourcing.

The **secrets of outsourcing** have been identified in "Supply Management" 29 June 2000, as follows:
- Concentrate of what do well and allow specialists in other areas to handle the non core services
- Adapt to new ideas and developments, as, what was acceptable in the past, may not be so in the future
- Choose a provider who understands all your needs
- It is crucial to fully know the current costs and service levels
- Ensure outsourcing delivers, planned benefits such as cost/service/time targets
- Acknowledge that information equals power in areas such as service level requirements
- Develop a strategic alliance with the provider, based on mutual trust
- Start with a phased controlled service with monitored cost/service levels at all stages
- Develop the right company culture which supports outsourcing
- Monitor the outsourced function with regular performance measurement

The important questions a business will need to consider, before outsourcing, can be asked as follows:
- Is it a non-core activity
- Can we release some capital
- Will we retain some operations in-house
- Will we retain management expertise
- What increased monitoring will be needed
- What are the risks of committing to one contractor
- Will flexibility be increased
- Will costs be reduced, whilst service is increased
- How will we account for future changes
- Are there any implications on the Transfer of Undertaking, Protection of Employment (TUPE) legislation

The suppliers of the outsourced service will have to be determined as being "capable".

Outsourcing is classic activity for procurement to be involved and the following **supplier criteria** can be studied:
- Financial Stability/Ownership/Turnover/Profitability

- Size/Equipment/Systems/Methods/Capacity
- Management Skills/Industrial relations/Contracts
- Referrals/Other Customers/Similar business handled
- 'Feel good factor'/Understanding/Easy to deal with
- Dependable/Reliable/Accreditation by an internationally recognised quality management standard

If it is then decided to examine outsourcing further, then the financial, operational and strategic advantages and issues will be raised; for example:

Financial Issues
- Capital can be released
- Off balance sheet finance is available
- Asset Utilisation's change
- Economies of scale
- Planned/Known costs are available
- Cost comparison must be comparing "apples with apples", for example by using Total Acquisition Cost (TAC)

Operational Issues
- Flexibility in 'spreading' peaks/troughs
- Response to special requests
- Management role changes
- Specialist knowledge is brought in
- Control (Management control must remain a core activity)

Strategic Issues
- After outsourcing, will some "in-house" expertise be retained so there is there still the ability to make changes
- Internal implications
- Spreading of risk
- Customer reactions (customer contact must remain a core activity)
- Fair and complete comparisons
- The outsourcing may assist in any internal change/new strategies/expansion

Finally, with any outsourcing, management must ensure that control is retained. Management needs to recall again here that the management cycle not only involves planning, organising, directing but also, controlling; outsourcing of control can cause problems, this must remain "core".

Information, Communication Technology (ICT) & E-business/E-procurement

All parts of the supply chain rely on ICT in the planning, operational, administrative and management processes. ICT provides integration, coordination and control mechanisms across a supply chain between all internal and external players. Information is required therefore at every stage of the supply chain and for all levels of supply chain planning.

Electronic business refers generally to commercial transactions that are based upon the processing and transmission of digitised data, including text, sound and visual images and that are carried out over open networks (like the Internet) or closed networks that have a gateway onto an open network (Extranet). Meanwhile, the CIPS definition of e-Procurement is; "E-Procurement is using the Internet to operate the transactional aspects of requisitioning, authorizing, ordering, receipting and payment processes for the required services or products."

E-procurement has been proven to provide a return on investment (ROI) of anywhere between 5% and 15% for many organisations and time savings in the procurement process of up to 75%. With these kinds of benefits, the impact on profitability can be immense as procurement savings drop straight to the bottom line. With e-procurement now available across the internet many companies and not for profit organisations are evaluating the available solutions for the first time and trying to assess the scale of benefit that will accrue to them. The concept of e-procurement has been around for a very long time. The idea that computer processing power and telecommunications could be brought together to assist in improving the process of corporate purchasing was first put into practice in the 1970s with the development of Electronic Data Interchange (EDI) software.

EDI however, really only offered a solution to large procurers, and only then when with their procurement from relatively large suppliers providing direct or strategic goods to the supply chain. Examples are the automotive manufacturers and their key component suppliers or the oil exploration companies and their service partners. The cost of EDI systems, with their underlying requirement for specialist networks, VANs (value added networking) and lack of interoperability between these VANs, made broadening the use of EDI to non strategic or indirect goods prohibitively expensive.

The adoption of the internet as a medium to supplant the VANs changed all of this. With a network that is instantaneously available world wide, 24 hours a day, and is inexpensive to access, it also requires no specialised training to use. Moreover, unlike the proprietary VANs, it is owned by nobody and is governed by standards for access, transferring and using data integration. The emergence of these standards – FTP, TCP/IP, XML and others provides for the first time a cost effective convergence of computing and communications to allow many buyers and many suppliers to interact electronically: the birth of the electronic, or "e" Procurement market.

E-Procurement therefore includes a range of technologies that apply the speed and uniformity of computer processing and the connectivity of the Internet to:
*   accelerate and streamline the processes of identifying and selecting vendors of goods and services;
*   placing, receiving and paying for orders;
*   assuring the application of purchasing rules, guidelines and discounts;
*   consolidating purchasing to achieve lowest prices;
*   reaching customers and offering goods and services for sale

Procurement encourages and facilitates procurer-provider visibility and collaboration that move both toward the ultimate organisational goal of Supply Chain Excellence. Good e-Procurement also requires a strong sense of collaboration that helps build stronger partnerships in which both sides prosper.

E-business applications

Some of the E-business applications are classified as Business to Business (B2B) and Business to Consumer (B2C):

- Business to Business (B2B) trading exchanges provide a two way on-line link between buyers and suppliers; they are now often referred to as a "marketplace". Suppliers can advertise their products and services through electronic catalogues; buyers can order from supplier catalogues, take part in auctions, or conduct tendering online. In industries with large numbers of buyers and suppliers, third parties generally organise and manage online forums. In industries with few buyers and a large number of sellers, the buyers often own and run the on line marketplace.
- Business to Consumer (B2C) where individual consumers and any system user can get up to-the-minute information, make enquiries, place orders and payments can be made on-line. Information about the current position and status of orders services can also be obtained.

Meanwhile some E-business examples follow:

Supply Chain aspect	Buying	Ordering	Designing products	Post sales
Information	Sharing with Suppliers	Visibility	Sharing with suppliers	Customer use records
Planning	Coordinating when to replenish	Forecast sharing/ agreements	New product launching	Service planning
Product flow	Paperless exchanges	Automated	Product changes	Automatic replacement of parts
KPIs	Compliance monitoring	Logistics track and trace	Project monitoring	Performance measurement
Business changes from "E"	On line "reverse" auctions, market exchanges	Click on ordering	Mass customisation	Remote sensing and diagnostics, download upgrades

It should be noted that buying on line, as with any other from of procurement, should still be subject to the assessment of risk. Additional risks with E-procurement methods may come from paying for an expensive E-procurement/reverse auction that does not produce commensurate savings, and if using an on-line E-marketplace, it is necessary to check and verify who has undertaken the prequalification of suppliers. With reverse auctions, the emphasis will be on clear simple specifications that tend to be more on a price decision, as for example is found with leverage and routine items. MEAT or "best value" is more difficult to access with reverse auctions, therefore requiring the use of more traditional procurement methods.

Costs and benefits

In a paper-based, manual system, the cost of procurement is significantly higher than most people realise. For example, the average administrative cost of a simple purchase order is between £75 and £125. Therefore, a purchase order for the purchase of a product priced at £10 actually costs more than £85. E-Procurement uses refined business processes and supplier relationships supported by technology to automate processes, eliminate the paper, and reduce errors, and it ultimately can cut the administrative cost of a purchase order by more than 75 percent. The purchase order that once cost a company £75 in administration now costs only £18.75 – a saving of £56.25.

E-Procurement applications can monitor contractual compliance. Additionally, e-Procurement reduces the requisition time up to 75 percent.

Shareholder value of E-Procurement

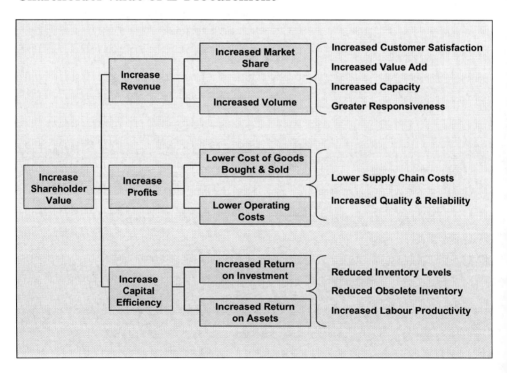

"Industry Week" magazine published the following research results in its "E-Procurement Explosion" article in May 2002:
- Hewlett-Packard (HP) saved more than 30 percent on advertising and $220,000 per quarter on electrical power. They claimed 20 percent to 25 percent increased efficiency due to a reduced number of purchase orders and administration.
- Lucent claimed 60 percent to 70 percent reduction in transaction.
- Texas Instruments reduced the cost of a purchase order from $80 to $25, Deere &

Co. from $97 to $22. 3M report costs went from $120 to $40 and errors from 30 percent to 0 percent.

• Owens Corning used auctions to cut negotiation time from two to three months to less than 90 minutes.

Case Study: IBM and E-Procurement

E-procurement is an area in which IBM is actively engaged. It says it has become a strategic necessity because so much business advantage can be gained. However, it does not feel that even after several years, it has tapped the full potential that e-procurement has to offer. The primary operational benefits that come from e-procurement are around catalogues, requisitions, approvals, purchase orders, delivery, invoices, payment and asset management.

Automating this procurement flow is critical to reducing expenses in the procurement process and minimising the cost of acquiring goods and services. Most purchases go through IBM's SAP system. The goal is for 80 percent of purchase orders to be "hands-free."

Results

The collective transformation process for procurement at IBM has paid off. The activities, beginning in the 1990s to today, have yielded tremendous improvements, including:

• Savings of more than $6 billion
• Maverick procurement reduced to less than 1 percent
• Client satisfaction improvement from 40 percent to 86 percent
• 99 percent of purchasing transactions are "hands free"; and 98 percent is conducted electronically
• Purchase order lead time down from 30 days to 1 day
  IBM estimates that operational efficiency alone contributes to approximately 10 percent of its cost saving efforts.

E-sourcing

The CIPS definition of e-Sourcing is:
"E-Sourcing is using the Internet to make decisions and form strategies regarding how and where services or products are obtained."

E-sourcing covers the parts in the buying process, which are at the discretion of the specialist buyers, which include knowledge, specification, requests for quotation/e-tender/e-auction and evaluation/negotiation contract. A good e-Sourcing practice is essential to making e-Procurement work. If you do not make the correct strategic decisions you will create a poor operational process.

E-Sourcing also provides a platform for delivering on promises of social responsibility; it provides accountability and visibility on why a company makes a decision to source products from their chosen suppliers.

E-Sourcing systems should therefore enable the sourcing team to:
- effortlessly analyse and model complex decisions in real time
- automate the contract life-cycle management including awards, rejections, amendments and renewals
- collaborate with the supplier, using a central system enables people to collaborate easily

E-Sourcing should deliver the following visible benefits:
- Real-time information; the sourcing team get visibility on contracts and spending patterns. Any planned improvement must ensure reliable up to date information for analysis purpose. A system can provide pre-qualified information about suppliers.
- Integrated process automation; taking time out of the sourcing process by reducing the amount of paper involved in the system. Typically such systems can distribute all requirements electronically.

E-sourcing can also be defined as providing accountability and visibility on why a company makes a decision to source products from its chosen suppliers. E-sourcing covers the decision and strategy of how and where a service or product is obtained. It therefore covers that part of the buying process that is implemented and controlled by the specialist buyer, including specification, requests for quotations, e-tenders, e-auctions and so on, up to the award of the contract. E-auctions should be part of the e-sourcing toolkit. If they are used to only drive down price, they will only have an effect in the short term. E-sourcing in e-procurement is then, is the process and operation of deploying these sourcing decisions and strategies within the organisation, typically by devolution to local users. E-procurement would then cover processes such as requisition again contract, authorisation, ordering, receipt and payment.

Too many people have tried to implement E-procurement without having an underpinning e-sourcing strategy in place first. The benefits of e-sourcing should therefore include:
- Real time information giving visibility on contracts
- Spending pattern and supplier performance
- Integrated, largely paperless, automation of the sourcing process
- Capability for analysis and modelling of complex decisions in real time
- Automated contract life-cycle management
- Enablement of collaboration with suppliers.

E-sourcing software and tendering

The e-sourcing software on the market is split into four loose categories.

1. The first is the tendering software that handles drawing up a contract within the buying organisation, as well as communication and negotiation with suppliers. This includes electronic reverse auctions or e-auctions.

2. Second, collaboration software helps organisations work with suppliers to draw up more efficient tenders, as well as publicizing changes in a tender.
3. Third, evaluation software helps users to trawl through competing bids, some of which may be thousands of pages long.
4. Lastly, contract management software reminds buyers when completed contracts are due for renewal.

All sourcing software should in turn be linked to the e-procurement part of the buying process, the actual buying, ordering and delivery of goods that takes place after a contract is signed.

One multinational drugs company finds 90% of its goods through e-sourcing and will run 2,500 auctions in 2005. It estimates the average saving at 19 percent. They firmly believe that the major share of savings do not come from auctions or competitive bidding techniques. Supplier collaboration is where the long term benefit is from. Lengthy relationships with suppliers rarely start well if they are preceded by an aggressive round of price cutting e-auctions.

The automation of administrative tasks, in the tendering process, for example, reduces process cycle times and the cost of tendering. Professor Andrew Cox, from the UK's Birmingham Business School, says that the real e-sourcing prize lies in improving supplier's process efficiency over a number of years, rather than simple reductions in the costs of goods and services.

E-procurement and Supplier Management

Whilst reverse auctions are successful, the real test for e-procurement is its ability to improve supplier relationships, according to a recent pronouncement from a senior US procurement figure, Daniel Enneking, vice-president of global operations and chief procurement office at NCR Corporation.

He told the Conference Board's 2003 Electronic Procurement Conference in Chicago not to get carried away with the success of e-auctions. He stated that the biggest challenge is expanding the use of electronic capabilities in the supply chain to improve supplier performance and management. Robert Waugh, chief sales and marketing officer at software supplier Bze Markets, also said that using software for supplier management was the next big step for companies after reverse auctions.

Enneking continued by warning that while e-procurement allowed greater tracking of costs, it was just an enabler for efficiencies. Suitable processes and people skills must be in place before electronic systems were implemented.

E-procurement within NCR, which has an annual procurement budget of about $3.6 billion on revenues of nearly $5.6 billion, had freed up his staff for more strategic work. NCR, well known as a maker of cash machines was working on extending e-procurement to include the sharing of manufacturing and design information.

E-procurement options

E-procurement automates the internal and external processes associated with buying, with added value increasing in line with the extent and sophistication of the electronic communication.

Catalogues
At the basic level, staffs are given access to web based catalogues, with goods and services are delivered direct to their desk. Electronic versions of existing supply catalogues are good for buying and selling commodity items from stock. Buyer and sellers can now have a one-to-one direct relationship. Efficiencies come from moving from paper-based post-contract process to electronic message passing. Implementing the capability to use electronic catalogue also facilitates participation in marketplaces.

Marketplaces
Whereas catalogue commerce is good for post contractual message passing, marketplaces are mainly good for pre-contract searching and negotiating for partners and prices. There are however some misconceptions about marketplaces. They do not help you manage the internal transaction processes better, but, they do support them by providing an excellent source of information about suppliers and access to multiple catalogues. They do not just provide auction facilities as 90% of the business going through them will be normal contracts based on improved collaboration.

Vertical marketplaces are electronic exchanges providing a range of capabilities (auctions, reverse auctions, dynamic bid and exchange, trade directories) within an industry. Horizontal marketplaces are electronic exchanges, usually offering a combination of information, contacts and the opportunity to buy and sell, based around either a community of users or a class of goods and services. Marketplaces may be private, available only to invited players, and/or public, open to any organisation (normally subject to some entry rules). Public marketplaces are good for buying and selling where there is no advantage from sustained buyer–supplier relationships. Private marketplaces are good for closer collaboration across the supply chain.

In all cases, the budget management, requisition authorisation and goods received paperwork (and even payment) is electronic. In many cases, tendering, contracting and opportunities for on-line auctions also feature. Buying is aggregated and management information is collected and processed centrally.

E-procurement: success factors and challenges to implementation

The following have been put forward as perceived barriers to electronic procurement:
* A "wait and see" attitude among firms in selecting e-marketplaces and procurement service providers;
* Concerns over security and confidentiality of the data needed to be exchanged in electronic environments;
* Reluctance of share data with trading partners;

- The "non-feasibility of custom made products" for pooling initiatives;
- Lack of standardisation; and
- Uncertainty over trust and commitment among trading partners.

Moreover, both small buyer and seller firms which the authors have talked to considered the following prohibitive and discouraging:
- The costs and development time required to set up online procurement systems, enabling these systems, and meeting workforce requirements of such systems;
- The lack of adequate security measures to protect data; and
- Trust issues between buyers and sellers.

In the same vein, managers of the seller firms also cited attitudinal resistance to change stemming from a number of concerns:
- The uncertainty over its ability to gain the expected return on investment to cover development costs;
- The work required to enforce business process changes called for by these systems; and
- Worker apprehensions about being replaced by automated procurement systems.

E-procurement legislation

E-procurement has been such a revolution for purchasers that uncertainty has been growing about which laws apply in cyberspace. However, e-procurement is still governed by existing law and purchasers should not forget good procurement /purchasing practices.

Apart from the laws that apply to purchasers in what may, guardedly, be called the 'real' world, there are key pieces of legislation that they need to be aware of.

Regulation of Investigatory Powers (RIP) Act 2000

This controversial piece of legislation in now in force and the act gives the authorities the right to intercept and/or monitor e-mails and Internet communication data. They would also be able, when circumstances required, to demand that the sender or recipient of an encrypted message hand over the code or decode the message.
Among the provisions of the act are:
- A maximum two year sentence for failure to comply with an order to disclose encrypted information.
- That the authorities can require public communications providers to allow e-mails to be intercepted and Internet messages monitored (this will usually require a warrant).

The act has been widely seen as interfering in the private transactions of businesses and individuals and has faced a barrage of criticism. It seems to be at odds with the government's intention to make the UK the best place in Europe for e-commerce and it has been suggested that internet service providers may migrate to the Republic of Ireland.

EU Electronic Signature Directive 1999/93

This was affected as part of the Electronic Communications Act 2000. The directive has three parts.

The first section relates to the establishment of a voluntary register of cryptographic support services providers. These services include the certification of signatures, key management and the time stamping of documents.

Part 2 provides for electronic signatures to be legally recognised as evidence in court proceedings. In the future, legislation is likely to be altered to allow the use of electronic communication in place of hard copy in a wide range of circumstances. The conveyance of public records and company reports and accounts are specifically under consideration.

The third part of the act contains a number of provisions, one of which is that users of encryption are under no obligation to deposit copies of their encryption keys with third parties. This appears to contradict the RIP Act, which says they are.

E-Commerce Directive 2000/31/EC

The directive sets out to remove barriers to the availability of information society services (ISS) within the European Union. They society is an EU description of the new digitally driven ways of doing business.

There are 5 main areas: the first is electronic contracts. Provision must be made for drawing up and concluding contracts electronically. Detailed procedures are set out to follow, although business to business partners can, if they agree, not adhere to them.

The second is transparency. ISS providers will have to make their basic business details readily available to customers and the relevant authorities.

The next area is commercial communications. These are defined as e-mail or web based advertising and marketing. They must be identifiable as advertising and their sourced named.

Codes of conduct are the fourth area. These are encouraged by the directive and also, when disputes arise between trading parties, it is recommended that they resolve their arguments outside the courts, rather than resorting to litigation.

The most contentious part of the directive concerns intermediary liability. It is made clear than an ISS provider will not be liable for the content of third party information that it transmits when:
- It is simply a conduit for such information (i.e. the ISS provider neither initiates it nor selects its recipients)
- It merely stores the information on a temporary basis for the sole purpose of subsequent transmission
- It merely stores the information at another party's request.

Distance Selling Directive 97/7/EC

This came into force in the UK as the Consumer Protection (Distance Selling) Regulations 2000 and covers business to consumer rather than business to business transactions. Under the directive, website designers and developers acting on behalf of suppliers must make certain information easily available to potential buyers, including:

- Identity and address of the supplier
- General terms and conditions of business
- Delivery costs
- Details of the terms applying to the return of goods
- The period for which the price or offer remains valid

In most cases, the buyer has a minimum of seven days to cancel the contract.

Draft EU regulation on jurisdiction and judgments

EU ministers have come to an agreement on this proposal and the legislation will decide which laws apply to a given transaction, enable aggrieved web purchasers to seek redress through their local courts and set up local arbitration. Companies using the web for buying and selling should always remember that e-commerce legislation supplements existing sale of goods acts, such as the Supply of Goods and Services Act 1982 and the Unfair Terms in Consumer Contracts Regulations 1994. It should not be regarded as a replacement.

Supplier Relationships and E-sourcing

As we have seen above, companies are increasingly looking at e-sourcing and reverse auctions as a means by which to reduce their procurement expenses and provide bottom-line savings to the organisation in a relatively short time. However, this has sometimes led to resistance among suppliers who believe that e-sourcing results in commoditization of goods and services, lack of appreciation of value added services, and in negative impacts on buyer-supplier relationships.

Whilst E-Sourcing and reverse auctions can provide benefits to buyers including process cost savings, reduction in search/information costs, and a more efficient procurement process; there is a potential that suppliers, especially those incumbent, will resist sourcing and reverse auctions in the belief that they lower profit margins and overlook value added services. Newer suppliers are more likely to view e-sourcing as an opportunity to expand their existing businesses without corresponding increase in their sales expenses. We therefore discuss below the various strategies that buyers can employ to maximise supplier participation in the reverse auction process as well as strategies suppliers can use in the short and long term to ensure that they are active participants in the strategic e-sourcing process.

Buyer Strategies

Buyers have a choice of working with a third party as an e-sourcing provider of licensing software or to conduct e-sourcing in-house. Companies in the initial stages of their e-sourcing efforts are more likely to benefit from going with a third part e-sourcing service provider to speed up their learning curve. Also, utilising a third party provider also helps to reduce conflicts of interest because most third part providers have a set of rules that must be followed by both buyers and sellers. These include rules about buyer intent to award the contract, the buyer bidding against suppliers to create artificial competition etc.

Choosing the right e-sourcing service provider is an important step in initiating an e-sourcing programme. In addition to strategic sourcing and reverse auctions expertise, technology and staying power, fit with company size and culture should be considered. A buyer should consider the provider's familiarity with the nuances of spend analysis, the identification of the right categories for e-sourcing, supply market analysis, the design of the right RFP, the ability to train suppliers, and the ability to provide operational support during the bidding event.

The buyer also should consider the service provider's experience with similar buyers. A service provider with a client base of Fortune 500 companies may use an approach that is not well suited to the needs of a mid size company with more limited resources. Finally, the buyer should understand the process by which service providers choose suppliers and ensure that appropriate suppliers are chosen. For example, some service providers may choose poor suppliers who do not match client needs, such as geographic proximity, regulatory requirements, ability to timely deliver a certain volume of goods or services etc.

Once the right partner has been selected, buyers can improve supplier participation in the reverse auction process by being proactive in the process. Close buyer participation that helps set the stage for a full fledged e-sourcing programme include spend analysis, identification of categories that are better suited for the e-sourcing process, proper timing of the events, appropriate lot and bidding strategies etc. Typically, indirect categories, MRO items, computers, office supplies, may be better suited for e-sourcing than direct materials. Buyers should improve supplier participation (particularly incumbents) by explaining:
*   The goals and objectives of the e-sourcing programme,
*   How the process will differ from the traditional process,
*   What the evaluation and selection criteria will be and
*   The time line for decision making.

Suppliers also should be notified if only pre-qualified vendors have been invited to participate. This is likely to be viewed positively by the suppliers and increase participation, especially if pre-qualification has been achieved through site visits to manufacturing locations or other audits. E-sourcing does not preclude establishing strategic relationships with select suppliers, but can be used as a first step in establishing such a partnership with competitive suppliers.

Supplier Benefits

E-sourcing can provide benefits to suppliers. These include a more transparent purchasing process, increased market reach, reduced customer acquisition costs and competitive pricing information. The e-sourcing and reverse auction process forces buyers to spend more time upfront in creating and communicating specifications, contract specifications, and delivery requirements, thus providing better information to the suppliers prior to the bidding process.

The e-sourcing process also tends to level the playing field for smaller companies with limited number of sales resources. Some suppliers have used reverse auctions to benchmark themselves against the competition and, if necessary look at approaches to obtaining more competitive pricing without compromising quality of products or services. As long as the cost of participating is less than the potential benefit from participating, a supplier will benefit from participating. There is clearly no benefit from not participating.

Supplier Strategies

Suppliers should be proactive in the e-sourcing process as well. They need to know the rules upfront that can include criteria for evaluation and award (lowest price versus best value), weights for each of the criteria, a timeline for decision making, and the reserve price (if any). Incumbents may have an advantage when they participate due to their previous relationship with the buyer. They also may have a better idea of the buyer's needs and requirements. Suppliers will generally find it advantageous to participate in the auction, because participation provides potential profit and additional information. Not participating generates no profit and no information. Suppliers should communicate issues and concerns in a timely and appropriate manner. For example, if there are anti trust concerns due to few suppliers of certain products, buyers can modify auction types to prevent revealing pricing information.

Suppliers should be careful not to get carried away in the reverse auction process by submitting a bid at a price at which they cannot supply the product/service profitably. For the long term, suppliers should attempt to differentiate their products/services in some way and ensure that this value is effectively communicated.

Collaborative commerce

Many buyers and sellers should be able to leverage e-sourcing to reduce their costs without negatively impacting the existing buyer-supplier relationships. After identifying the appropriate e-sourcing partner, effective communication is key both among buyers and suppliers. The marketplace enables information sharing and process synchronization in a true e-business context, delivering seamless integration across the supply chain. Collaborative commerce has arrived.

Case Study: Higher Education E-Procurement

The University of Salford has developed an e-procurement marketplace primarily for the University Sector. The marketplace, known as HEeP, uses internet technology, is innovative and facilitates collaborative e-procurement in the Higher Education Sector.

The HEeP marketplace is a low cost solution which in time will provide major benefits in improving the effectiveness of University purchasing and in reducing the costs of transactions. The HEeP project's aim is to be the primary internet marketplace for e-procurement activity in the Higher Education Sector.

The UK Higher Education Sector comprises in excess of 170 institutions (Universities and Colleges) with a combined annual spend on goods and services in excess of 4.5 billion pounds. In recent years the Sector has improved its purchasing arrangements and has collaborated through seven regional purchasing consortia to develop contracting.

A myriad of national, regional and local contracts exists to cover the majority of supplies and services but contract compliance by institutions is generally unsatisfactory. Existing procurement processes are typically manual and paper based and transaction costs are estimated to be between 35 pounds and 50 pounds per purchase. Such costs can be significantly reduced by avoiding the need to repeatedly key in the same data to different systems.

A number of e-procurement systems have been tried by individual institutions but no single solution, prior to HEeP, has generated widespread support.

The HEeP marketplace provides significant benefits to the Sector by delivering a marketplace to support real time electronic trading between institutions and their suppliers. HEeP's "thin" marketplace delivers real efficiency gains by streamlining the procurement and transaction process which in turn reduces costs and enables both institutions and suppliers to make financial savings.

Another feature of HEeP is that it provides much needed management information regarding the acquisition of different goods and services. This purchasing information will in due course enable the Sector to improve its contracting arrangements further for example by identifying opportunities for more local contracts to be combined into regional contracts and for more regional contracts to become national contracts, thus delivering economies of scale.

The HEeP marketplace is designed to facilitate and automate the processes by which institutions procure goods, namely:
- Identify suppliers who are contracted to supply them particular goods and services
- Locate the appropriate areas on those suppliers e-commerce websites
- Raise purchase requisitions on their own finance systems so that the purchases can be awarded formal approval
- Send confirmed purchase orders to suppliers' back office systems to initiate dispatch of the goods
- Receive supplier invoices and upload them into their finance systems so that payment can be made.

E-auctions and the procurement of services

A common misconception of e-auctions is that they are chiefly suited to the sourcing of material "products" and preferably, commodities.

While commodities undoubtedly lend themselves to sourcing via online bidding, there is now very clear evidence to indicate that e-auctions can, and do, produce excellent results in the purchasing of services. Indeed, it is in the area of services purchasing that the most explosive growth in the adoption of this process is being seen. E-auctions are becoming such a popular tool for the sourcing of these categories for the following reasons.

First, every substantial business has a need to buy general services, from car fleet management to security to cleaning to office supplies. For some businesses these purchases are "core"; for the majority they are not considered strategic. The levels of spend are, however, often quite considerable. With any large spend, the supply base will be very keen to compete for business.

Second, there is invariably considerable scope to improve the services procurement processes and thereby to deliver surprisingly large savings. For many companies, direct procurement was initially far more sophisticated and controlled than was the case for indirect. This is still true for many businesses.

Third, the fact the demand for purchased services is so broad has lead to the development of significant supply base capability. In many services sectors, the supply bases are still extremely fragmented. This invariably means that the supply market is highly competitive.

A further essential ingredient is the fact that, with professional input, services requirements can be extremely well specified. Indeed, selecting online bidding for the negotiation phase of the tender exercise often drives greater clarity in specification. It is vital that suppliers participating in an e-auction are clear about what they are bidding to supply. With a commodity, specification is relatively straightforward, the only major differences often being the packaging and delivery arrangements. But even purchases at the other end of the "complexity spectrum" can be well specified and successfully auctioned.

Indeed, the specification can vary from bidder to bidder. For example, when Ford bids to supply a medium sized car it is probably a Mondeo, whereas Vauxhall would offer a Vectra, each with a specification list pre-agreed with the buyer. Another charge sometimes levelled against e-auctions is that "they're all about price". This is not the case. Whether or not a tender project involves the use of e-auctions, an optimum result will only ever be delivered in non price factors are given due consideration alongside the price elements.

After an e-auction, the buyer is left with a series of written "best bids" from suppliers. In the vehicle example cited above, the buying company will be left with a decision probably based on weighted parameters, but within which price (or whole life-cycle costs) have been determined via a highly rigorous process – the e-auction. The experience of many of the author's clients as users of e-auctions, then it quickly becomes clear that without unlimited resources, a traditional tender process could not possibly enable parties to make as many revisions during the negotiating process as they can within an e-auction. The process saves significant resources as well as driving a better deal.

Finally, there is the hard evidence. Thousands of separate projects have seen e-auctions deliver fantastic results in the sourcing of services. Not only have buyers been able to discover new suppliers and price levels, but it has opened the way for vastly improved levels of quality and service.

Against e-auctions

An e-auction is a good way to buy commodity goods and some commodity services. But it is an unsuitable way to buy a service that cannot be simply described and instantly delivered. Every problem can look like a nail when on e is armed only with a hammer and it is not just complexity, but a series of factors, that limit its use.

Other dimensions that make services less suitable for e-auctions include intellectual property and switching costs, as well as the fact that service contracts are not covered by any equivalent of the Sale of Goods Act or the concept of "fitness for purpose".

Services frequently require ongoing definition and negotiation. Improved efficiency is often reasonably expected and buyer and seller have to achieve continued savings through some form of gain share. This dimension of a purchase can be negotiated competitively but it seems hardly suited to the frenzy of an auction.

Imagine, for example, the purchase of a facilities management service in which the vendor must invest months trying to understand the local situation. Many will take a lot of time working to develop proposals. But this becomes more difficult to maintain if the final stage is a dog-eat-dog affair after the buyer has absorbed all of the supplied know-how. Opportunities for continuous collaboration on cost reduction and benefits sharing are ruled out.

The relationship between a vendor and customer goes through a power shift during a negotiation. The buyer's power is greatest at the start and declines as commitment increases. The e-auction delays this, until power shifts suddenly and completely. Some vendors are getting expert at exploiting this by bidding low to get the business and then cashing in through extortionate charges for changes.

Better suppliers may even refuse to enter a tendering process that ends in a gladiatorial contest. The cost of preparing proposals and bids can be high. Risking everything in a sudden death may simply not be worth it. And those vendors that do take part and face the prospect of an e-auction at the end are likely to hold positions in reserve, protecting their information and their best and final offer until the endgame. This may reduce the worth of any requests for information and requests for proposals that precede it.

Competition is not always perfect, especially in services, and bidding process can be more rigged than a wrestling match. In one case, a buyer of a temporary staff agency service went straight to auction on the total mark-up, missing the fact that local agencies had got used to margins for overheads and profit that were three times the norm. We should not lose sight of where most value is added in service buying. Research shows that two thirds of all potential savings come from persuading the internal client that a standard service will do the same job as the specified exclusive one. More than two thirds of the remaining potential can be achieved through traditional means, with a real time bidding process.

Deskilling of purchasing, by going straight to auction, helps to leverage scarce resources but it also contributes to the exclusion of purchasing from the big decisions of the day. There are few examples of e-auctions for outsourcing HR or finance services and, unfortunately, not even many cases where purchasing is consulted about such strategic outsourcing.

Case Study: BA and E-Procurement of Services

British Airways has cut its European public relations spend by 25 percent after holding an e-auction.

Previously, the airline's PR work for 28 European countries was shared between three agencies. Two agencies retained the business, on three year contracts; a departure from the previous annual rolling basis.

There was some concern by PR people at first in that an e-auction would take that human contact aspect out of dealing with suppliers; an antithesis to PR and marketing people.

The process made them extremely focused on their specifications. They had to be, because PR services are not like cleaning or catering where the job is tangible and can be clearly defined. It also saved them probably four to five days work that would have been meeting suppliers to negotiate deals.

A mock e-auction was run two days before to get people used to it.

BA's procurement director, said the e-auctions are part of the airline's purchasing strategy, established in 2003 to save 300 million pounds from its 4 billion pound procurement budget.

They have met the target for reduction in suppliers to 2,000 which is about right for a company like BA with an 8 billion pound turnover. Three years previously they had around 14,000 suppliers.

Case Study – Shell

Oil giant Shell is expecting to process 90 percent of its global spending electronically by the end of 2007. This is a huge undertaking and is forcing many of their suppliers and competitors to rethink their own procurement strategies.

As the costs of implementation have reduced greatly over the years, this has made it very difficult for Shell's suppliers to resist the development. For Shell, currently a leader in its industry in e-procurement development, a possible 1.5 – 2 percent saving in its global procurement cost has provided the main thrust to the business case.

Further efficiencies will come from increased contract compliance, lower supply chain costs, increased global reach and the removal of 'non-value adding steps' to the internal procurement process.

Shell have said that positive changes for Shell's suppliers will include quicker payment, vendor maintained catalogues that allow suppliers to own and maintain their own data, further integration and collaboration within the supply chain and an increased profile with other companies that can support e-procurement.

Mini Case Study - Shell

The authors have also accumulated considerable experience with The Shell Group & SPDC Nigeria in particular and the following paragraphs share this knowledge.

In pushing for online bidding, the company aimed to, as much as possible, cut out the human element in handling bidding processes and give a level playing ground for contractors in a manner that was quick, convenient and unwaveringly transparent.

They were faced with key questions:
*   which product(s) do they select for bidding,
*   how do they align the online bidding activity with current Tender Board approval processes,
*   how do they get the buy- in of local contractors
*   how do they manage the bandwidth and internet accessibility problems?

The team zeroed in on products with the following attributes,

*   Availability of many suppliers
*   Ease of specification
*   High spend/value
*   Possibility of significant savings

For the local contractors to buy in into the process, an awareness session was conducted showing the potential of online bidding for them. They were also able to use an "internet café" set up in the Shell offices. The gains of online bidding showed up the very first day. The savings in the final bid price translated to 9% when compared to the historic price offered for the same goods in the conventional Tender Board process.

A second session for another product was held along the same lines in which 10 suppliers participated. The savings was 40.6%. Another nine suppliers took part for a third product, which made savings of 14.2%.

E-auctions; some other reported savings

E-auctions can cut the cost of council goods and services by an average of one quarter, according to figures from the Regional Centres of Excellence.

Results from the first wave of the national programme of e-auctions show they delivered an average saving of 27 %. The nine e-auctions held in 2005 – 2006 generated savings of 12.9 million pounds from set up costs of 137,000 pounds, a gain of 94 pounds on every pound spent.

Corporate social responsibility

There are many views on what CSR is. The narrowest view is the classical view by the economist Friedman is that the corporate responsibility of business is to increase its profits. The owners of the company who are supposed to be interested in profit maximisation are the turning point of the decisions made by the company. Social responsibility is considered here, to be primarily the responsibility of the government.

A broader approach is the stakeholder perspective; here, companies are not only accountable to the owners of the company, but also to the stakeholders. The argument is that stakeholders influence the activities of the company and/or are influenced by the activities of the company. Companies are, for example, accountable to politicians who can curb the activities of the company by introducing a bill.

The broadest approach is the societal approach in which companies are considered to be responsible to society in general. The view is that companies are part of society. They need a "licence to operate" from society. Today companies representing this approach are characterized as "good corporate citizens".

Carroll focuses in on the essentials of the above three approaches. He considers the role of companies today as a role which includes four dimensions:
*   economic
*   legal
*   ethical
*   philanthropic

Carroll also focuses on the stakeholders of the company as he sees that social responsibility is a diffuse and almost non-operational concept, unless organisations learn to "unfold stakeholder thinking".

The European Commission also links CSR to the stakeholder approach. CSR is a concept whereby companies integrate social and environmental concerns in their business operations and in their interactions with their stakeholders on a voluntary basis (EU Commission, 2001, p.6). The definition is used by leading companies in Europe and is considered as the basis of the European CSR policy.

One of the most referred to definitions is by the World Business Council for Sustainable Development (WBCSD, 1999) that defines CSR as "the continuing commitment by business to behave ethically and contribute to economic development whilst improving the quality of life of the workforce and their families as well as of the local community and society at large".

The CSR concept is still developing and has not reached the maturity stage. It consists of a number of free standing and competing ideas that have not been sufficiently integrated into a broadly accepted and robust theory. In particular, there is an absence of consensus regarding the elements (steps) underpinning the processes of corporate social responsibility. Therefore, the analysis presented in this section is to seen as work in progress and subject to change as the CSR concept climbs the maturity curve.

Other CSR Definitions

There are many definitions of Corporate Social Responsibility (CSR). One such definition is as follows: "The firm's consideration of, and response to, issues beyond the narrow economic, technical, and legal requirements of the firm to accomplish social benefits along with the traditional economic gains which the firm seeks."

Another definition offers the following: "An ethical organisation is one that is able to reflect appropriately and evaluate its actions in the context of an ethical domain, within the process of organisational decision making. In attempting to do so, the organisation must grapple with the problem of multiple agency-constituency roles."

Many correspondents argue that pressure for CSR emanates from multiple stakeholder groups including customers, employees, suppliers, community groups, governments and institutional shareholders. CSR here is concerned with treating the stakeholders of the firm ethically or in a socially responsible manner. Stakeholders exist both within a firm and outside. The aim of social responsibility is to create higher and higher standards of living, while preserving the profitability of the corporation, for its stakeholders both within and outside the corporation.

This is pragmatic and acknowledges the importance of economic performance, it recognises that firms serve a broad range of stakeholders, and it highlights the importance of striking a balance between economic performance, meeting the stakeholders expectations and responsibility towards society. CSR can only flourish if its protagonists recognise the importance of economic performance.

CSR values

The following values underpin the CSR concept:
*   Seeks to understand and meet the needs of stakeholders including that of customers, owner, employees, suppliers, and the society at large;
*   Integrity of individual and collective action;
*   Honour;
*   Fairness;
*   Respect;

- Participation;
- Individual and collective responsibility to others.

Waddock and Graves (1997) empirical research showed a positive association between corporate social performance and financial performance. The outcome of studies examining the link between CSR and financial performance is however indeterminate with other studies in identifying this positive link and finds no link and in some cases, a negative link. Martin-Castilla (2002) argued that CSR serves the long term interest of the firm by aligning the interest of the firm with that of its stakeholders.

Elements of CSR Process

Elements of CSR Process	Description
No-Harm	This principle draws upon the rights philosophy by demanding that the firm should not engage in any action that leads to harm.
Transparency	This principle draws on the liberty and informed choice theory. That is full disclosure and provision of information to all parties so that they are able to take decisions that do not compromise their welfare
Voice	This principle requires that stakeholders' interests are protected through visible and active participation in the decision making process at all levels.
Equity	This is derived from the theories of rights and justice and its aim is to ensure that there is perceived equity in the actions of business.
Benefit	The need to examine the benefits of an action, that is to say, if a certain act is carried out, who wins, who stays the same and who loses from it? What are the gains and losses?
Integrity	This requires integrity of action in all forms
Liberty	This is based on the liberty theory of ethics by stressing the right of the individual freely to engage in or disengage from transactions with the firm.
Care	This is focusing on protection and promotion of positive rights by the firm.

Source: Table Adapted from Ahmed and Machold (2004)

Checklist: Drivers behind Corporate Social Initiatives

- Gaining a competitive advantage
- Emerging morals and ethics – although some people still believe that an organisation exists solely to maximise shareholder value, many more have come to the conclusion that this should not be at the expense of the environment, community or society in general
- Thinking in terms of engagement and not speedy solutions – for example, acting

with only the shareholders in mind will create a gap in commitment between employees and investors
- Understanding that society and economics are inextricably linked – just as social situations impact upon the economy, the economy also has an effect on society. This is the view of Mintzberg who vehemently opposes the argument that a company exists purely to create profit for its shareholder; he believes that companies must accept the part they play in society

Critical Success Factors

- Connect with your organisation's core values and competencies
- Respond to moral pressures – although your response may not be completely to the liking of any pressure groups, it will demonstrate that you are prepared to listen and, in most cases, compromise
- Measure your success

Case Study: CSR and Business in the Community (BITC)

Twenty five years ago a group of British companies decided to improve the way that business affects society. They set up Business in the Community (BITC), an independent charity to inspire, engage, support and challenge companies to continually improve the impact they have on society. It now has 750 member companies, including 71 of the FTSE 100, and its combined membership represents 12.4m people in 200 countries.

The creation of the Corporate Responsibility index began in 1998 when it was decided that companies needed a way to measure and report on responsible business practice. The purpose of the Corporate Responsibility Index is the only index that measures the impact businesses have on the staff they employ, and the societies in which they operate and on the environment.

Business in the Community (BITC), emphasises that corporate responsibility is not just a "feel good" exercise but is of strategic and financial importance to every business and is vital that the momentum behind CSR is maintained. Companies that do not keep a grip on working conditions, the activities of their suppliers or pollution are more likely to be prosecuted, shut down by the authorities or boycotted by the public. Overall, there has been a substantial increase in the number of companies with policies and targets in the public domain, especially on hum rights, standards in the supply chain and in the work place.

The companies in the CSR Index are committed to measuring and controlling their social and environmental impact. Companies that have taken part said it led to business advantages, including cost savings, an improved corporate image, better recruitment and greater efficiencies.

But there are still some of Britain's biggest businesses who do not take corporate social responsibility seriously. Companies are recognizing that a genuine commitment to responsible business can be a source of innovation that produces new opportunities. BITC's Company of the Year – Marks and Spencer   has made sustainability and corporate citizenship an integral part of the M&S brand as well as a key part of its commercial recovery.

Environmental issues as a CSR driver

Environmental concerns are reflected in reducing waste. It has been estimated that most companies underestimate the true costs of their waste by a factor of 20. True costs can equate to 4% of turnover of which about 1% could be saved by waste minimisation, for example, one company, specializing in the management of industrial fluids, converted from steel storage to plastic drums. With plastic drums used over and over, the company saved approximately $1.8 million annually and significantly reduces the volume of discarded containers.

The "making waste work" initiative has identified the Four "R's" for the reduction of waste. These are:
- Reduce the amount of waste
- Reuse items i.e. plastic reusable packaging rather than cardboard
- Recycle items i.e. at recycling depots or recycling companies
- Repair items, i.e. increase maintenance and avoid scrapping

The Procurement Department is often most suitably placed within the company to contribute to overall environmental performance. Green issues have to filter down from a company to its suppliers to be effective and there are at least three good reasons for companies to try to influence their suppliers to improve their environmental performance:
- Obtaining better service or reduced prices from suppliers
- Responding to life-cycle demands from customers
- Maintaining or enhancing the corporate image

Many larger companies have already seen returns (cost avoidance, cost minimisation and environmental liabilities) from waste minimisation. Key to the success of a waste minimisation programme is supplier involvement. This means that suppliers are not faced with unreasonable demands and puts a proportion of the innovation in the hands of suppliers who have the greatest technical knowledge of their product. In the case of a SME procurement company dealing with a larger selling company, it also assists in the dissemination of best practice.

Checklist: common considerations for procurement professionals undertaking waste minimisation and pollution control:
- Purchase of recycled products; increases market for recycled products and strengthens the developing infrastructure
- Purchase of recyclable products: products with greater percentage of recyclable materials or more easily recycled materials increase post use recycle value and encourage recycling

- Purchase from suppliers with preferred environmental status; provides impetus for suppliers to pursue environmental initiatives
- Purchase products manufactured with renewable resources; minimise depletion of non-renewable natural resources
- Specify or purchase reusable packaging; reuse on site, at other facilities, or return to the original supplier for reuse
- Purchase materials that are environmentally friendly or neutral
- Purchase products that are manufactured with environmentally superior processes for example, powder coating versus spray painting reduces air emissions
- Reduce the number of different or incompatible materials; facilitates recycling, coloured paper reduces value of recycled office paper, labels/stickers that are difficult to remove inhibit recycling

Environmental evaluation criteria

What are the likely criteria to be applied in assessing a supplier's environmental performance? It is not possible to be too specific, but there are some general headings, to be analysed and supplemented, which can be given.

There are likely to be four main headings which provide a high level taxonomy in relation to environmental issues. These are as follows:
- Regulatory compliance
- Environmental effects and performance measures
- Existing environmental management procedures
- Commitment to management and process improvement

The first heading will encompass the various legislative and regulatory issues. Some will be mandatory conditions for supplier approval. Other criteria under this heading, though not mandatory, may nonetheless have a high weighting, both within this high level category and for the overall evaluation. For mandatory criteria, it is likely that buying organisations would withhold approval/negotiation until such time as the supplier did fulfil the mandatory conditions.

The second category of environmental effects heading covers the various effects and performance measures, such as ecotoxicological information, volatile organic compounds records, etc.

The third category heading covers the existing management procedures relating to the existing set of products and processes. This will involve environmental effects register maintenance, energy conservation policy, etc.

All of the above headings will relate to specific products or sets of products and bout in materials and components relating to the transformation processes involved in the business covered. The final category covers the commitment to continuous improvement in both management and transformation processes. These will apply to the supply company irrespective of the various product and materials which are supplied.

Case Study: Nissan UK

Nissan manufacturing UK's environmental journey began several years ago and, initially, was brought into focus by a need to comply with legislation. Achieving this soon brought all functions, including our suppliers, together on activities designed to meet requirements but at no on cost.

They set out to look at it from the total business need. Foremost was the instruction to meet environmental legislation but at no cost. Achieving this requires savings to be made elsewhere to offset against legislative demands. First, they had to identify and understand all the drivers of the activity. A list was compiled including total detailed costs expended within each category. This involved collaboration with suppliers of components and packaging in order to detail and calculate all costs, including secondary costs.

For example, if they received the components in cardboard box packaging from a supplier and the intention was to delete the cardboard and use a returnable stillage, it took not only the cost of the cardboard versus the cost of the new stillage but included such issues as time saved on decanting the cardboard box to present the components to the assembly line versus the ability to present the new stillage direct to line side. Also, by working with the supplier of the component, they calculated any benefits in their manufacturing and used those to reduce the piece cost. Also, eliminating decanting operations improved the welfare of employees by reducing heavy lifting operations. This reduces potential for industrial sickness which is a cost to the company.

A further example is dealing with the safe transportation of airbags. An airbag contains explosives which are subject to handling and transportation legislation. There are also environmental issues should there be an incident in transit. The initial packaging was aimed at meeting those issues. However, it was expensive and created waste from the protection involved. The new method for delivery was developed jointly with the supplier. The benefits it will bring are:

Benefits
- Elimination of supplier packaging (environmental waste)
- Reduction of disposable packaging (wastes)
- Improved compliance with legislation on transportation of hazardous goods (environmental issues)
- Elimination of decanting operations (safety and cost)
- Prevention of dust ingress (quality improvement)
- Reduced handling requirements (safety, employee welfare)

They have also worked on other issues with suppliers, such as recycling (for example, of plastic fuel tanks); reduction of process waste; paint technology and elimination of environmentally unsound materials. All achieved reduced costs.

179

The environment is best dealt with not as a specialised activity, but as a natural part of business. It is not an obstacle to performance but an important driver in obtaining business advantages. The public do not buy items solely because they are green; they buy them because they are better quality and lower cost as well as green.

Nissan's Waste Strategy
- Conform with all government and European legislation
- Adopt proactive introduction of strategies to conform with future legal requirements
- Introduce and maintain cost reduction exercises aimed at achieving waste elimination
  and improving effective waste management
- Monitor and control current day to day waste stream activities
- Adopt a programme of continuous improvement.

CSR and the Supply Chain

Of all the challenges facing organisations, established and maintaining responsible business all the way down the supply chain, remains one, of the most exacting and complex.

Ensuring that perhaps thousands of suppliers comply with your corporate responsibility codes is hard enough; in an ever more globalised economy the difficulty is compounded by differences in culture and language.

Case Study: Waitrose

Supermarket chain Waitrose (part of the John Lewis Partnership) sells 18,000 different products, sourced from 1,500 suppliers in more than 60 countries, all of which must sign up to the ethical and environmental requirements of its Responsible Sourcing Principles.

Waitrose says: "It's all very well having best practices but you must also ensure your suppliers interpret them in a consistent fashion. It's very easy for different cultures in different countries to interpret things in different ways. Even for something as straightforward as stipulating that workers must not be exposed to hazardous conditions".

Establishing workable codes of conduct and a streamlined compliance process only go so far in fostering more responsible business from your supply chain. However, giving incentives to suppliers is becoming as important as setting out clear rules. "There should be a carrot as well as a stick. Achieving better compliance should not just be about enforcement, it should also be about working with suppliers to improve working conditions and fostering long term relationships." The payback for Waitrose is abundantly clear, "Where there are good labour standards, there is better productivity and better quality."

"If you are buying in China, but don't understand the working conditions there, you are not a responsible business." B&Q similarly note that; "If you look after your people, you get better productivity. If you are managing the work with your suppliers well, you get better quality products."

"We do it first and foremost because it's the right thing to do, but the business benefits are also clear."

Think of a typical existing supply chain. The products are conveyed from suppliers to original equipment manufacturers (OEMs) and then on, via various other intermediaries, to the end user, who finally disposes of it.

This concept is changing and those involved in supply management arena are witnessing the dawn of the "closed loop supply chain". The most obvious example of the closed loop model is the disposable camera. A customer buys the camera, which can only be used once, with a film already inside. The customer returns the camera for developing; the manufacturer retrieves the camera and then either services it and repackages it for further use or disassembles if for reusable components.

Today, makers of printers, such as Xerox, and of refrigerators, are arranging their supply chains in similar ways, coming full circle to reap economic and ecological benefits. Undoubtedly, these benefits and pressures have been the main forces behind the closed loop shift.

In EU, the Waste Electrical and Electronic Equipment (WEEE) Directive aims to reduce waste by promoting reuse, recycling and other means by which products can be salvaged to minimise the impact on the environment. Private householders are to be able to return waste goods without charge and manufacturers must meet collection and recycling targets. Producer responsibility is backed up by measures such as disposal bans, increased disposal tariffs, restrictions on waste transportation, emission control and waste prevention.

This has dramatically altered the traditional linear supply chain model in which, once upon a time, vendors would sell their products to customers and it would be up to shoppers to dispose of their refrigerator, oven or printer at the municipal dump. WEEE changes all this, and manufacturers are now seeing a new end to the supply chain as they take back products at the end of their lives. This presents not only a logistical problem in clearing the equipment away, but also a cost.

This offers manufacturers an opportunity to recycle the parts they produced for the earlier product. By incorporating the recovered parts into the supply chain, they are "closing the loop" and bringing the product full circle. To make this process work, advances in design are needed to make the product "reusable". But because products will be used again rather than created from scratch, factory emissions and energy consumption will be cut. Supply chain cots are directly linked to its processes, and operating a closed loop model contributes towards cheaper processes.

But for any closed loop supply chain to be successful, manufacturers must look at how they manage the entire life-cycle of a product. Companies must evaluate the environmental burden associated with a product, process or activity. Legislation such as the WEEE directive will mean that manufacturers have to look closely at forward and reverse supply chain processes to minimise environmental impact, energy use and wastage. The benefits of a closed loop supply chain in terms of both economic gain to the company and a positive impact on the environment are clear.

When changing any established supply model, there are a number of issues that need to be resolved. Xerox, identified a number of barriers to implementing an extension to the return and recycling process, these included:

- Customer related issues, such as the acceptance of recycled products and the need for simplicity in the returns process;
- Product related concerns, for example, product design, access to technology and the labour intensive nature of the return and recycling process;
- Internal factors, such as the allocation of costs and financial benefits;
- External factors, such as meeting legal obligations regarding disposal and the public image of the recycling industry in general.
- A consultation period with suppliers is important to get the best value from the relationship.

Xerox now reuses 70-90 percent by weight of machine components, while meeting performance specifications for equipment with all new parts.

The Green Supply Chain

Procurement managers are entrusted with the task of procuring a wide variety of raw materials, components, consumables and packaging materials required to run the industrial enterprise and produce finished goods to satisfy market demand. They have a vital role to play in giving their company the competitive edge in the market place by adopting environmentally sound policies and practices. Purchase decisions, besides other considerations, must also be environmentally sound and every link in the supply chain tuned to this philosophy.

They must impress upon their managements that in the present climate of private enterprise, consumer driven competitive marks and increasing public awareness, a proactive approach to the environmental issues will be beneficial. Adoption and use of environmentally sound technologies and manufacture of eco-friendly products will lead to overall reductions in cost. With increasing public awareness consumers may even be willing to pay a little extra for green or eco-friendly products.

For a proper appreciation of the ecological soundness of a purchase decision and its likely impact on environment, an in depth study and analysis of the complete life-cycle of the product needs to be carried out. This concept, called the "cradle to grave" approach, must examine the cumulative impact on the environment that the product generates, right from the stage of extraction of its raw material up to its final disposal after completion of economic life-cycle.

This cradle to grave analysis will study and assess the environmental impact of:
- The raw materials used
- Manufacturing/production methods/processes employed
- Energy consumed
- Modes and quantum of transportation used
- Pollutants and wastes generated by the manufacturing process
- Type of packing used, scope of its reuse/recycling
- Final disposal of the product after expiry of its useful economic life

To be able to carry out such a life-cycle analysis, the procurement manager must study and understand the entire manufacturing cycle and discuss the subject with the manufacturer and/or supplier of the raw material/component.

The supplier of the component must be taken into confidence and the objectives of the exercise explained to him. It needs to be conveyed to the supplier that the proposed study will be equally beneficial to him and will in no way affect his business prospects. On the contrary, it will help him improve quality and consumer acceptance of his product and reduce overall cost by minimising energy consumption, reducing waste and generation of pollutants and reuse/recycling of hitherto discarded products. With the introduction of partnership sourcing and the reduction supplier base, it should be possible to have a proper interaction with the suppliers to obtain the requisite details for life-cycle analysis.

Checklist: Elements for Life-cycle Analysis (LCA)

The following are the important elements that need to be considered in LCA and details gathered about them from the supplier or other source of information.

Raw materials
What are the raw materials used in the manufacture of the product and is their consumption optimal? Is the raw materials derived from a renewable or a non renewable resource and how can its impact on environment be minimised? Use of raw materials such as lead, mercury, and nickel, found to be carcinogenic, must be avoided where possible.

Energy consumption
Is the manufacturing process energy efficient? Presently most of the energy is produced from non renewable resources. It is therefore imperative that use of energy is optimised and non renewable resource conserved.

Manufacturing process
Is the process of manufacture efficient in use of raw material/energy/labour and does it employ environmentally sound technology. Does it create excessive pollution and generates toxic

wastes? Manufacturing technologies have been a major source of environmental degradation. Manufacturing processes using potentially harmful ingredients such as cyanides, chlorine and asbestos need to be avoided. It is better to use clean technologies to reduce pollution rather than using cleaning technologies, to remove pollutants which have already been generated. Use of clean technology will prove to be cost effective besides being environmentally friendly.

Another important point to be examined is whether the technology employed permits use of recycled raw materials. This is an important consideration as it will reduce the need for virgin raw materials and lead to cost reduction and other benefits.

Waste reduction
Waste during manufacture is very costly and must therefore, be eliminated or minimised. It not only represents poor quality but is also a source of employee demoralization.

Reuse/recycling of by-products of production process
Are the wastes and by products of production process recycled or reused so as to recover material and energy, thereby minimising down stream pollution? Reuse of reclaimed water, oils and lubricants etc can lead to considerable savings and also reduce environmental contamination.

Packaging
Primary and protective packing contributes substantially towards total cost and their disposal presents problems. Use of reusable or recyclable packing needs to be encouraged. With the advent of partnership sourcing and limited supplier bases, the use of reusable and returnable packing can be expanded, resulting in cost reduction and minimising the need for disposal of packing materials. As far as possible, use of recyclable and or bio-degradable packing needs encouragement to reduce the mountains of packaging rubbish.

Final disposal
Recycling and disposal of the product at the end of its useful economic life is the last stage in the cradle to grave approach. Can the product be recycled for use as raw material? If not, is it bio-degradable? Will its disposal by dumping pollute the environment? All these aspects need careful evaluation as there is an emerging concept that producers are liable for final disposal of their products even after they have been transferred to others. Such concerns arise from the difficulties experienced in disposal of products such as nuclear wastes, used auto tyres and certain on recyclable plastics which can not be easily disposed of in an eco-friendly manner.

The result
Having carefully examined the important parameters, based on the data obtained from the manufacturer and/or supplier, the parameters which have a predominant environmental impact can be identified. The importance and role of these can then be discussed with the supplier to enable him to incorporate the necessary changes in the raw material, manufacturing process, packing to make the final product more environmentally friendly. The procurement manager will have to act as a guide and facilitator to enable the manufacturer to incorporate various changes and derive full benefits from the life-cycle analysis.

CSR in Global Supply Chains

Corporate Social Responsibility (CSR) in a general sense reflects obligations to society and stakeholders within societies impacted by the firm. To illustrate the increasing importance of CSR with respect to supply chain management, consider the case of Wal-Mart and the Kathie Lee Gifford line of women's clothing. Despite the fact that items with the Kathie Lee Gifford brand carried a "made in the USA" label, news items started appearing in 1996 suggesting that the garments were actually being produced in Honduran sweatshops. This news about its suppliers damaged the Wal-Mart brand name and tarnished its reputation. The Wal-Mart case is not an isolated one.

However, recently, Wal-Mart has been aggressively pursuing a variety of environmental strategies that have profoundly impacted its highly integrated global supply chain. The company will invest $500 million in sustainability projects that already involve its vehicle fleet, energy usage, packaging, agribusiness, organic clothes and food, and eco-stores themselves.

The trend towards embracing CSR has become so significant that Hau Lee, a global authority on supply chain management (SCM), claims that socially responsible supply chains are, indeed, a new paradigm.

"…implementing CSR initiatives within supply chains effectively (involves) ensuring supplier compliance."

Many issues are involved in implementing CSR initiatives within supply chains effectively, not least of which is ensuring supplier compliance. Recently, firms have come under pressure to raise the level of supplier monitoring as a means of increasing such supplier compliance. For instance, the International Labour Organization (ILO) initiated the Better Factories Program to raise working conditions in Cambodia's garment factories. Relying on unannounced visits to factories, it monitors a 500-item check list, notes progress made in remedying problems and reports its findings publicly. Its success is attributed to the fact that all factories are involved and share a similar set of objectives, it is transparent and credible to foreign buyers, and meets the needs of the workers.

High levels of monitoring may also carry unintended consequences relating to managing the exchange relationships that make up a supply chain. Research suggests perceived fairness can improve commitment and trust within buyer-supplier exchange relationships, which have been repeatedly shown as important to achieving the level of interaction and knowledge exchange necessary for high performing supply chain relationships. Several factors drive firms to accept responsibility for managing supplier CSR, including customer and stakeholder expectations and the potential threat of legal liability.

Firms primarily use three instruments in implementing socially responsible behaviour among their subcontractors:
*   Social labels
*   Socially responsible investment
*   Codes of conduct

Social labelling informs the public of the firm's compliance to an established set of criteria, and tends to be more effective in certain situations than in others. Labelling seems to work more efficiently in export markets involving the retail trade, and is often associated with niche products aimed at affluent consumers who are not price sensitive and are willing to trade price for support of the espoused social issue. For instance, Starbucks might label its coffee as being grown by producers who received a premium price because Starbucks negotiated directly with the source. That premium is then passed onto the consumer.

Socially responsible investing arises when financial decisions are based on achieving a socially desirable end and acceptable economic returns. For instance, large state pension funds in the USA, such as California's, have for a number of years invested in companies that align with the fund's position on certain social issues. American universities also have directed investments in their endowment portfolios to support certain social programs and avoided investing in companies that espouse views contrary to the school's moral conscience. However, in practice, very few funds own enough shares to affect the stock prices of non-conforming companies.

Codes of conduct are applied to corporate policies and actions rather than to goods, and imply that the firm observes and/or enforces the policy advocated. For instance, Levi Strauss' 1992 code stipulates that it will seek to do business with partners that do not use child or forced labour, do not discriminate, and do not use corporal punishment.

Cisco began the process of addressing both human rights and environmental issue in 2004. They adopted a code for suppliers that outlined standards to ensure safe working conditions, where workers are treated with dignity and respect and manufacturing processes are in conformance with stated environmental considerations. The code also includes the expectation of full compliance with host country's laws and regulations, as we as compliance with internally accepted standards.

Codes of Conduct

Adopted in 1998, the International Labour Organisation (ILO) Declaration on Fundamental Principles and Rights at Work is an expression of commitment by governments, employers' and workers' organisations to uphold basic human values that are vital to our social and economic lives. The Declaration covers four areas:
- Freedom of association and the right to collective bargaining
- The elimination of forced and compulsory labour
- The abolition of child labour
- The elimination of discrimination in the workplace.

High monitoring levels lead to buyer/supplier conflict, militating against the trust and commitment integral to successful performance. A firm cannot manage its supply chain partners if it has not articulated precisely what its intentions are, what it is doing itself and what it expects from its suppliers and its suppliers' suppliers. Codes of conduct represent the efforts of each company to put into writing a statement or set of expectations regarding supplier corporate social responsibility.

There can be no ambiguity as to what the goals are, the penalties for those who violate the letter and spirit of the code, and resources are available to help suppliers (current or potential) become and remain compliant. Accuracy of information is essential as are consistency in criteria used in selecting and evaluating suppliers, as well as the need for objective (i.e. unbiased) application of the criteria.

Any action that encourages involvement or participation in supply chain issues will go a long way to building commitment and a common CSR vision. To complete the circle, a corporate policy of statement of the buying company's commitment in the form of a corporate social responsibility report should be developed and endorsed. Companies such as Disney, Gap and McDonald's Corporation publish CSR reports that both illustrate their commitment to their codes of conduct, and also highlight the benefits they derive from their efforts. More important, they measure the effectiveness of those efforts, and embrace those supply chain partners whose behaviours epitomize CSR.

An Environmental Management System

An Environmental Management System (EMS) is defined as:
"A method of controlling and regulating the organisation's environmental concerns"

The International Standards Organisation; ISO 14001: Environmental Management System standard states:
"The EMS includes organisational structure, planning activities, responsibilities, procedures, processes and resources for developing, achieving, reviewing and maintaining the environmental policy".

In turn the standard then clarifies that the following is involved:
- Aspect covered are; Activities, products or services that can interact with the environment
- Impacts are; Any change to the environment adverse or beneficial
- Objective; Overall goal arising from the environmental policy – quantifiable where applicable
- Performance; Measurable results related to the control of environmental aspects, based on policy, objectives and targets
- Policy; Statement of intentions and principles – provides a framework for action and for the settings of objectives and targets
- Target; Detailed performance requirement that arises from the objectives
- Interested party; Individual or group concerned or affected by the performance of an organisation
- Pollution prevention; Use of processes, practices, materials or products that avoid, reduce or control pollution

Checklist: the benefits of EMS

- Avoiding fines and prosecutions
- Reduced operating costs

- Reduced wastes
- Compliance with environmental legislation
- Reduced insurance premium
- Increased public/customer relations
- Satisfying stakeholder demands
- Integration of improvement efforts

ISO 14001 is an Environmental System Standard and when adopted by an organisation can be assessed by an independent third party who will check conformity to the standard. If the organisation achieves certification the EMS has been independently verified and attained a recognised level of environmental Management.

ISO 14001 sets out the following five principles for a successful EMS
- Commitment and policy
- Planning
- Implementation
- Measurement and evaluation
- Review and improvement

Checklist: Initial considerations for Implementing EMS

Commitment from management is a key factor to the success of an EMS who needs to develop awareness and understand of:
- Why the organisation needs an EMS
- The benefits
- The goals and objectives
- The links with other objectives

Senior management has the responsibility for:
- The environmental policy
- Environmental reviews
- Appointment of an environmental representative and team
- Ensure adequate resources are available to support them

Undertake an Initial Environmental Review (ER), this ER helps the environmental team to:
- Compile a register of significant environmental aspects and impact (Cause & Effect)
- Prepare an environmental policy
- Develop objectives and targets

An ER typically covers:
- The significance of the above
- Quantifies emissions, discharges, wastes, energy usage
- Identifies cost saving opportunities
- Identifies the "must do's" for legislation and regulation (law)
- Provides an overview of site activities
- Reviews current environmental system documentation

The Environmental policy should state:
- A commitment to compliance with environmental legislation
- A commitment to continual improvement
- A commitment to preventing pollution

It must be:
- Written and communicated
- Specific to the organisation
- Signed and approved by the person with the highest authority and responsibility for the site
- A controlled document

The responsibility of the Environmental representative is important, as ISO 14001 states: "An organisation should establish and maintain a procedure to identify and have access to legal and other requirements that the organisation subscribes to that are applicable to the environmental aspects of its activities or services".

This is usually satisfied by a register of legislation which typically includes:
- The main law or code
- Secondary legislation
- Guidance on the legislation
- Summary of requirements
- Implications for the organisation
- Who are the regulatory authority or equivalent

An Environmental Management Programme is usually in two parts

1) Outlining the environmental controls:
- Operational procedures that affect environmental performance
- Risk assessments (R-Probability x Consequence)
- COSHH register/controls
- Emergency preparedness procedures
- Organisation/responsibility charts
- Environmental policy

2) Setting Objectives and Targets
- Objectives are set out in reference to initial environmental review, register of legislation, assessments of significance and the environmental policy
- Targets are the clear and concise operational requirements relating to the objectives
- Targets should be realistic and measurable, time scaled and assigned to an individual or team

Senior management of an organisation must review the effectiveness of the EMS and whether action is required to take into account.

- Changing environmental legislation
- Modified customer expectations
- Stakeholder pressures
- Failure to achieve objectives or targets
- Required changes to operations
- The results and recommendations of audits.

Monitoring and measurement of activities that can have a significant impact on the environment must take place. This is documented and carried out by trained operational personnel.

Adequate awareness and training must be delivered to communicate and support the environmental management system policy, goals, management of objectives and targets. Training must be relevant to the management of significant aspects and impacts at all levels and positions that affect the system performance and should be delivered to support the Environmental Management System.

Environmental Audits

There are three levels of audits;
1)   Internal audit, the self assessment
2)   Customer audit of your organisation and vice versa
3)   Independent of the company

The first two audits use experienced and trained auditors with appropriate knowledge experts when required. They have a schedule to audit and document the audit process by checking check at all levels, for example:
- policy
- objectives/targets
- operations
- documentation
- ISO 14001 compliance/implementation

Finally they give feedback to managers responsible and management meetings.

The third and independent audit is called the certification audit and is conducted against the requirements of ISO14001. It uses completely independent assessors and a certificate system that provides proof of compliance to a standard. They are usually conducted twice per year.

Summary

With approximately 50% -70% of turnover as bought-in goods for many companies, the Procurement and Supply Chain functions are most suitably placed within the company to contribute to overall CSR and environmental performance. Many larger companies have already seen returns (cost avoidance, cost minimisation and environmental liabilities) from waste minimisation. Small and medium sized companies are also beginning to change.

Key to the success is supplier involvement. It means that suppliers are not faced with unreasonable demands and puts a proportion of the innovation in the hands of suppliers who have the greatest technical knowledge of their product.

Supplier development

As a business's needs, supplier goals and objectives change constantly, it is unlikely that the capabilities of a supply base and the requirements of a buyer organisation will naturally align for any prolonged period of time. Supplier development aims to create and sustain alignment between a buyer organisation and a supplier for the benefit of both parties.

Supplier development has been described by many of the companies as supporting the supplier in enhancing the performance of their products and services or improving the supplier's capabilities. An amalgam of various definitions by consultant colleagues of the authors produces a definition of supplier development as:

"A long term cooperative effort between a buying firm and its suppliers to upgrade the suppliers' technical, quality, delivery and cost capabilities and to foster ongoing improvements."

Supplier development is meanwhile defined by the authors as:

"Any effort of a buying firm with a supplier to increase its performance and/or capabilities and meet the buying firm's short and/or long-term needs."

Portfolio analysis

Clearly when a typical supplier base can consist of thousands of suppliers, effort should be focused on those key categories of spend that are most likely to delivery significant additional value to the business, as developing current or potential suppliers can be resource intensive. Using portfolio analysis, such as Kraljic, to segment spend, is a relatively straightforward to determine the most appropriate categories and, therefore, identify those suppliers to engage in a supplier development programme.

At this stage, some other factors should also be considered, such as the expected benefits from supplier development for the buyer organisation and the supplier's ability to develop and change. Also, another consideration is the cost of development for both the buyer and supplier to ensure that there is an acceptable return on investment for both. Buyers need to protect themselves from supplier power, and long term relationships built up through supplier development programmes may be a way of achieving this. This is because the expenditure is large enough to encourage supplier participation and the category's supply market is difficult to buy in, so the relationship tends to be seen as long rather than short term.

The stated commitment to a supplier development initiative means that is highly likely that the relationship between buyer and supplier will progress and migrate "up" the relationship spectrum.

A well structured supplier development programme should link the achievement of specific performance deliverables to discrete "steps" in this relationship migration, where suppliers receive benefits for delivering on their commitment to change and develop.

Added value supplier development

A number of different offerings can add value to the relationship and could help to compensate for any price increases or offset them. Examples include:
- Joint focus on identifying and solving the shared problem together
- Incentivised performance and shared risk and rewards
- Product innovation, assistance with research and development or even outsourcing responsibility for development
- Scheduling delivery in order to support product availability
- Consignment stock or simplified ordering and invoice processes
- Packaging waste reclamation, reduction or both
- Improvements and developments in product yield
- Higher quality levels

There are many ways to increase the value that suppliers can deliver. Active participation internally from teams identifying whole life-cycle advantages, which are linked to strategic needs, is one of the best ways to ensure the supplier development programmes work.

One of procurements basic objectives is to maintain a network of capable suppliers. Yet many purchasers view their suppliers' performance as lacking in critical areas of quality and cost improvement, delivery performance, new technology adoption, and financial health.

As today's firm's focus on their core competencies, they become more dependent on their suppliers to meet ever increasing competition. To compete in their respective markets, buying firms must ensure that their suppliers' performance, capabilities and responsiveness equals, or surpasses that experienced by the buying firm's competitors. Thus, many buying firms actively facilitate supplier performance and capability improvements through supplier development.

In practice, supplier development activities vary significantly, ranging from limited buying firm efforts that might include informal supplier evaluation and a request for improved performance, to extensive efforts that might include training of the supplier's personnel and investment in the supplier's operations. The focus of many supplier development activities has been a short term focus, targeted at improving suppliers' product or service performance, instead of it being a long term focus on improving suppliers' capabilities.

Supplier development activities

Buying firms may use a variety of activities to develop suppliers' performance and/or capabilities. These activities include:
- Introducing competition into the supply base
- Supplier evaluation as a prerequisite to further supplier development activities, raising performance expectations

- Recognition and awards
- The promise of future benefits
- Training and education of the supplier's personnel
- Exchange of personnel between the buying firm and the supplier
- Direct investment in the supplier by the buying firm

It is a fact that the success of buying firms' supplier development efforts varies. This result raises the question of what factors are responsible for supplier development success. Further, what factors may inhibit successful supplier development? Supplier development is often a manifestation of a buying firm's proactive stance or attitude towards supply base performance.

Lack of buying firm power, measured in terms of the percentage of a suppliers output purchased by the buying firm, has been cited as one reason suppliers seem to be reluctant to participate in supplier development efforts. Lack of effective communication has also been cited as a barrier to supplier development, as has lack of buying firm credibility.

Firms may engage in supplier development as a reaction to competitive markets. Firms may also seek competitive advantage from strategic supply initiatives such as supplier development because of competitive pressures such as shortened product life-cycles, fast changing technologies, ever increasing quality levels and cost cutting by competitors. Thus, firms that face relatively high levels of market competition may put more effort into their supplier development efforts. However, do firms that put forth greater supplier development efforts reap greater benefits? The answer is overwhelmingly "yes".

Supplier Development Practices

Supplier development is becoming increasingly important since supplier switching (i.e. searching for alternative sources of supply and sourcing the product from a more capable supplier) might not be viable due to unavailability of alternative suppliers or due to excessively high switching costs, and the vertical integration (i.e. bringing the needed product in-house by acquiring the supplier or setting up manufacturing capacities internally) might require substantial investment and be in contradiction with firms' intentions to focus on their core competencies.

The basic notions of supplier development can be traced back to 1943, when Toyota joined a supplier association (renamed thereafter Kyoko Kai) to assist a number of subcontractors in the Tokai region in improving productivity. From then on, supplier associations within the Toyota supply network and collaboration between Toyota and its suppliers grew constantly. With some exceptions, such supplier development played little part and was not widespread in the Western economy until the 1990s. Since then, firms in the automotive industry pressed ahead with this practice and turned it into a popular and powerful approach to improve supply chain performance in Western industries.

Other chronicled examples of supplier development practices applied subsequently by firms outside the automotive industry are, for example, Harley-Davidson, Digital Equipment Corporation, Motorola, or Marks & Spencer.

Reactive and Direct supplier development

Firms taking a 'reactive approach' measure only when there is poor supplier performance and to eliminate existing deficiencies therefore when problems have already occurred. By contrast, with a strategic approach firms try to improve supplier performance actively and for the long term; before performance problems actually occur.

Supplier development can be distinguished by the role the buying firm plays and according to the resources committed to a specific supplier. In the case of "direct" or "internalised" supplier development, the buying firm plays an active role and dedicates human and/or capital resources to a specific supplier. Direct supplier development includes activities such as on site consultation, education and training programmes, temporary personnel transfer, inviting the supplier's personnel, as well as the provision of equipment or capital.

The firm must safeguard its supplier specific investments, for example by establishing long term buyer supplier relationships. The buying firm commits no or only limited resources to a specific supplier in case of "indirect" or "externalised" supplier development. Instead, the firm offers incentives or enforces supplier improvement and hence makes use of the external market to encourage performance improvements. This is frequently done by assessing suppliers, communicating supplier evaluation results and performance goals, increasing a supplier's performance goals, instilling competition by the use of multiple sources or promising future business.

Checklist: Supplier Development Practices

- Buying from a limited number of suppliers per purchased item
- Supplier performance evaluation and feedback
- Parts standardisation
- Supplier certification
- Supplier reward and recognition
- Plant visits to suppliers
- Training to suppliers
- Intensive information exchange with suppliers (i.e. sharing of accounting and financial data by the supplier and sharing of internal information such as cost, quality levels, by the supplier)
- Collaborating with suppliers in materials improvement and development of new materials
- Involvement of suppliers in the buyer's new product development process.
- Sourcing from a limited number of suppliers.
- Parts standardisation complements sourcing from a limited number of suppliers by increasing the volume orders with specific suppliers.

Supplier development and purchasing performance: a structural model.

Proper management of supplier relationships constitutes one essential element of supply chain success. As we have mentioned above, buying firms faced with problems of deficient supplier performance and/or capabilities can implement a wide range of supplier development practices such as supplier evaluation and feedback, supplier recognition and supplier training, in order to upgrade the performance and/or capabilities of the weakest links in their supply chain.

We can view supplier development at three levels – basic, moderate and advanced:

1) The basic supplier development model applies to those supplier development practices that require the most limited firm involvement and minimum investment of the company's resources (i.e. personnel, time, and capital) and are thus likely to be implemented first in an effort to improve supplier performance and/or capabilities. These basic supplier development practices include evaluating supplier performance, providing feedback about the results of its evaluation.

2) The moderate supplier development refers to supplier development practices characterised by moderate levels of buyer involvement and implementation complexity, therefore requiring comparatively more company resources (personnel, time and capital) than basic supplier development practices. The supplier development activities considered to have moderate levels of involvement and implementation complexity include visiting suppliers' plants to asses their processes, reward and recognition of supplier's achievements in quality improvement, and supplier certification.

The collaboration with suppliers in the improvement and development of new materials and components completed the moderate supplier development construct. This practice contrasts with the involvement of the supplier in the buyer's new product design process which requires a higher level of involvement and implementation complexity and therefore is considered in the advanced supplier development construct. Hence, the moderate supplier development construct included measures of visiting suppliers to assess their facilities, rewarding and recognising supplier's performance improvements, collaborating with suppliers in materials improvement and certification of suppliers through ISO 9000.

3) The advanced supplier development model pertains to those supplier development practices characterised by high levels of implementation, complexity and buyer involvement with suppliers, therefore, requiring a greater use of company resources (personnel, time and capital) than moderate and basic supplier developments.

Supplier development practices that have shown high levels of implementation, complexity include training suppliers and involving suppliers in the buyer's new product design process. Supplier involvement in the buyer's design process is also linked to other supply practices, in particular, a collaborative atmosphere. A cooperative climate between suppliers and buyers can be achieved by intensive information exchanges such as suppliers releasing internal information (e.g. costs, quality levels) and buyers having access to a supplier's accounting and financial data. This type of communication with suppliers requires a high level of inter-firm involvement and consequently was included in the advanced supplier development construct. The advanced supplier development model included measures of training provided to suppliers, supplier's involvement in the buyer's new product design process, sharing of accounting information by the supplier, and sharing of cost and quality information by the supplier.

Checklist – Supplier development phases

1. Basic supplier development
- Suppliers are informed of their performance (quality, delivery, cost, etc.)
- We maintain relationships with a limited number of suppliers (3 or less for every purchased material).
- We use standardisation of raw materials and parts.
- There is a procedure for supplier quality qualification.

2. Moderate supplier development
- We visit suppliers' factories to assess their facilities.
- Purchasing collaborates with suppliers in improvement and development activities for new raw materials and part.
- Suppliers are recognised and rewarded for materials quality improvement.
- Suppliers are certified ISO 9000.

3. Advanced supplier development
- The company provides training to its suppliers.
- Suppliers participate in the company's new product development process.
- Purchasing has access to suppliers' internal information (production costs, level of quality).
- Purchasing has access to suppliers' external information (accounting information).

Relationships among supplier development activities

Trent and Monczka (1999) argued that sourcing from a limited number of suppliers is a first step towards the implementation of more complex supply chain practices. This is because practices requiring closer interaction between buyer and supplier, such as involving the supplier in the product design process, are not feasible with a large supply base.

Supplier evaluation allows the buyer to identify what supplier performance indicators and/or capabilities need to be improved. Using this information enables the buyer to make a better decision about the kind of supplier development activity that needs to be implemented.

For example, if the quality of materials needs to be improved, the buyer could collaborate directly with supplier in materials improvement, or provide training on quality management to suppliers. Similarly, if the focus is to improve on-time delivery, the buyer could share production information with suppliers. Additionally, the reward and recognition of supplier performance improvements is not possible without continuous supplier performance evaluations.

Empirical research has shown that the evaluation of suppliers through site visits, and the use of a supplier reward and recognition system, improves supplier performance.

Global supply networks

The development of suppliers within global supply chains provides many advantages to a company. These advantages include amongst others:
- Reduced component and/or tooling costs
- Improved product quality
- Greater product flexibility.

The initial problems however faced by many companies are that most of the local suppliers do not have the technological, resource and logistical capabilities that could support the company's operation.

However, by integrating local suppliers into the network and then working with them to develop selected product lines, it is possible for local suppliers to achieve a level of quality, cost, delivery and flexibility which can meet the company's immediate and long term needs. It will often be important to allow local supplier the time to develop their manufacturing operations to meet the demand pressures.

The development of an effective supply chain system is created through a strong working relationship being developed between the customer and its supplier. This relationship is aimed at developing its future technical and organisational capabilities, as well as providing advice and support towards ensuring product cost, flexibility and delivery reliability is achieved.

Supplier Development Methodology

Some companies have addressed the area of local supply chain development through and approach a structured development programme. During this programme the selected local suppliers are initially termed associate suppliers. These 'associate' suppliers work alongside established suppliers and incrementally take on increased volumes of product as their technical and logistical capabilities increase. The development of the associate supplier approach is based on three major stages, namely:
- Technical development
- Capacity development
- Logistical development

Firstly, the technical capabilities of the company are developed prior to concentrating on their capacity and logistical capabilities.

The second stage of the development process aims at ensuring that the associate supplier can manufacture the products under the increasing volumes required to become a full supplier whilst maintaining product quality at every stage. For instance, the associate supplier will be given between 5 and 10 percent of the volume requirements of the established supplier in order to test the process capability and logistical capacity of its system. Working with the process engineer, the company will be given increased product volumes as and when the system is capable of achieving the volumes under repeatable quality levels until the agreed capacity quota is reached for the company concerned.

Finally, the logistical system is refined. What is particularly interesting is the ability to continually drive costs down year by year and to improve on the company's supply flexibility and delivery frequency. The company becomes a fully fledged company when the process engineer is happy that there is suitable technical and logistical capacity within the company for further expansion over successive years.

Below is a summary diagram of a structured supplier development approach:

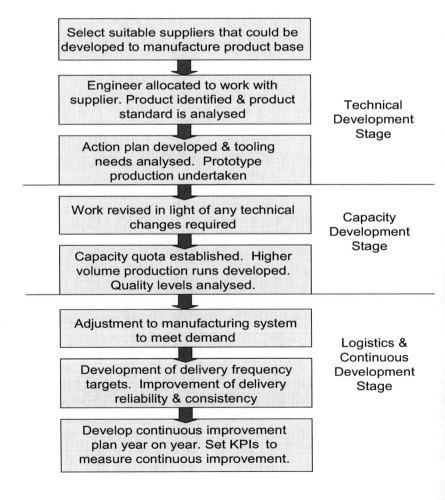

Relationship Positioning Tool

Now let us look at the developments in supplier relationships and how supplier development can improve overall performance in the supply chain. Some Companies have been frustrated in their attempts to increase their own competitiveness by the poor performance of other members of their supply chains. Whilst the focus of their attention has been directed forward towards their customers, they have failed to recognise the considerable advantages to be gained from closer involvement with their supplier.

The goal here is simply, to have all of the companies in a supply chain behaving as the best do, for example, 100 percent quality and delivery, all at a reducing overall cost. Such a chain would operate with minimum lead time and maximum response to final customer demand. Clearly, if 70% or 80% of your final product cost has been contributed by your external suppliers, there is considerable scope to work together to see out and develop opportunities for improvement.

The Positioning Tool (PT) is a technique which measures the relationship between a firm and its supplier. It identifies the strengths and weaknesses in the customer supplier relationship and encourages discussion between customer and supplier company personnel in a way that avoids blaming individuals. It enables the customer and supplier companies to create a joint agenda for improvement activities, including supplier development and buying organisation development.

The "management' of parties you do not own cannot be dictated but must be gained through a willingness to collaborate. Attitudes of collaboration, sharing and open communication need to replace traditional adversarial practices, which tended to assume that product, services, suppliers and employees, are interchangeable and easily discarded when times are difficult.

Managers involved have two difficulties:
- Understanding the full range of issues inherent in managing their supply links
- Knowing where to start to make the changes necessary to increase the effectiveness of their supply links through supplier development

The Positioning Tool (PT) addresses both these difficulties, by analysing the current situation between a company and a supplier and pin pointing aspects of the relationship which needs to be improved.

Adverse variations from targets for quality, delivery and cost with respect to supplied goods are unwanted wastes and indicate weaknesses in the performance of the relationship. Similarly, the relationship has to be effective in a way which ensures that continuous improvement through innovation of the supplied goods take place.

The potential of the relationship to continuously improve to meet present and future demands with respect to quality, delivery, cost and innovation is therefore dependent upon the:
- strategy developed by the customer
- capability of the supplier

The strategy developed by the customer, is measured in terms of the attitude adopted towards the supplier, how the customer's requirements are specified and how these are supported through systems and people.

The capability of the supplier is measured in terms of:
- Overall company profile
- People skills and organisation
- Process capability
- Supplier management

Additionally an important aspect of the customer's ability is to create a flow of information to the supplier, which provides a basis for the effective transfer of goods/services and the sharing of knowledge and ideas.

Similarly, the supplier's must also have the ability to create a flow of information to the customer. Again, the information issues are:
- Technical
- Involvement
- Business
- People

Just as the major contributory factors are made up of major roots such as company profile, people, process, and supplier management, the elements of the PT "Tree" model divide into minor roots. For example, under supplier capability, process we have:
- Design
- Plant capability
- Plant capacity
- Systems
- Process range
- Flexibility
- Lead times

In a similar way, each of the other major roots under the major factors is fed by a hierarchy of minor roots. As for any analysis procedure, data has to be gathered to provide a base of information on which the identification of strengths and weaknesses can take place. Two questionnaires, one for the customer and one for the supplier, gather over 300 pieces of data. Each response to a question is scored against "best practice". From these collected scores, the strengths and weaknesses of the relationship can be identified and areas for improvement identified on both sides.

By opening up the possibility of a free and open interchange of views on the PT results, to which both have contributed but which have been evaluated by a third party comparing with the industry best practice, the exercise rapidly develops into a mutual self help process in which both sides see value, since they have already recognised that each must change to some degree to effect the best possible improvements.

Action Time: Electric Motors Ltd. (EML)

EML have always produced electric motors, however, the company has recently made a strategic decision to move into the electronic components segment, where one of the key components will be the central processor. The quality and cost of the central processor will therefore be vital to the overall competitiveness of EML's final product.

The Head of Procurement has been asked to devise a pricing strategy for this key item. Traditionally, the Company has used a tender and bid methodology for all its key items. This time, the Head of Procurement has decided to carry out an initial analysis of the market and to discuss with design and engineering their requirements in terms of the central processors performance and requirements and market knowledge.

Task
In order that the pricing strategy can be determined, what questions should be put on the agenda at the meeting with design and engineering?

Action Time: P & C Ltd.

P&C are an international company producing a wide range of packaged foods. The central procurement group (CPG) carries out procurement of raw materials and packaging. CPG do not enjoy a good reputation within P&C for the following reasons:
*   Many plants have excessive inventory of some items, yet often run out of others items
*   Costs continue to rise
*   Quality rejects are increasing

Externally, CPG uses an adversary approach with suppliers, who, often complain about poor information from CPG. The P&C inbound supply chain is long and complex with transactional procurement from many suppliers, due to CPG policy of awarding on the lowest price and maintaining supplier competition.
This means suppliers hold high inventory levels to protect against sudden increases in demand from CPG. Meanwhile suppliers are aware that with P & C, large sales promotions are planned months in advance.

Task
What improvements would you suggest and why?

Action Time: Soaps Ltd.

Soaps Ltd. produces a range of domestic and industrial soaps and detergents. It has enjoyed a strong position in the marketplace for many years. However, the market has recently become increasingly competitive, with new entrants to the industry.

These have entered the industry through the own brand sector with the production of generic detergent products for the industrial sector. The new entrants have very low costs, are highly efficient and compete effectively.

Soaps Ltd. needs to become a leaner and lower cost producer. One of the ways in which the board feels that it can become more cost effective is by placing greater concentration upon its core activities and by making more efficient use of its procurement power. The board is also interested in the supplies side of the organisation and the contribution that it may make to increased efficiency and profitability.

As a first step towards increasing efficiency, a decision has been made to outsource a number of activities that are seen as non-core. These include services such as security, catering, freight transport, warehousing, and information technology (IT) in the first phase; followed later by other suitable functions,

As the recently appointed procurement manager, you are worried that the exercise is to be conducted by the functional department concerned, with little, if any, input from you. You feel that this increases the risk of poor decisions being made, particularly in the conduct of the exercise, the selection of suitable suppliers, and the resulting standards of performance by those suppliers.

You are well aware of the problems of sourcing suppliers and managing contracts, but are concerned that there is a general lack of awareness of these problems within Soap Limited. Prior to introducing new measures for improved efficiency, you have undertaken an initial survey of the procurement function. This indicates the following:
*   Purchase orders are all treated in the same manner regardless of value or type.
*   Some aspects of the inventory control system and ordering system have been computerised but some have not.
*   Suppliers are selected on the basis of past performance and/or the lowest price, and relationships tend to be short term and adversarial.
*   Inventory levels are high and records are not always accurate.
*   Items are frequently purchased by user departments without reference to the procurement department.
*   There is very little attempt at proper forecasting of demand.
*   Batch size tends to be large due to long changeover times in the production process.

As the newly appointed you will need to undertake the following tasks,

Tasks:
1) What do you see should be the role of sourcing and procurement in Soaps Limited?
2) What sourcing and procurement processes and procedures should exist?
3) How will you manage the risks and spend whilst satisfying customer and suppler requirements?
4) How will you measure and control the procurement and procurement function?

Appendix 1: Review Questions

The Procurement Process – Some review questions to ask

- What are the annual spend and requirements of the purchasing portfolios?
- Is there a programme to reduce the procurement lead times?
- Is component variety limited by looking closely at users specifications (avoiding brand names) and duplicated purchasing?
- What are the supplier assessment methods and supplier management policies?
- Do all communication processes deliver understanding?
- What codification is used?
- Is supply chain management used?
- Is end-to-end product evaluation used by applying the total costs of ownership (TCO)?
- What programme is there to develop relationships with users/customers and with external suppliers?
- Is there a culture of Total Quality?
- Have buyers changed from being reactive order-placers to be proactive commodity managers?
- Should you outsource or manage procurement yourself?
- Is there a programme to reduce the supplier base to a small number of qualified suppliers fully integrated into the business?
- Is there a culture of continuous improvement?
- Are alternative suppliers approached?
- Are quotations obtained from a number of sources?
- Are all purchase requisitions/purchase orders properly authorised?
- Does a policy exist for inviting bids/estimates/tenders?
- Are safeguards in existence to prevent the procurement of excessive quantities?
- Is the procurement department given a sound forecast of materials and other requirements in good time to enable them to be bought on favourable terms?
- What are the ordering costs against stockholding costs?
- Do buyers have the authority to speculate in commodity markets?
- What are the suppliers financial and credit ratings?
- What credit terms are offered?
- How do these compare with other suppliers' credit terms?
- How do they compare with the suppliers' cash flow needs?
- What are the cost implications of overdue deliveries?
- Are the prices competitive (given quality levels)?
- What controls do suppliers have over their activities?
- Is sufficient information available, by specific cost element, to know the reasonableness of the price quoted?
- Is the price reasonable in terms of competition?
- What is the supplier's current financial position as shown in their most recent balance sheet?
- What are the suppliers' current and projected levels of business?
- Are price breakdowns by cost element on fixed price contracts furnished?

- Will designated individuals in the supplier's organisation be specified from whom the buyer can obtain relevant information and data?
- Are there any special handling, packaging or shipping requirements that may delay delivery?
- Are spares involved, and are they allowed for in the supplier's plans and schedules?
- Do they demonstrate ability to meet the schedule and lead times?

Appendix 2: Further information

Institutes

Chartered Institute of Purchasing and Supply: www.cips.org
(There are also hundreds of links available from this site)
Chartered Insatiate of Logistics and Transport: www.ciltuk.org.uk

Journals/Magazines

Logistics Business: www.logisiticsbusiness.com
Logistics Europe: www.logisticse.com
Logistics Manager: www.sevenkingspublications.co.uk
Supply Management: magazine of Chartered Institute of Purchasing and Supply: www.cips.org
Supply Chain Business. www.supplychainbusiness.com

Appendix 3: Abbreviations

ABC   the 80/20 rule or Pareto analysis (often called ABC analysis)
Av.D   average demand
BOM   bill of materials
CR   continuous review
DV   demand variability
EDI   electronic data interchange
EOQ   economic order quantity
ERP   enterprise resource planning
FOQ   fixed order quantity
FOT   fixed order time
FMS   fast, medium, slow
ICT   information communication technology
IT   information technology
ITT   invitation to tender
JIT   just in time
KPI   key performance indicator
LCC   life-cycle costs
LIFO   last in first out
LT   lead time
LTV   lead time variability
MEAT   most economically advantageous tender
MRP   materials requirements planning
MRPII manufacturing resources planning
MTO   make to order
MTS   make to stock
OEM   original equipment manufacture
OTIF   on time in full
PESTLE political, economic, social, technological, legal, environmental
PTN   post tender negotiation
PR   periodic review
Q   quantity
RFB   request for bid
RFI   request for information
RFQ   request for quote
ROCE   return on capital employed
ROL   reorder level
ROP   reorder point
RP   requirements or resource planning
SCM   supply chain management
SKU   stock keeping unit
S/L   service level
SLT   supply lead time
SLTV   supply lead time variability
SS   safety stock

TAC   total acquisition costs
TCO   total cost of ownership
TQM   total quality management
VOT   variable order time
VOQ   variable order quantity
WEEE   waste electrical and electronic equipment
WIP   work in progress
WLC   whole life costs
VMI   vendor managed inventory

Bibliography

Angeles R, Nath R. (2007). Research Paper in *Supply Chain Management*. International Journal 12/2 104-115. Emerald Group Publishing Ltd.

Arminas D. (2003). E-Procurement and Supplier Management. *Supply Management*. April 2003.

Arminas D. (2005). E-Procurement of Services, BA case study. *Supply Management*. May 2005.

Audit Commission, The. (1998): *A Fruitful Partnership: effective partnership working.*

Boyd. D E, Spekman. R E, Kamauff. J W, Werhane. P (2007). *Long Range Planning: CSR in Global Supply Chains: A Procedural Justice Perspective.* www.sciencedirect.com. February 2007.

Burnett,K. (2001). E-Procurement Legislation. *Supply Management*. Feb 2001.

Carroll, A.B.(1991).The pyramid of Corporate Social responsibility - toward the moral management of organisational stakeholders. *Business Horizons*. vol34.

Castka P, Bamber C.J., Bamber D.J., and Sharp J.M. TQM AND CSR. (2004). *The TQM Magazine*. Volume 16 – Number 3, pp. 216-224. Emerald Group Publishing Ltd.

Duffy, R.J. (2007). Purchasing and Supply Solutions *"Operational Excellence in Procurement"*. Centre for Advanced Purchasing Studies.

Ghobadian, A., Gallear, D., and Hopkins, M. TQM and CSR Nexus. *International Journal of Quality & Reliability Management*. Vol 24, No. 7 2007, pp.704-721. www.emeraldinsight.com.

Gray, R. (1996). No Back-Seat Driving. *Supply Management*. 5th Sept 1996.

Hatton, J. and Young, W. (2004). E-auctions and the procurement of services. *Supply Management*. June 2004.

Hemmings, M. (2004). Closed Loop Supply Chains. *Supply Management*. February 2004.

Kraljic, P. (1983). Purchasing Must Become Supply Management in *Harvard Business Review.*

Emmett, S. (2002). *Improving Learning & for Individuals & Companies*. Capita.

Emmett, S. (2005). *Supply Chain in 90 minutes*. Management Books 2000.

Emmett, S. (2005). *Excellence in Warehouse Management*. Wiley.

Emmett, S. (2006). *Logistics Freight Transport - national and international.* Cambridge Academic.

Emmett, S & Crocker, B. (2006). *The Relationship Driven Supply Chain; creating a culture of collaboration in the chain.* Gower.

Emmett, S & Granville, D. (2007). *Excellence in Inventory Management - how to minimise costs and maximise service.* Cambridge Academic.

Emmett, S. (2008). *Excellence in Supply Chain Management - how to understand and improve supply chains.* Cambridge Academic.

"Focus" (CILT magazine). September 1996.

"Gulf Today". 2 August 2005.

"Human Resources" . November 2004.

Krause, D.R. and Ellram, L.M. (1997). Success Factors in Supplier Development. *International Journal of Physical Distribution & Logistics Management.* Vol 27 No. 1, pp. 39-52. MCB University Press.

Lloyd, M. (1994). How green are my suppliers. *Supply Management.* Oct 1994.

"Logistics Europe" magazine.

Macbeth, D.K., Ferguson, N., and Neil, G. (1993). PSERG 2nd International Conference.

Martin-Castilla, J.I.(2002). Possible ethical implications in the deployment of EFQM excellence model. *Journal of Business Ethics.* Vol 39.

Mehta. S.K. (1994). *Green Supply Chains Purchasing and Supply Management.*

Supply Management. 20th September 2007.

Mylius, Andrew 2005; "A Game of Two Halves" in Supply Management 6 October 2005.

Norman, D. (1996). Window of Opportunity. *Supply Management.* 5th September 1996.

"Partnerships with People". DTI. (1997).

"Partnering Works". The Housing Forum Report. (2003).

"Purchasing and Supply Solutions". *The Irish Journal for Supply Chain Management Best Practice.* 2007.

Sanchez-Rodriquez, C., Hemsworth, D., Martinez-Lorente, A.R. (2005). The effect of supplier development initiatives on purchasing performance: a structural model. *Supply Chain Management.*

Shell Case Study. (2004). *Supply Management.* June 2004.

Stone, A. (2007). Net Closes on Suppliers. *The Sunday Times.* 6th May 2007.

The Sunday Times. Companies That Count. 6th May 2007.

The Sunday Times. 18 February 2007.

Supply Management. 29 June 2000.

Thomas, A., Barton, R. (2007). Integrating local suppliers in a global supply network. *Journal of Manufacturing Technology Management.* Vol. 18 No.5, pp. 490-513, Emerald Group Publishing Ltd.

Vail, S.D. (2005). E-Sourcing. *Supply Management.* July 2005.

Waddock, S., Graves, S. (1997). The corporate social performance-financial performance link. *Strategic Management Journal.* Vol 18.no 4.

www.buyitnet.org

www.pilottaskforce.co.uk

Index

Bulk buying/supply 5, 14, 24, 61, 131
Business to business (B2B) 157
Business to consumer (B2C) 157
Buyer dominant 49-50, 136 (see also: Best Practice)
Buyers/Buying 1-2, 4-6, 10-11, 19, 31, 33, 43, 48-50, 52, 64, 82-83, 85, 87-88, 90, 112, 114-115, 129-130, 132, 135, 137, 150-151, 156-157, 159, 166-167, 170, 185, 191, 193-194, 196 (see also: Best Practice)
Buy-make-move-sell 11

Capacity 80-83
Capital investment 3-4, 26-27, 97, 153-154, 158, 194-195
Car manufacture 6, 12, 25, 136, 156, 169, 193
Care of substances hazardous to health (COSHH) regulations 78, 188
Cartels 136
Case studies 6-9, 16-17, 31-32, 35-36, 85-86, 115-116, 121-125, 140-142, 146-148, 151-152, 159, 167-168, 171-172, 176-177, 179-181
Cash flow 110
Cash-to-cash cycle time (C2C) 110
Catalogues 162
Cause and effect 188
Caveat emptor 82
Central tender committee (CTC) 56
Centralisation/Decentralisation 5-6 (see also: Policies and Processes)
Chartered Institute of Purchasing & Supply (CIPS) 82, 131, 156, 159
Cleaning 3
Codes of conduct 185-187 (see also: Supply chain code of conduct; Best Practice)
Coding – see Product coding
Collaboration 33, 145, 157, 160-162, 194-196, 199
Collaborative approach 58, 71, 133-135, 137-140, 143, 145, 194 (see also: Best Practice)
Collaborative supply chains 14, 101
Collateral contract 84 (see also: Contracts; Best Practice)
Commission on European contract law 88-89 (see also: Procurement cycle: order and post-contract steps)
Communication 21, 24, 44-45, 104, 111-112, 143, 167, 193
Companies 80, 96, 150, 153-154, 160, 165-167, 173, 176-178, 182, 186-187, 190, 196-200
Competition 2, 47, 109, 129-130, 136, 143, 170, 192-193, 199
Competitive advantage 14, 193
Competitive bidding – see Bids/Bidding
Competitive bidding/tendering – see Tenders
Complaints – see Defects
Conformance 43, 57
Consideration 82-83
Construction 3, 143
Consumer needs/Consumer demand 10-11, 86-87, 157
Continuous review 92, 98 (see also: Procurement cycle: order and post-contract steps)
Contracts (Rights of Third Parties) Act (1999) 85

Contracts 42-43, 54-57, 63, 77-91, 100, 114, 117-118, 132, 143-145, 153, 160-162, 164, 166, 170 (see also: Best Practice; Procurement cycle: order and post-contract steps)
Copyright 87-88
Copyright Designs and Patents Act (1988) 88
Core business/activity 34, 153-155, 169
Corporate social initiatives 175-176 (see also: Best Practice)
Corporate social responsibility (CSR) 129, 173-178, 180-182, 185-187, 190 (see also: Best Practice)
Corporate strategy 17-18
Cost and freight (C&F) 150 (see also Cost, insurance and freight [CIS])
Cost price 3, 5, 64 (see also: Purchases/Purchasing; Policies and Processes)
Cost, insurance and freight (CIF) 150-151
Costing 52, 60-61, 65, 96, 131, 184 (see also: Procurement cycle: order and post-contract steps)
Cost-plus 132, 136
Costs 1, 3-5, 14-15, 17, 19, 21-22, 29, 34, 46, 48, 57-58, 64, 71, 96-97, 103, 106, 110, 112, 121, 125, 131-132, 134, 139, 143, 151, 153-155, 158-159, 163, 170, 177, 181-182, 184, 187, 190, 194, 196-199 (see also: Best Practice; Procurement cycle: order and post-contract steps)
Counter-offer – see Offer
Critical/Critical items 19-20, 30, 32, 96, 137-138, 176 (see also: Best Practice; Policies and Processes)
Culture 145-146, 149, 154, 166
Customer demand/needs 2, 12, 22, 43-44, 64-65, 78, 134
Customer relationship management (CRM) 188
Customer Service 24, 54, 68, 145, 150, 182
Customers 1-2, 4-5, 9-13, 16-18, 22, 24, 27, 31, 43-45, 49, 60, 64, 77, 89-90, 92, 99, 109-110, 112-113, 131, 134, 136, 143, 145, 155, 170, 181, 190, 199-200
Customs 79
Cycle stock 24, 29 (see also: Stock; Stockholding)

Decentralisation – see Centralisation
Decoupling points 23, 29
Defects 3, 22, 83, 86, 102, 107
Delivery 2-5, 10-11, 14, 21, 41-44, 49, 53, 62, 65, 77, 91, 94, 100-102, 106-107, 110-112, 150, 165-166, 169-170, 191-192, 197, 199 (see also: Policies and Processes; Procurement cycle: order and post-contract steps)
Demand 2, 19, 22-26, 28, 93, 99-100, 129-130, 136, 169, 197, 199 (see also: Policies and Processes; Procurement cycle: order and post-contract steps)
Demand chain 10-11
Demand variability 93-94, 97
Design(s) 1, 3-4, 19, 22, 46, 77, 88, 131, 157, 166, 181, 195
Deterioration 3, 26 (see also: Defects)
Discounts 107, 130
Dismantling/Disposal 3, 57-58, 183-184 (see also: Best Practice)
Disputes 82, 84, 88, 117-121 (see also: Procurement cycle: order and post-contract steps)